A Guide to Research in Music Education

5th Edition

Roger P. Phelps
Ronald H. Sadoff
Edward C. Warburton
Lawrence Ferrara

The Scarecrow Press, Inc.
Lanham, Maryland • Toronto • Oxford
2005

SCARECROW PRESS, INC.

Published in the United States of America
by Scarecrow Press, Inc.
A wholly owned subsidiary of
The Rowman & Littlefield Publishing Group, Inc.
4501 Forbes Boulevard, Suite 200
Lanham, Maryland 20706
www.scarecrowpress.com

PO Box 317
Oxford
OX2 9RU, UK

British Library Cataloguing in Publication Information Available

Library of Congress Cataloging-in-Publication Data

Phelps, Roger P.
  A guide to research in music education / Roger P. Phelps ; Ronald H. Sadoff, Edward C. Warburton, Lawrence Ferrara.— 5th ed.
     p. cm.
  Includes bibliographical references (p.   ) and index.
  ISBN 0-8108-5240-3 (hardcover : alk. paper)
  1. Music—Instruction and study—Research. I. Sadoff, Ronald. II. Warburton, Edward C. III. Ferrara, Lawrence. IV. Title.
MT1.P5 2005
780'.7—dc22
                                                                    2004010739

Contents

Figures

Preface

It has been thirty years since the first edition of *A Guide to Research in Music Education* appeared in print. The second edition (1980) saw a version in Japanese. The third edition was issued in 1986 and the fourth in 1993. Ever-changing philosophies, concepts, and techniques, as well as phenomenal advances in technology, have led to considerable rewriting and literature updates to keep up with the rapid advances in music education and the arts.

I am grateful to Professor Lawrence Ferrara, who applied his broad knowledge and skills to chapters 3 and 4. Professors Ronald Sadoff and Ted Warburton, with their knowledge and experience in the arts, collaborated on the new chapter 8 on technology and music education. It has been my privilege to write and update the other chapters.

We hope you will find the updated fifth edition practical and easy to understand, as well as stimulating and nonthreatening.

Roger P. Phelps
Cary, North Carolina

Acknowledgments

Lawrence Ferrara dedicates chapters 3 and 4 to his wife, Kathryn Evans Ferrara, for her love and support. He extends thanks to Professor Philip Taylor of New York University for his reading and numerous suggestions regarding chapter 3 (Qualitative Research). Thanks also go to Professor Charles Varela, University of Illinois at Urbana-Champaign, for his substantial help in the formulation of chapter 4 (Philosophical Inquiry). In addition, he acknowledges Roger Phelps, professor emeritus, New York University, for his important role as a teacher and mentor.

Roger Phelps dedicates his chapters to his loving wife, Dr. Mildred Wade Phelps, who offered encouragement and many helpful suggestions. Acknowledged also is assistance from library staff members at Meredith College and North Carolina State University in Raleigh, the Charlotte-Mecklenburg Library, Charlotte, and the very helpful library staff members in the School of Music and the Jackson Library at the University of North Carolina at Greensboro.

Chapter 1

Selecting a Research Problem

Change is omnipresent, ongoing, and difficult, if not impossible, to stop. Likewise, change and research are intertwined and directly related to one another. Seeking answers through research may be the result of change, or change can be the result of research. Change may be beneficial or detrimental, depending on the direction. The focus of change, says Fabun, can be controlled and can be changed in the direction one desires to go.[1]

On a positive note, changes in the treatment of persons with certain cardiac problems have resulted in the implantation of stainless steel stents in diseased arteries, which means a better quality of life for persons with clogged arteries. These life-saving results likely would not have been possible without research and testing by cardiologists and biomechanical professionals. Negatively, the early twenty-first century witnessed catastrophic changes worldwide on September 11, 2001, when terrorist attacks leveled New York's World Trade Center and heavily damaged the Pentagon in Washington, D.C. The precision with which these dastardly attacks were carried out showed evidence of careful research and planning by the perpetrators. The result was the loss of life for several thousand innocent individuals. Drastic political, sociological, and psychological changes have occurred in the aftermath of September 11. These attacks have led to increased security at airports, train stations, bus terminals, municipal buildings, nuclear power plants, and other places that will affect the lives of people for many years to come. The positive and negative examples just given illustrate different outcomes based on research and change.

1

The research process can be an intriguing one for the experienced researcher as well as for the research novice. Upon completion of the research, personal satisfaction will come from uncovering new knowledge, refining older long-held precepts, or finding answers to vexing questions. By then you probably will be an experienced researcher. Bogdan and Biklen put it this way: as an experienced researcher you will establish an agenda, and you should know what to study and how to do future research.[2] Asking questions is the key to delineating a good research problem, says Wiersma.[3] Also in accord are Ary, Jacobs, and Razavieh, who affirm that one of the most significant phases of research is the selection and formulation of a research problem.[4] Almost as detractors, Altick and Fenstermaker claim a good researcher is one who approaches research as a skeptic.[5] Leedy gives a hypothetical example of a vague and unsatisfactory problem statement relating to an early vocal music form: "Palestrina and the motet." With more specificity, the formerly broad statement becomes a viable study to analyze and compare the motets of Giovanni Pierluigi da Palestrina (1525?–1594) with those of William Byrd (1542?–1623).[6]

Beginning researchers sometimes wonder in what direction their research should go. Several possibilities exist for doing aesthetic inquiry in the arts, including music, or possibly in researching classroom problems using descriptive techniques. Topics utilizing philosophical, historical, qualitative, quantitative, or experimental/quasi-experimental procedures should not be overlooked either if one has an interest in pursuing research in one of these categories. After studying this chapter, you should be able to focus on a possible research topic and formulate a tentative idea of the method (or methods) for tweaking that research idea. The specifics for applying the chosen method(s), however, must wait until later chapters.

DEFINITIONS OF RESEARCH

In this book the term "research" refers to (1) identification and isolation of a problem into a workable plan, (2) implementation of a plan to collect the data needed, and (3) presentation of the collected data into a format to be made available to others. This chapter will deal with the first part of the definition—identification and isolation of a problem. Later chapters will present procedures and techniques for obtaining data and reporting these facts. The term "research" has many meanings, some general, others more specific. In an ambivalent sense, if someone wants to do "research" on a puzzling question, in what context is the term meant? Often in a nonacademic setting it means nothing more than trying to cope with a situation and does not imply the careful investigative process so important for good research.

Hittelman and Simon define research as "the systematic attempt to (a) collect information about an identified problem or question, (b) analyze that information, and (c) apply the evidence thus derived to confirm or refute some prior prediction or statement about that problem."[7] A less technical definition is offered by Tuckman, who reports that research is seeking answers to questions.[8] The deductive-inductive method is used by Best and Kahn to relate research to the scientific method.[9] Time can be saved in focusing on a research problem, state Mauch and Birch, if the researcher knows what restrictions may be found in the proposed study.[10] Graziano and Raulin write that the process of inquiry is a specific thought process.[11] Research is systematically collecting and analyzing data for a specific purpose, according to McMillan and Schumacher.[12] Crowl believes research is more than locating and evaluating materials that relate to a topic.[13] There is no one procedure for planning research, write Cohen, Manion, and Morrison. They believe this is governed by what is appropriate for one's purpose.[14] Madsen and Madsen's definition of research is how one thinks rationally and objectively.[15]

The definition of music education research that is operational throughout this book is as follows(*research is a carefully organized procedure that can result in the discovery of new knowledge, the substantiation of previously held concepts, the rejection of false tenets, and the formal presentation of data collected.*)

RESEARCH CONCEPTS

The researcher in the arts and music can anticipate encountering certain terms and/or concepts relating to procedures of research. Those that refer only to specific types of research will be discussed in appropriate chapters in this book. Others, which are common to all types of research, follow. An understanding of these terms is important to the logical organization of a research study.

When matriculated, especially at the doctoral level, students are required to make a distinction in their program of studies between an emphasis that will enable them to pursue a project with a *pure* research emphasis and one that may be labeled *applied*, usually referred to as *action* research. Action research can be used at all levels of instruction in order to improve performance, state Gall, Gall, and Borg.[16] Pure, sometimes known as "basic" or "fundamental" research, is based on the accurate reporting of results, usually with little or no attempt to incorporate practical applications of the findings of the research. Those who read the reports are expected to make whatever use or application of the data that seems appropriate to their own situation. *Pure* research, often concerned with the development of a theory or model based on previous models, is desirable in almost all fields of endeavor, but frequently is not the type to produce answers to questions facing arts educators in the classroom. A history of eighteenth-century English secular choral music most likely would be classified as pure research, provided the study was conducted according to the tenets of "basic" research. Applied, frequently labeled "action" research, is conducted in such a way that the investigator includes practical suggestions for applying the results of the study to a teaching situation. An anthology of eighteenth-century English secular choral music would be classified as applied research because an anthology, by implication, may consist of compositions that have been collected and edited for a specific group, with rehearsal suggestions also incorporated in the study. The anthology quite properly could contain a history section, but this factor alone is not significant enough to change the character of the research, since the focus of a study of this type is to present practical suggestions for utilizing the results.

Clarke composed choral settings to selected psalms based on Jamaican folk melodies, rhythms, and harmonies for an action research project. He reviewed three centuries of Jamaican history and culture to determine the influence of African and European immigration to that Caribbean island. Nine psalm settings were arranged for three voice parts with piano, guitar, and percussion accompaniment. The settings, explains Clarke, are appropriate for Jamaican students in secondary schools, churches, or music festivals.[17]

Of the research methods discussed in this book, experimental/quasi-experimental, quantitative, and descriptive studies would usually be classified as applied research and historical, philosophical-aesthetic would fall under the pure research rubric. Beware, because it is dangerous to assign any one of these methods to either pure or applied research. How the research is conducted and the results obtained should determine which category the studies fall under. The purpose and the data collected ought to indicate how the research is classified. Pigeonholing can be frustrating, but researchers who, during the process of planning, consider their research with either a pure or applied emphasis will find it much easier to organize and develop.

"Qualitative" and "quantitative" are terms frequently referred to in research jargon and may have different meanings. As used in this book, they refer to procedures for looking at information. In the former, research results are largely subjective, that is, not easily translated into scores, whereas in the latter, objective data based on the scores of some type of measurement are given. If one were to count the number of bassoon players in all the public schools of a given state, qualitative data could be obtained. In other words, "kinds of information" rather than their evaluation. The mere counting of bassoonists would not indicate how proficient these bassoonists were. Some type of objective evaluation of the proficiency of these bassoonists would be necessary—this would result in quantitative data, a most desirable practice when it is possible to do so. Leedy ascribes qualitative research to inductive analysis and deductive analysis studies to those that are quantitative.[18]

While it is possible for a research project to be so organized that it would contain only qualitative data, it would be virtually impossible for a study to contain quantitative but little or no qualitative data because even in research where data obtained are the result of some type of measurement, narrative is necessary to explain the theoretical rationale for the research, and a rationale is a type of research.

In reviewing research in music education, sometimes one can find studies that contain qualitative data only, with quantitative data omitted, when there is every indication that both types should have been included. Such research is weak usually because the investigator has not proceeded thoroughly and carefully to the next significant step of quantifying information. For instance, a qualitative study might be undertaken to learn which school systems in a given state have instrumental music programs. These data, readily available by questionnaire (written or online), could be useful to school administrators who do not have an instrumental music program.

They could then report to their boards of education that such a program is needed if students in the community are to receive the same cultural experiences that youngsters in neighboring school systems have. To music teachers, by contrast, these data might be relatively useless because they give little or no indication of the actual content of the instrumental music programs surveyed. They merely indicate the presence or absence of instrumental music in the school systems reviewed. Music directors more likely would be interested in determining how the curricular offerings in their schools compare with those of other schools.

Since music is largely concerned with the development of skills, the question of competence in performance often arises. This problem is largely quantitative, and answers would depend on using a specialized instrument of measurement in conjunction with a questionnaire. Such an investigation would be proper under certain conditions. The investigator would need to establish criteria for comparison in order to ascertain how well the groups performed. Researchers who organize their projects to obtain quantitative data are in a much better position to produce a significant piece of research when qualitative data also are obtained. It should be clear by now, that both qualitative and quantitative research may produce valid results, although different techniques are used for each.

CATEGORIES OF MUSIC EDUCATION RESEARCH

Most research studies in music education fall under one or a combination of the following categories: aesthetic-philosophical, descriptive, historical, experimental/quasi-experimental (sometimes called behavioral). Or the research might be a combination of one or more of them. (Procedures for obtaining and treating data in these methodologies are enumerated in later chapters in this book.) Occasionally music researchers engage in research across different fields, for example, combining music or arts with psychology or therapy.

A purview of standard textbooks in educational research will likely reveal a discussion of the descriptive—with its many components—experimental/quasi-experimental, and historical methodologies, but unfortunately aesthetic and philosophical procedures often are missing. Texts on musicology and other specialized music topics normally include procedures for conducting historical research but say little, if anything, about the other possibilities discussed in this book.

Philosophical inquiry, or research, is mentioned in some older research texts, but many educational researchers have either denied the existence of philosophical inquiry as a separate type of research or suggested that its use was so extremely limited as to be hardly worth serious consideration. Several writers consider philosophical inquiry to be no different from the process of the scientific method and reflective thinking, to which it is closely related, to be sure. Rainbow and Froehlich are among recent researchers who devote an entire chapter to philosophical inquiry.[19] The American Educational Research Association (AERA) also has recognized that philosophical inquiry is a valid method for obtaining information. *Complementary Methods for Research in Education*, edited by Richard M. Jaeger, contains a chapter by Michael Scriven entitled "Philosophical Inquiry Methods in Education."[20] In music education, philosophical inquiry normally relates to a comparison of ideas, and it can be a very fruitful technique.

Some recent thinking, however, suggests that there is no separate philosophical inquiry methodology; it is part and parcel of aesthetic inquiry because of the ideas that are compared both aesthetically and philosophically. Such is the approach fostered by Lawrence Ferrara, one of the coauthors of this textbook. (His approach is discussed in chapter 4.)

Aesthetic inquiry (or research) is a designation normally reserved for the study of the beautiful in the arts. It may consist of a comparison of art objects, or to a comparison of ideas using aesthetic and philosophical approaches. To be specific, in music, it may relate to learning about a composer or a composer's music, or to any investigation that focuses on music. This type of research has received considerable emphasis in performance-oriented programs, those offered for the D.M.A. or the Ph.D., for example. When concerned with the study and analysis of certain compositions of a composer, including the composer's role in the mainstream of music history, it may be regarded quite properly as quasi-musicological in scope. Many possibilities exist in the aesthetic type of research for a music educator who has a good aesthetic, theoretical, philosophical, and musicological background. The largely impersonal nature of behavioral research, which has become quite prominent in music education, appears to be losing ground to the more personal approaches that are possible through the application of aesthetic-philosophical procedures.

Qualitative research, found in some of the newer research textbooks or more recent editions of textbooks by McMillan and Schumacher and Tuckman, may be combined with descriptive research, or listed as a separate entity, especially when the qualitative research has a strong social-science base. The qualitative method deals with topics that are ethnographic, sociological, or involve some kind of fieldwork.[21] Bogdan and Biklen, in *Qualitative Research for Education*, include both phenomenological and "ethnomethodological" approaches. Ethnomethodology refers to the kind of methods researchers use to obtain their data.[22]

Since the techniques, philosophical bases, procedures, and characteristics of each of the research methodologies referred to earlier will be presented in detail in subsequent chapters, they will be referred to here only in passing. Any study, of course, may incorporate some parts of other research types, as noted earlier, but the main emphasis of such a study will be upon one of the types just noted. The organization of research largely determines the format under which the research will be conducted. Historical research will emphasize authenticity and credibility of data. A descriptive report contains data on some current observations, whereas experimental (behavioral) and quasi-experimental studies usually will concentrate on techniques that involve statistical comparison of variables. Understandably, labels associated with a given research report should not become a fetish, because the essential factor is *the way the research is organized and implemented, and findings reported.* Categorization, however, is helpful in determining procedures that will be or have been followed in a research project. Research could be labeled aesthetic-philosophical, aesthetic-descriptive, aesthetic-historical, aesthetic-quasi-experimental, or any other combination. Using an aesthetic-descriptive approach, a music or other aesthetic topic might be investigated by a researcher using descriptive techniques, and in the aesthetic-quasi-experimental mode, an aesthetic topic could be investigated using quasi-experimental procedures. Most research is rarely developed exclusively with one methodology at the expense of others. By analogy, no person is completely an introvert or an extrovert; personality traits label one as being inclined in one direction or the other. To cite another example: a computer-generated musical tone identified as A may have a frequency of 220 hertz (Hz). When the sound is analyzed by the computer, it may be found to possess minor amounts of energy present for E (966 Hz), or $C_{\sharp}$ (1,100 Hz), yet the tone is perceived as A because it is the dominant sound. Another study might include both historical and philosophical concepts yet be regarded as essentially experimental. Background information on the experiment proposed or on theories on which it is predicated could be philosophically based. Regardless of the kind of organization, the research must meet certain rigid criteria if it is to be solid. Results of any of the types of research identified largely depend on the skill and acuity of the researcher, not exclusively the study's organization, because even the best organized research plan can be useless if it is not implemented by an investigator who utilizes good research techniques.

EXPANSION OF DEGREE PROGRAMS

In past years teachers of public school music were trained not only in the more formal normal schools and teachers colleges but also in teachers institutes, singing schools, and military music schools. The need for more specialized training led to extension of two- and three-year programs in normal schools offering no degree to advanced graduate school curricula culminating in some form of doctorate. About seventy years ago many state departments of education began to mandate at least a baccalaureate degree as a prerequisite for a teaching certificate. Since the end of World War II, the increasing demand on the part of state departments of education for a minimum of a master's degree as the requisite for permanent certification has resulted in monumental growth in graduate programs in music and other fields of education all over the nation as well as other parts of the world. A few master's programs offer extra course work as an alternative to the usual thesis. Other institutions give students a choice of some type of creative endeavor (composition, arrangement, recital, field work) in lieu of a thesis. The option of either extra course work or a project of some kind has advantages. Experiences by the authors in advising students at both master's and doctoral levels, however, suggest that graduate schools should consider the feasibility of requiring some type of written requirement involving research for all master's degree candidates. Not only can these students expand their knowledge and receive intellectual stimulation, but they also will have had some practical research experience should they eventually pursue a doctorate.

There is great proliferation of degree designations in master's degree programs—Master of Music, Master of Arts, Master of Science, and Master of Music Education, among others. Sometimes a graduate student in music may believe that the Master of Music is superior to the Master of Arts. One cannot always tell by the degree designation the actual quality of master's degree programs. The reputation of the institution, the faculty involved in the program, and the success of graduates are important criteria to consider, as well as the accrediting associations to which the institution belongs. A good source of reference for master's theses completed is *Master's Theses Abstracts*, which has been published since 1951–1952.[23]

Sometimes a graduate student will use a pilot study to determine the feasibility of pursuing the proposed study in greater depth. Howe's research, "Some Effects of Sequential Music Tasks on the Cognitive and Social Skills of Learning Disabled Adults," is an example of this kind of pilot study. Howe's subjects (Ss) were nine learning-disabled adults enrolled in an intensive job training program. Various musical tasks were given to the Ss, using Orff-Schulwerk instruments. Both the musical and social skills of the Ss showed marked improvement.[24]

The demand for academic standing beyond the baccalaureate degree began in the 1920s. Until World War II, the master's degree was generally considered to be the terminal degree for music teachers, even at the college or university level. At that time many college and university professors had an extensive background in professional performance or had a high standard of training at a music conservatory where a degree usually was not awarded, the rigid training being the criterion for obtaining a university teaching position. It often was assumed that musicians were "doers" rather than "thinkers." Work beyond the master's degree (or conservatory nondegree programs) was believed to be unnecessary because "thinkers" usually were researchers and "doers" often were not. In the past fifty or sixty years, however, the pressure for advanced degrees on college and university music teachers by administrators has caused a rethinking of graduate music education, with the result that many postbaccalaureate students now anticipate the master's degree as a transitional step to the doctorate. An aspirant for a teaching position at the college or university level can hardly hope to achieve tenure or rise above the level of Instructor (or occasionally assistant professor) without an earned doctorate.

Jones and McFee, writing in the *Handbook for Research on Teaching*, point out that dissertations in music education largely have been quantitative in scope, based on research methods from general education and psychology.[25] Studies on curriculum in music education, note Jones and McFee, essentially have been directed toward developing performance skills. In comparing music and art education, the same authors indicate little agreement on goals and objectives of instruction by art and music educators. On the positive side, the nod was given to music educators who were more in agreement than art educators in regard to methodologies needed to provide answers to research questions.[26]

If you have examined college or university vacancy lists on the Internet, or otherwise, it should be patently clear that among the application requirements the phrase "doctorate required or preferred" stares at you boldly. The by-product of coercion by higher education administrators for an earned terminal degree has been a doctorate with emphases different from those of the traditional Ph.D. or Ed.D. This has been true in specialized fields such as music and the other arts, where the Ph.D., the typical research doctorate, often is not equated with the kind of scholarship possessed by musicians and other artists. One of the newer degrees is the Doctor of Arts (D.A.). Dressel reports that the D.A. was originally conceived as a degree for practitioners rather than for the research-oriented specialist.[27] Thus it would appear that the D.A. would be the logical degree for the practicing musician to pursue.

To indicate diverse approaches to doctoral degrees, in the following sections several recent dissertations are identified for the D.A., D.M.A., Mus. Doc., D.M.E., Ph.D., and Ed.D.

Richard B. Hunan, for his D.A., examined online trombone journals to ascertain which specific methods dealt with credibility, accessibility, and performance in electronic journal publishing.[28] Several universities desired a more specific degree so curricula were developed leading to the D.M.A. (Doctor of Musical Arts). James L. Fern, used CD-ROM and MIDI techniques in his D.M.A. study to develop and test a computer-based software program for teaching jazz improvisation.[29] The Mus. Doc. (Doctor of Music) traditionally has been an honorary degree conferred on outstanding composers, conductors, and performers. It is possible, in some universities, to earn the

Mus. Doc. An annotated bibliography of original, twentieth-century compositions for trumpet with concert band accompaniment was the focus of Bryan W. DePoy's research for a Mus. Doc.[30] Another fairly new degree is the D.M.E. (Doctor of Music Education). Kimberly Ann McCord, for her D.M.E. research, observed, described, and analyzed the behaviors of children with learning disabilities who composed music using a MIDI keyboard with a synthesizer and software program developed by the researcher.[31] Susan W. Hines used motoric and nonmotoric music instruction in reading and mathematics to examine the achievement of learning disabled children in kindergarten through ninth grade for her Ph.D. dissertation.[32] Burnout was the focus of Katherine L. Hendry's Ed.D. dissertation. Using the Maslach Burnout Inventory, Form ED, she measured emotional exhaustion, depersonalization, and personal accomplishment concerns of selected vocal and instrumental educators.[33]

With few exceptions, all doctorates require some type of terminal project in written form, be it a dissertation, composition, project, or whatever form the creativity takes. Increasingly, doctoral students are using the Internet and other technological tools for their research. Richard D. Repp, in a Ph.D. study, used the Internet and auto-accompanied software with spectral analysis to determine their effectiveness in undergraduate voice lessons.[34]

The Doctor of Arts is a more flexible, interdisciplinary, and individually oriented program of studies enabling a researcher to relate music to other arts more efficiently than the traditional Ph.D. or Ed.D. Sometimes there may be confusion between the designations D.A. and D.M.A. Check carefully to make sure the institution you plan to enter (or already attend) offers the degree that best fits your needs, be it the D.A., D.M.A., D.M.E., Mus. Doc., Ph.D., Ed.D., or any other degree designation.

A possibility for research might be to compare music performing groups in private schools (both secular and religious) with comparable groups in public schools. Another possibility is to compare music instruction in charter schools with the teaching of music in private and/or public schools. One might ask: "Is the learning environment for band or choral students better in private and charter schools or in public schools?" "If there is no difference, why not?" "What factors seem to be important if there is a difference?" "What tools or instruments may be utilized to compare these groups?" "Are they different from those used in other schools?"

Using computers as the primary mode of teaching and learning, "virtual charter" schools and "Web academies" are on trial in Colorado, Minnesota, and Wisconsin. Students isolated geographically can use the Internet to interface with teachers who may be miles away. Whether or not cybernetic instruction will result in more effective, efficient learning than traditional classroom instruction still needs to be determined.[35] At the time of this writing there do not appear to be many opportunities for research into "virtual charter" school instruction and learning for music researchers because of the "one-on-one" teaching situation, making it difficult to obtain enough subjects (Ss) for comparison. Even more important, though, is the accessibility of the data.

Sometimes it is believed that the Ph.D. is superior to the Ed.D. This is not necessarily true. The main distinction between the two degrees ought to be the kind of project to be completed. The Ph.D. frequently is concerned with the development of a theory or model philosophically, some kind of qualitative or descriptive observation, or a report on some historical or aesthetic activity. Action research for the Ed.D. usually is a practical project that one can take directly to the classroom. Martella, Nelson, and Martella say that in action research the scientific method is used to solve problems in the classroom.[36] Here are some hypothetical examples of the difference between the Ph.D. and the Ed.D. Suppose you were to develop a model to teach music to multiply handicapped children. This research probably would be in the realm of a Ph.D. study because the model should be theoretically based and would of necessity be process oriented. On the other hand, a series of lessons for multiply handicapped children in music likely would be classified as action research, appropriate for the Ed.D. or another doctoral degree designation. In this instance what a person had outlined and developed could be taken directly to the classroom. This would mandate that it be tested to determine its applicability to the appropriate population. Of the newer degrees, D.M.A., Mus. Doc. emphasize performance or other skills, but essentially steer clear of the "action" research concept. Regardless of the degree designation, results of the research are what is important. Some institutions do not offer certain degrees because they are not authorized to do so by an overseeing agency such as a board of trustees. As already stated, this is not to infer that one degree is superior to any other. The standards expected for any of these degrees should be consistent; the methodology and kind of results sought should be the difference. The egregious canard that the Ed.D., D.M.A., and Mus Doc. are inferior to the Ph.D. should be expunged from the literature and from the minds of those who hold such views. Holders of the Ph.D. also should not look snobbishly down their noses at any of the newer degrees if the research is of high quality. Research is not a game of trying to determine who is more intellectual than someone else!

Some universities permit a variant of the Ed.D., referred to as the "Alternative Ed.D.," which stresses the development of a product, a series of position papers, or the completion of a textbook, to cite three examples. The Alternative Ed.D. format is not used much by researchers in arts education; it includes title, problem statement, subproblems, significance of the study (including relevance to one's field of study), methodology, annotated bibliography, and relevant personal and professional experiences. In this proposal, note that the term "annotated bibliography" is listed, making this component different from the standard bibliography in the traditional Ed.D. or other doctorates. "Annotated bibliography" replaces the "related literature" and "bibliography" sections found in other proposals. The Alternative Ed.D. proposal (or design) normally exceeds no more than ten pages, exclusive of annotated bibliography and professional experience.

While doing some research, Phelps came across an interesting and tantalizing incident of memorabilia, the Doctor of Pedagogy degree. This designation was used frequently in the late nineteenth and early twentieth centuries. Such a degree was awarded to one John J. Dawson by New York University in 1895, only five years after the School of Pedagogy was established, the first school to award degrees in education.[37] (This dissertation will be discussed in greater depth in Chapter 7, "Historical Research: Concepts and Techniques.") Hug reports that the Department of Music Education (now the Department of Music and Performing Arts) was established by Hollis Dann (1861–1939) in 1925.[38] What is even more unusual is that two doctoral dissertations with a music education emphasis had already been written before the Department of Music and Music Education was founded in 1925.

A review of *Comprehensive Dissertation Index (CDI)* for 1861–1972 reveals another dissertation was completed in 1895 by Thaddeus L. Bolton for a Ph.D. at Clark University. Bolton's dissertation,

"Rhythm," dealt with teaching rhythm to children. Thus Bolton and Dawson must be considered pioneers in research relating to music teaching. It is interesting that the 1895 *CDI* reference for Bolton does not also include Dawson's name!

With few exceptions, all earned doctorates are based on the acceptance of some kind of "creative" project as part of the requirements for the degree. Therefore students in music education as well as other disciplines find themselves faced with the often frightening reality of engaging in research. Many times selection of an acceptable topic becomes an unnecessarily long and tedious process, one that could be shortened considerably if reflective thinking were used to identify and proceed with a topic that is meaningful and interesting. When seeking a research idea, avoid asking your adviser: "What do you want me to do?" The usual response is a snide answer such as, "Well, there are many students who would like to get a doctorate!" The necessity for doing one's own thinking is emphasized by Koefod, who observed that an excellent research report is the hallmark of this kind of investigation.[39]

COMMON WAYS TO OBTAIN RESEARCH INFORMATION

Three common ways used to obtain information on a research topic are (1) trial and error, (2) serendipity, (3) review of literature in one's field. If you are a teacher, solutions to some of your dilemmas may have been found by trial and error, trying one strategy, then another, until eventually an approach is found that appears to be satisfactory, at least on an interim basis. This trial-and-error strategy does not fall under the accepted heading of "research."

Serendipitous discoveries have accounted for some of the greatest advances in the scientific world; however, very few solutions to problems faced by music educators have been the result of serendipity. (The term "music educators" is used throughout this book in a very broad sense to mean those who teach music of any kind at any level.) The word "serendipity" is derived from the Three Princes of Serendip, as told by eighteenth-century British novelist Horace Walpole (1717–1797). As they sailed the Indian Ocean, these three princes of Serendip, known formerly as Ceylon, and now as Sri Lanka, were constantly finding things they did not expect. One prime example of serendipity in the scientific world will suffice. The discovery in 1928 by Alexander Fleming (1881–1955), quite by accident, of that marvelous antibiotic penicillin. Fleming, from his research on influenza, observed, by chance, that spores from the *Penicillium notatum* had wiped out a culture of staphylococcus bacteria, which led him to see the powers of the mold from which penicillin is made.[40]

A fairly recent serendipitous discovery, related to a connoisseur of the arts, was the accidental finding by James Gilbreath and Douglas L. Wilson of Thomas Jefferson's (1743–1826) classification catalog of his personal library. Jefferson's catalog had been assembled by Nicholas P. Trust, his private secretary, and prepared for publication in 1815 by George Watterson, Librarian of Congress. Gilbreath, history specialist at the Library of Congress, and Wilson, Knox College professor, discovered that Jefferson's personal catalog had been mistakenly bound in the front of the Watterson catalog. Jefferson placed his books in three categories of knowledge: history, philosophy, and fine arts. His fine arts collection included books on architecture, painting, sculpture, and music. Watterson's arrangement, disapproved by Jefferson, involved an alphabetical listing of all entries.[41] (Recall that many of the holdings of the Library of Congress were destroyed when the British burned Washington, D.C., during the War of 1812. Jefferson subsequently sold much of his personal library to the Library of Congress.)

To approach serendipity from a hypothetical viewpoint, Sir Arthur Sullivan (1842–1900) wrote a vocal composition entitled *The Lost Chord*. The discovery of this "lost chord" would have been the result of serendipity had the traditional system of harmony developed by Jean-Philippe Rameau (1683–1764) not been so well established already that a "new" chord was impossible. Any significant research findings, except those resulting from serendipity, are careful and deliberate and then a critique follows. This cycle follows several times before results are achieved. Since problems and changes are ever present, humanity will continue to be challenged to draw upon its ingenuity for solutions in the future as it has in the past. The continuum is endless because as answers to questions emerge through various research procedures, new and additional challenges arise as humanity moves up the ladder of progress. Only when the hunger to improve is satisfied will mankind's quest for knowledge cease.

Emphasis in this book is on the third of these ways commonly used to obtain research topic information; namely, the development and implementation of a carefully organized plan of research. These procedures will be discussed at length in chapters that follow this one.

The selection of a feasible research topic is of prime importance. Here is an example: a Unionist Civil War buff (also called the War Between the States) who is thinking about combining music and Civil War events might want to examine the role of Colonel (later Brigadier General) Benjamin J. Grierson, a former music teacher from Illinois. Colonel Grierson's successful raids of sixteen days in Tennessee, Mississippi, and Louisiana in 1863 diverted the attention of the Confederacy from General Ulysses Grant's (1822–1885) siege of Vicksburg, Mississippi. A researcher might ask, What was Grierson's role as a music teacher? Where did he teach? What did he teach? Did he enlist in the Union Army or was he drafted? What musical activities did he engage in during his service with the Union Army? Was Grierson involved musically after his discharge from the Union Army? Grierson, a composer and arranger, is said to have played several instruments. On patrol he reportedly entertained himself and his troops within earshot by strumming on a jaw's harp as they rode along.[42]

Taking a Confederate point of view of this fratricidal brotherly conflict, Ferguson investigated the musical and military contributions of bands of the Confederate States of America. About 2,400 bandsmen served in 155 bands for the Confederacy. During combat they usually served as hospital corpsmen and surgeons' assistants. Bands from Louisiana, North Carolina, and Tennessee, about which little had been written previously, were included in Ferguson's research.[43]

As pointed out earlier in this chapter, the human race is instinctively committed to change, for without it, survival for any length of time is virtually impossible. The "greenhouse effect," pollution, Anthrax scare, SARS, West Nile virus, and other life-threatening events are a cause for concern. Research by dedicated investigators will be needed to curtail, or at least arrest, these disturbing disasters in the world. The human race does not yet appear to go the way of the prehistoric brontosaurus and the fabled dodo bird, whose disappearance from the face of the earth has been attributed to environmental changes. Even a cursory glance at a music history textbook will reveal names of instruments that are no longer in use: the ancient Greek cithara, the medieval shawm, the ophicleide of the nineteenth century, and others. Or witness the changes in instrumentation for instruments formerly found in bands and orchestras of the last one hundred years. A late-nineteenth- or early-twentieth-century band score might call for the soprano saxophone (which has been revived in some contemporary jazz ensembles), the E♭ mellophone, E♭ cornet, D♭ flute and piccolo, and others. The E♭ alto clarinet, after a period of disuse, seems to have had a revival of interest and use by contemporary band arrangers and composers. Why are some of these instruments not in vogue today? That is a serious question research may or may not be able definitely to answer. Nevertheless, the current use or disuse of some of these instruments in contemporary ensembles is no reason for failure to learn about them. Any person well read in music—or any discipline—is expected to be familiar with significant developments (and even those less significant) and events pertinent to his or her field. How does one best acquire this knowledge? The answer is through research.

The term "research" can be an awesome and frightening one at times. Students have entered some of these authors' research classes with fear and trepidation because the world outside of academia frequently stereotypes a researcher as one who is isolated from society; one who spends time turning knobs, mixing chemicals, or holed up in front of a computer. Is the music educator expected to go into seclusion to search for solutions to problems? The answer, of course, is no. Fortunately, research need not be something to dread; it even can be fun!

Repeating a previous statement, change is ever present not only in society but also in education, bringing with it new problems to be solved. Already observed is that the quest for solutions to problems may be labeled "research" in the proper sense of the word. Educators may seek answers to some classroom problems by applying the results of completed research. Some solutions to problems may result from less formally organized procedures. Kelley, writing several years ago, stated a premise that still is valid today, that research actually is a process of evolution.[44] Here is an example: the clumsy five-key eighteenth-century clarinet of Johann C. Denner (1655–1707) would be repugnant to the contemporary clarinetist, who performs on an instrument containing up to twenty keys and rings. Is it possible that the cithara, shawm, or ophicleide could have been modified and improved to keep pace with changing aesthetic and musical concepts? This conjecture hardly seems appropriate; the record is clear. Obsolescence and usefulness are both the result of change, but for different reasons, many of which likely will never be known. Research may hasten either one or the other. From a practical standpoint, research is concerned with utility—or should be—although from a historical perspective, obsolescence might provide appropriate research opportunities for many studies.

SELECTION OF A TOPIC

It is a "given" that a master's thesis or doctoral dissertation is expected to make a contribution to knowledge. Before settling on a topic, some consideration needs to be given to the *purpose* of the research. Other than the obvious—to obtain a degree—you need to ask yourself, Why am I doing this research? Will the research improve my perspective on education? Will the research supplement my resume and enable me to obtain a better position? A positive or negative answer may be given to each one of these questions, but the fact still remains that a research topic still needs to be identified, and one that is oriented toward your goal of providing information in your field relating to the chosen topic.

As a starter, here are some specific questions relating to your *purpose* for the research as well as adding new knowledge to your field: What am I interested in? Are there classroom problems that might be resolved by research? Am I sure I possess the background necessary to successfully complete the research? Is the topic I propose one that is supported by my adviser and/or department? Has the proposed research been done before? How can I be sure I can obtain all the data I need to complete the research? There are no complete answers to these questions, of course, but they can stimulate your mind and help you focus on the proposed research.

Davis and Parker identify several sources of possible topics. Those relevant for music researchers are (1) current problems in the classroom, (2) suggestions for further research found in completed theses and dissertations, (3) suggestions from authorities in the field, and (4) procedures generally accepted as valid, but without substantiation.[45] Problems encountered in the classroom may not lend themselves to formal research procedures. Earlier it was noted that answers to classroom problems cannot always wait for the usual development of a research proposal and its implementation. Why do students use and abuse drugs is not one that can be answered quickly. It is too complex and involves the assistance of many professionals working together with the teacher.

It is rare to find a thesis or dissertation that does not include a section (final chapter) containing suggestions for further research. These chapters can be lucrative sources for possible topics. Then there are several sources that include titles of completed research. Among the most valuable for music students are *Dissertation Abstracts International (DAI)*, *Master's Abstracts*, and *Doctoral Dissertations in Musicology (DDM)*. Using the lists from these sources, it is possible to review the abstracts online. The titles are indications but not complete ideas of what still remains to be accomplished.

Research suggestions often are presented by authorities in the field as they lecture at conferences, in the classroom, or by personal conferences with them. It must be assumed that they are leaders in the field and as such can offer concrete suggestions for topics that need to be researched.

Teaching techniques and approaches often are handed down from one generation to another. Some of the "techniques" are time tested, but this does not necessarily mean they have been evaluated through careful research processes. While not numerous, such ideas can be fruitful sources for research. Tuckman reports that the selection of a research problem or topic is one of the most difficult in the entire research process, and one to which little guidance can be given. Yet, he does offer encouragement that a problem may be expressed as the relationship that exists between one or more variables.[46]

A respected, concise account of topic selection takes into account the relationship that should exist between student and adviser. Although written several years ago, these axioms by Chambers still are appropriate today.[47] Paraphrased from the *Phi Delta Kappan*, Chambers writes that graduate students should (1) avoid asking their advisers for "assigned" topics, but rather seek those that are in accord with their own interests and initiative; (2) select subjects that are in harmony with their interests and background instead of those that are suited to the "predilections" of their advisers; (3) manifest erudition by not expecting their advisers to serve as "intellectual nursemaids"; (4) define their problems clearly; (5) become familiar with the literature in the field to ascertain what has or has not been done; (6) determine what methods, techniques, or instruments will be needed; and (7) find out whether field trips or visits to museums, libraries, private archives, and other repositories of information are necessary. After continuing with suggestions for student-adviser conferences and for writing up the study, Chambers concludes by stating: "Research is not necessarily as complex, difficult, mysterious, or esoteric as a pedantic attitude can make it seem. In common with all things that are really great, it is essentially simple in concept. It has been comprehensively and simply defined in eight words as 'the orderly treatment of data to answer questions.'"[48]

Referring to Chambers's first point, topics that are "assigned" by advisers have validity *only if you are interested in the subject and can involve yourself wholeheartedly in it.* By analogy there are too many exercises in music theory that result in a mediocre or mechanical sound because the persons writing them have not been given the freedom to express themselves in a manner that is meaningful and significant to them. This obviously does not imply that all rules and principles should be abrogated. Guidelines certainly are needed, but students need to be encouraged to express themselves in a manner that is in accord with their own initiative and creativity. All too prevalent are research projects in a "series," usually at the master's level, which are "assigned" by advisers to certain of their students. A group of studies of this type might focus on a general title, such as a survey of elementary private instruction books for specific instruments, with students examining and comparing materials for each instrument of the band or orchestra. Such projects, if well organized and implemented, can be beneficial to students in instrumental techniques classes who are unfamiliar with these publications. It is in this spirit, one would hope, that advisers make such assignments. Koefod takes a less optimistic viewpoint when he states that students beg for this kind of assignment because they have been led to believe that this is the way to find a research topic.[49] Whether the "assignments" are voluntary or involuntary, the results will usually be of little value unless the researcher is interested and completely immersed in the subject, which is Chambers's second point. The process of reflective thinking, to be discussed shortly, will be more effective when the choice of topic is the result of your own initiative, since the decision undoubtedly will be one of the most important to be made in your educational career, and thus should be predicated on something in which you are intensely interested.

Chambers's third point, referring to advisers who serve as "intellectual nursemaids," is both amusing and tragic. The implication is that students will merely put the "flesh" on "skeletons" constructed by their advisers. An adviser can no more do your reflective thinking than take your examinations. Advisers should direct their attention to questionable patterns of thinking and organization of items of various kinds. Suggestions by advisers should be practical, relevant, and within the framework of the research proposal. Their comments should be viewed as suggestions, not mandates, with full responsibility for accepting or rejecting them resting with you, upon whom the onus eventually falls for defending your research.

Fortunately, many students give considerable thought to potential topics prior to enrollment in a graduate program. Others depend on expediency, mandate, suggestions from an adviser, or some extrinsic factor in choosing a research topic. Such ambivalence can hardly result in anything more than inferior productivity. You should choose a topic for investigation in which you have an interest, one you can claim as "your own." It is inconceivable that one would want to become involved in research in which one is neither totally engrossed nor in general agreement philosophically. Administrators generally recognize that personnel perform tasks more efficiently in areas in which they are competent and interested. In the interest of educational efficiency, good administrative practice dictates that such predilections be honored whenever possible through appropriate assignments. Why should involvement in research operate under different procedures? As if in reply, Kelley notes that the conduct of worthwhile research is not easy, and he deplores those who dismiss its importance too lightly.[50] Because the selection of an appropriate topic is so significant, it will be treated more comprehensively in chapter 2.

Chambers's fourth point relates to defining a problem clearly. It has been gratifying to the authors of this text to observe that the quality of research in music and the arts has been rising over the years. This is hardly to proclaim that research in the arts is without fault. Akin to that of education in general, some studies in music education and the arts have been open to question. Some of the criticism is justified. Actually, there are innumerable problems in education and the arts significant enough to be solved. Might it not be more useful to concentrate on those that are of immediate concern and have practical value for the busy educator? When realistic solutions for those have been found, then some attention may be given to other topics of less import to educators. Realistically, it must be admitted that some of the most critical problems in education do not lend themselves to easy and quick solutions. The time schedule of a researcher and possible financial subsidization both are frequently limiting factors. Times change, of course, so some solutions may neither be found nor needed for certain complexities. You might ask, why engage in research if it will not be beneficial or the results will be inconclusive? Significant research rarely results when answers to problems are obtained in haste.

A review of literature is the fifth concern of Chambers. Even a cursory review of the studies published for the last several years in the *Journal of Research in Music Education (JRME)* would reveal a large number that involve behavioral approaches to music education problems. The preponderance of behavioral studies is substantiated by Jones and McFee.[51] Yarbrough came to the same conclusion in her content analysis of articles published in 2002 for the *JRME* for a fifty-year period. She found that descriptive and experimental (including behavioral) studies, in that order, comprised over 76 percent, historical and philosophical 16 percent, and qualitative and other for 8 percent. It is possible that editorial policy may have resulted in the high percentage for experimental and descriptive research. Or, those involved with other types of research simply did not write articles for the *JRME*.[52]

Methods and techniques constitute Chambers's sixth category. The experimental approach has been used largely because it is believed that the most valid data can be obtained by using the behavioral method for problem solving. This is almost like saying, "Now I have a working knowledge of the behavioral approach so I must find a research topic to fit this methodology." Or, could it be that this is an attempt to overcome the inferiority complex musicians sometimes have had for so long because their colleagues in the behavioral and pure sciences have dismissed their efforts in music-education as supercilious at best? One axiom that any fledgling researcher needs to keep in mind is this: *Selection of the topic should come first; the methodology to deal with that problem should come next.*

Should an experimental or quasi-experimental approach be used where quantification of data will be by statistical concepts, or should a more qualitative methodology be used employing aesthetic, philosophical, or historical techniques? These latter approaches usually would involve visits to repositories of knowledge, Chambers's last point. Now it is true that the results of behavioral or experimental research usually do result in data that are very objective, but they sometimes can be rather artificial and arbitrary. Many answers unquestionably can best be obtained with experimental techniques; however, answers to some questions can better be received using other methodologies. The careful structuring of research projects in music education and the arts, regardless of the methodology used, should be accompanied by a subsequent meticulous implementation of the research plan to bring about valid and objective results that, when interpreted and disseminated, will be meaningful and practical to both researcher and research consumer.

THE SCIENTIFIC METHOD

In order for research to be judged solid, it must consist of at least three steps: (1) logical organization, (2) objective implementation, and (3) precise interpretation. Logical organization involves a thought process that enables one to develop an effective research proposal, design, or prospectus, which normally begets a thesis, dissertation, or grant proposal. Once the proposal is developed and approved, the actual implementation of the research plan can proceed. This involves objective procedures identified in the proposal to collect and correctly interpret the data obtained. This may involve some narrative presentation, with or without examples, statistical evaluation, or computer printout of data. It is always possible that some of these steps—organization, implementation, and interpretation—may not be accurate as initially set up. Even a well-organized proposal may not be implemented effectively, resulting in questionable data. Both organization and execution must be of the highest order. There are instances where both the organization and implementation are of the highest order, but the interpretation leaves music to be desired.

It seems almost redundant to mention that the investigator is crucial to the success of all research. The researcher must be both inquisitive and critical as well as be able to ascertain what research approach is feasible. As Barzun and Graff succinctly put it, the scientific method enables a researcher not only to identify a problem but also to identify the objective of the research.[53]

To the musician, largely trained in nonverbal left brain, right hemisphere skills, the concept of undertaking research may seem extraneous, based on training and musical development. Musicians often have been accused of failure to follow the logic of a researcher and consequently have neglected to take advantage of research that can provide practical answers to some of their problems. In addition, musicians often have not been trained to think logically and be able to apply the tenets of the scientific method. The scientific method is paramount to the thought process of the physicist, mathematician, empirical researcher, and others whose training has been in the physical or social sciences. Leedy states that the goal of the researcher is reached when the problem is identified using the scientific method and data are collected to resolve the problem.[54]

Precepts of the scientific method, which is a way of thinking, were initiated and originally utilized by researchers in the natural sciences, principles that now have been applied to research in almost all disciplines. Unfortunately, music educators frequently have believed that the scientific method should be incorporated only with certain types of research. This misconception evidently has been due to a misunderstanding of what the scientific method connotes. (Each of the methodologies discussed in this book needs to incorporate concepts of the scientific method. Of course, some modifications may be necessary.)

There is no mystery about the scientific method. It is rarely a situation where one is closeted in a laboratory, shutting out the outside world to conduct some top-secret experiment. With "tongue-in-cheek," musicians should be used to the "closet" because many hours will have been spent by most of them in small practice rooms blowing, pressing, bowing, or using whatever technique is necessary to produce sounds. This type of seclusion is neither the method of science nor of the scientific method. "Scientific method" is the concepts and procedures of science developed by Francis Bacon (1561–1626) and others in the seventeenth century and later, which have been adopted by other disciplines. The scientific method emphasizes strict controls within the particular discipline. Both the music philosopher who examines and evaluates ideas and the behavioral music researcher who compares variables in an experimental or quasi-experimental situation can use the concepts of the scientific method.

Stated in its simplest terms, the definition of the scientific methods used in this text is *an investigation that is logically organized, objectively implemented, and precisely interpreted.* Almack clearly defined the scientific method as the precise search for knowledge.[55] A more complex definition, one more acceptable to behavioral scientists, is given by Kerlinger, who says that scientific research is a very carefully organized and critical investigation of the hypothetical relationship among various factors under review.[56]

According to Mason and Bramble, the scientific method entails a series of procedures that are independent and extend over one another to systematically obtain knowledge. To put it another way, it is a thought process for doing research.[57] Munro defines the scientific method as a genetic approach to psychology, as distinct from an explanation of a work of art in psychological terms, which might not be adequate because the identity, form, or potential value of the work cannot be understood clearly and appreciated. He believes a careful thought process—application of the scientific method—can enable a person not only to understand the creative and appreciative process, but also to determine how aesthetic productions are either good or bad.[58]

Best and Kahn write that the terms "research" and "scientific method" are considered to be synonymous by some educators. They identify the scientific method as consisting of problem identification, hypothesis formulation, observation, analysis, and conclusion.[59] Although the foregoing definitions are somewhat different, they all have in common the idea that some type of careful thought process is necessary to carry out the research, regardless of the techniques used.

It is noteworthy that all the cited references place emphasis on the scientific method as *an objective thought process*. The onus is upon you, the researcher, to organize your study so that objectivity will be the foremost and ultimate goal. Objectivity for philosophical research obviously will not be the same as it will be for an experimental study, but it is still possible to obtain a certain degree of objectivity in philosophical research. The scientist's basis for objectivity originally stemmed from certain assumptions regarding natural phenomena. The philosopher, as well as the natural scientist, might regard these "natural phenomena" as "commonsense" assumptions. The German word *Wissenschaft*, which literally means knowledge and science, is a good illustration of this application of the scientific method. A train, bus, or airline schedule (or timetable) contains the "science" facet of *Wissenschaft* because the information is organized and verifiable in the structural method of science. Knowledge, however, does not occur until it is verified that the means of transportation just referred to did indeed depart or arrive on schedule. Unless this is done, one cannot have "knowledge" and can only assume these modes of transportation will be punctual. To give another oversimplified example, the scientist and the philosopher assume that the sun will rise and set at certain specified times on any given day in the future because of past experiences. They cannot prove, moreover, that these phenomena will take place in the future. An assumption can be made only because these phenomena have happened in the past. In designing and developing a machine, manufacturers normally do not demonstrate beforehand that every machine of that type will respond in the same way if certain conditions relative to its operation are met. They can only assume such will occur in view of previous experiences with this machine under comparable testing conditions. Such assumptions are accepted as true without the necessary validation, say Graziano and Raulin.[60]

Even the music educator who finds the realm of science to be an anathema should have no difficulty in applying the scientific method. Many researchers in music actually have been using some of these concepts, perhaps without realizing they are based on the "scientific method." Science and philosophy are compatible in regard to the premises on which knowledge is based, even though their respective techniques for obtaining data are different. Unfortunately, the philosophical aspect of the scientific method has not been used as widely in music education as it should be. Note these illustrations. How many students who write exercises in conventional Rameauan four-part harmony really understand the philosophical and acoustical reasoning behind the axiom prohibiting parallel fifths? Students may write exercises that are technically perfect, but do they understand why they sound so good? Do bassoonists who are trying to produce a "resonant" tone understand the scientific ramifications of timbre? Their teachers may give them certain practical suggestions for reed adjustment or for embouchure development that could result in significant improvement in tone quality, but still may be unable to analyze why this transformation takes place. Some music educators will argue that the development of practical skills should come first. Then, if time and inclination are present, philosophical and theoretical concepts may be introduced.

In the natural and physical sciences, where reflective thinking and an "intellectual" approach normally are an adjunct to instruction, the scientific method is not foreign to most graduate students who initiate a research project. Observing the desirable fusion of skills and theory, Good states that philosophy minus science is handicapped, and science is empty without philosophy.[61] Since computers, even at the elementary school level, are common, is it unreasonable to anticipate that the logical and creative skills of current and future graduate students should be at a higher level than was true twenty or thirty years ago?

Music is a skill; consequently, graduate students in music who have spent endless hours in practice rooms may be intellectually handicapped. Yet if research is to be successful, some intellectual activity is necessary. This intellectual process often is referred to as "critical" or "reflective" thinking. *Metempirical* is a philosophical term that refers to obtaining information solely through reasoning, whereas observation and measurement characterize the *empirical* method. Take the example of a hypothesis, one of the benchmarks of experimental research. A hypothesis just does not suddenly appear; it is formulated for testing as a result of reflective or critical thinking. Otherwise the rationale for the hypothesis may not be feasible. Yes, the behaviorist also uses reflective or critical thinking.

As already observed, logical thinking is necessary if one is to develop, implement, and report the results of research. Logic is not a popular subject in most schools and the subject usually is reserved for those who plan a career as a philosopher, mathematician, computer technologist, or religious leader. Why should musicians be exempt from using logic? You will recall that a good research project depends on the logical development of a problem that can then be effectively implemented and reported in an objective manner. Writing a few years ago, Searles lists four reasons, still relevant today, for using logic to develop a research project: (1) it enables one to understand the deductive and inductive processes of logical inference; (2) logic makes it easier to differentiate between emotional appeal and rational conviction; (3) it assists a researcher to critically appraise assumptions and presuppositions that serve as bases for arguments; and (4) logic enables one to focus on the ambiguity of words, thus resulting in more effective use of linguistic symbols.[62]

REFLECTIVE THINKING

To repeat, it is necessary to use reflective thinking to formulate a problem into a pliable, workable format. This initial phase of research unquestionably is one of the most important, yet it frequently is treated perfunctorily.

Concepts of reflective thinking may be traced as far back as the deductive method used by Aristotle (384–322 B.C.) and other Greek thinkers. *Deduction* is reasoning from general to specific (or particular). This concept of reasoning marked one of humanity's earliest attempts to think through problems. As an oversimplified example of deduction, note the choral director who hears some unusual sounds coming from the group and tries to determine what causes them. It turns out that the altos were singing E♭, not E; the tenors forgot to sing F♯, and the accompanist was one measure off from the group. Deductively, the choral director in this absurd example has observed several problems and has been able to correct them by identifying specific weaknesses. In the research proposal, to be discussed in the next chapter, the process of delineating a general problem statement and then formulating specific, or subproblems, is analogous to deductive reasoning.

Syllogism is another example of this Greek concept of deductive problem solving. In categorical or formal syllogism, the most common form of syllogism, the formula for an argument consists of three propositions. The first two, known as major and minor premises, are assumed to be true and lead to the third proposition, known as the conclusion. No attempt is made to prove or disprove the major and minor assumptions. It is important to remember that the major and minor premises must be accepted as true without question; otherwise the conclusion cannot be valid. An example of categorical or formal syllogism follows:

Major premise: All musicians are talented.
Minor premise: Conductors are musicians.
Conclusion: Conductors are talented.

In examining the logic of this syllogism, one assumes that the musicians concerned are talented or they would not be musicians and that the conductors could not conduct unless they had musical training and were musicians. The conclusion, then, is obvious. Characteristic of any syllogism is the identification of three factors, each of which is repeated twice. In the foregoing example, "musicians," "talented," and "conductors" each appear two times. Because of the acceptance of faulty assumptions, some syllogisms do not result in valid conclusions. Consider this example:

Major premise: A trombone is a brass instrument.
Minor premise: A brass instrument has valves.
Conclusion: A trombone has valves.

The major premise is true; the minor premise only partly true. Most brass instruments contain either piston or rotary valves; however, the trombone (with the exception of the largely obsolete valve trombone) does not. The conclusion, therefore, is not tenable.

There are many classic anecdotes about those who dared to use logic different from the deductive method as late as the seventeenth century, and who were reprimanded severely. Observe the announcement by Galileo (1564–1642) that while searching the heavens with his new telescope he had discovered four moons revolving around the planet Jupiter. This announcement was received skeptically by many of his peers. One fellow professor even stated that since Aristotle had not mentioned these moons before, they could not possibly exist. Others declared that since the moons were not visible to the naked eye, they did not exist at all. Such was the stranglehold the Greek system of Aristotelian logic had on scholarship up to the seventeenth century, the time of Francis Bacon (1561–1626), who disagreed with the prevailing concept of blindly accepting deductive theories simply because they had been passed on as truth by "authorities."

This uncertainty about the truth of a generalization led Bacon to develop the type of thinking known as *induction*, or reasoning from the specific to the general. It was assumed that because of reasoning based on specific items, generalizations could then be made about similar or related, but unobserved, facts or events. This kind of reasoning is used occasionally by music teachers. Look at this simplistic example. In rehearsal a band director may conclude that the group will perform badly after observing several specific deficiencies *before* the group starts to play. First, it is evident that the oboists do not have their reeds completely inserted in the casing, which will result in intonation that is consistently flat. Some of the French horns appear to be using an E♭ slide even though the music is written for F horns. The percussion section may have the wrong music in front of them. These examples, like the deductive one, are preposterous, but illustrate that the band director has observed several deficiencies and as a result inductively has generalized that unsatisfactory sounds will result if the musicians performed under the conditions just described, even though the band has yet to play one note of music. Researchers involved with formulating a research proposal may have in mind specific components to be researched, but they then must inductively derive the general statement, the *gestalt*.

More recently researchers have been using a combination of the two concepts, commonly referred to as the "deductive-inductive" process, also known by the term "general-to specific-to general." Charles Darwin (1809–1882) is generally recognized as the first person to successfully combine the idea of Aristotelian deduction with Baconian induction. According to Best and Kahn, Darwin, in stating his theory of the origin of the species, formulated through the deductive-inductive approach a process that now serves as the basis of the scientific method.[63] A simple illustration will suffice. After hearing a beginning string class perform badly, the string teacher analyzes the performance of these students, inductively observing deficiencies and correcting them. Finally, as a result of an inductive analysis of each student's performance, the teacher can deduce what will result if changes are not effected. Ary, Jacobs, and Razavieh indicate that Darwin's approach to the deductive-inductive process is in accord with the scientific method, the most appropriate one for procuring valid information.[64] Application of the deductive-inductive concept should make it easier for an investigator to formulate a research idea and then implement it. The deductive-inductive process of logic should make it relatively easy to organize a research study reflectively.

The basis for reflective thinking and the scientific method, according to Gall, Gall, and Borg, clearly adheres to the five steps for problem solving originally proposed by John Dewey (1859–1952).[65] Researchers in many fields of education still hold this distinguished educational philosopher in high regard. Dewey's five steps, as paraphrased, include (1) recognition of need, (2) isolation of the problem, (3) postulation of a solution, (4) accumulation and codification of data, and (5) confirmation and experimental substantiation of hypotheses.[66] To Dewey's original five, other educational philosophers, such as Kelley, have added another: appraisal of the solution in light of future needs.[67] Not only do these six precepts form the basis for the delineation of a problem, but also they may be employed for the implementation of the research. These six steps, then, form the basis for the *formulation, implementation,* and *promulgation* of a research idea. To put it another way, they constitute a "method" for research in a general sense.

The following question is often asked: If the hypotheses are rejected in research using directional hypotheses, does this mean the research is invalid? The answer is probably not. One can learn from a situation such as this. It may mean the level of significance was too restricted for comparison of the variables used in the research. Conversely, negative information often can point out weaknesses in logic or method. Tuckman states that if one is looking for a relationship between some variables and none is found, the weakness may be in the methodology employed rather than in what is hypothesized.[68]

The scientific method and reflective or critical thinking should not alarm a researcher in music education; rather, these concepts need to be understood and used. Today, when so much emphasis is placed on technology, the sciences, and other disciplines, one can ill afford to proceed with a project that is not *logically organized, objectively implemented,* and *precisely interpreted.* A researcher usually will need considerable assistance and guidance to realize these objectives, especially if his or her undergraduate training has emphasized "skills" at the expense of a "systematic" and "intellectual" approach to learning. A college or university that does not provide intelligent and perceptive leadership to graduate students in research is derelict in its duty to train today's and tomorrow's leaders in music education and the arts. This does not imply, of course, that students who comply with certain academic requirements automatically will receive their degrees. The determining factor simply should be whether or not you will be able to produce a piece of research that at least meets minimum standards prescribed by the institution granting your degree. You are entitled to competent advice and guidance to reach your goal.

Formulating a problem is the most important initial step in research. It was highlighted earlier in this chapter by stating that a research problem based on reflective or critical thinking is much easier to bring to a satisfactory resolution than one that is not. The most profound as well as the least significant problems may prove to be disconcerting to music educators, but if ways are found to resolve these dilemmas, their teaching could be more effective. The realization that many problems still remain for a researcher in music education has both positive and negative aspects. Most impelling, perhaps, is the negative connotation, because it suggests that conditions, however they may be defined, could be better for all concerned if solutions were forthcoming. On the positive side, graduate students may become duly apprehensive lest someone preempt their topic and complete their research first. So they apply themselves in an overly diligent manner. Such zealous misgivings usually are needless because, as most completed research bears out, the same problem can be approached differently by other researchers. In addition, when one problem seems to be solved, others turn up that were not apparent earlier.

Even though research activity in music and the arts seems to be quite high, and although solutions to many previously disturbing problems have been found by an ever-increasing number of investigators, there are inconsistencies wherein the results obtained either have been inconclusive or unconvincing. Perhaps it is one of the ironies of research that indecisive answers frequently arise when a researcher fails to give enough thought to the organization of the problem. In the desire to begin collecting data as soon as possible, researchers may begin the actual search process before comprehending the significance of the research. An unorganized accumulation of data can be the result of this kind of impulsive action. More than one adviser has had to remand students to the reflective or critical stage because they had begun to obtain disparate data with no other reason than it was interesting to do so. Research data by themselves are virtually worthless unless there is a rationale for interpreting and using them. Commenting on the importance of circumspect attention to the problem, Hopkins and Antes report that studying educational problems using the scientific method not only can solve problems but also create new knowledge.[69]

Involvement in research can be a most absorbing and gratifying experience, especially if an understanding and application of concepts of reflective or critical thinking as embodied in the scientific method are uppermost in the mind of the researcher. Since the setting for research actually begins with a problem that may need to be clarified or refined before it can be solved, a discussion of this initial phase of research will be deferred until the next chapter, because it is of such importance to warrant a separate in depth treatment.

INITIAL CONSIDERATIONS IN THE
SELECTION OF APPROPRIATE LITERATURE

It is incumbent on you to familiarize yourself with the literature of your field. Advisers sometimes are distressed when students come to them for advice on a red-hot idea before they have examined the literature to determine whether the proposed study is feasible. A preliminary search could eliminate many projected topics, leaving you free to devote your energies, and those of your adviser, to topics within the realm of possibility. It is inconceivable that two individuals may be proceeding with the same topic unbeknownst to one another. Although the likelihood of this is slim because of the many online literature sources available today, Good and Scates give an account of two music-education research studies conducted on the same national organization, although they were not completed at the same time. The studies were completed in different sections of the United States even though the institutions were only three hundred miles apart. The initial research was completed five years before the second. The study could easily have been located if the second investigator had perused *Doctoral Dissertations Accepted by American Universities.*[70] Consulting online sources such as *Dissertation Abstracts International (DAI)* and *Comprehensive Dissertation Index (CDI)* should make it easier for you to avoid duplication of topics. The question may be raised, why is it necessary to avoid duplication of topics? It is considered to be a violation of research ethics to deliberately duplicate a research study that already has been completed unless it is a replication study, usually characteristic of the medical and physical sciences.

After your topic has been tentatively approved by your adviser, it is necessary to carefully consider and make a projection of the methods, techniques, equipment, and instruments (if any) used to bring the research to a successful completion. This might involve the use of aesthetic or philosophical inquiry techniques, questionnaires, or certain standardized tests or instruments of your own devising, or special equipment such as computers, synthesizers, or other devices. Need for these items will be determined partially by the methods or procedures chosen. A researcher using qualitative methods might use interviews (in person or via the Internet), case studies, or even philosophical tenets. A true experimental study might not use a questionnaire; a quasi-experimental project, however, could use this instrument.

Research that has a historical, philosophical, or even a qualitative bent usually would call for information obtained from various repositories (libraries, museums, archives, historical societies, private collections, etc.). Since historical procedures will be treated in detail in chapter 7, mention will be made here only in passing. You need to know where specific sources are located. If visits are involved, plan them according to such considerations as financial resources, time available, and hours the repositories are open. Usually it is next to impossible to conduct systematic and exhaustive historical research without this kind of planning. Field studies, such as visits to schools, colleges, and universities, often are mandatory in descriptive research when comparisons are made between curricular offerings or programs of music education, or any other subject. To determine why string programs may be successful in one school system and not in another can hardly be done by means of a questionnaire only. Questionnaires, interviews, observations, and personal visits probably will be needed to garner enough data to make valid statements when comparing schools or school systems. With the increasing use of computers, a golden opportunity exists for a researcher to interface with interviewees in a quantitative research setting.

FORMULATING A RESEARCH PROBLEM

When you have a general subject in mind, it is necessary to proceed through several steps before you reach a point at which your research is well defined as practical and capable of implementation. Writers of research textbooks offer excellent suggestions relating to the formulation of a research problem. Wiersma avers that good research is not possible without asking the right questions.[71] Almack suggests including what already is known and what needs to be learned, consistencies that are evident, and suggestions for implementation received from various sources.[72] Leedy suggests that it is imperative that you "formulate a problem that is carefully phrased and represents the single goal of the research effort."[73]

Certain questions must be asked about the problem you have under consideration. The answers will go a long way toward determining whether to proceed with the plan, modify it, or discard it entirely.

By posing and answering general questions, it is possible to proceed to more specific items in an attempt to delineate a problem even more clearly. For purposes of illustration, begin with a hypothetical topic such as a history of music in the United States. At first glance, the topic may appear to be a good one for a graduate student, especially at the doctoral level. Before proceeding it would be necessary to consider such questions as the following: Will this research cover all phases of instrumental, vocal, opera, symphony, chamber music, music education, etc.? Will it be concerned with performance, teaching, or both? What years will serve as limits of the study? What kinds of information will be sought? Where may the desired information best be obtained? How will the phrase "music in the United States" be interpreted? Will the research involve only native-born Americans? Will it include the role of music publishers? Will the compositions mentioned be analyzed or identified without comment? Will the research include artists and performing groups from other countries who have performed in the United States? Will I collect and catalog manuscripts (MSS) or facsimile copies of works by American composers? What attention will be given to reviews of performances presented by artists in various cities? How can gaps still remaining in American music history best be determined?

Almost immediately it should be apparent that "a history of music in the United States" is a subject that consists of many components, each of which might be a topic worthy of investigation. Delimitation, or focusing on a workable topic, is of extreme importance for research to be successful and cannot be overemphasized. While there certainly are enough research topics to go around, graduate students sometimes become unduly apprehensive that all topics in which they are interested soon will be fully explored, as was mentioned earlier in this chapter.

The following fourteen steps are suggestive of those you might keep in mind as you focus your attention on the hypothetical research problem on American music just noted. The feasibility of any research proposal may be determined only after similar procedures have been followed. In other instances the impracticability of an idea as originally conceived will be apparent quite early as projected procedures become apparent. If you decide to proceed with your original topic, it may be necessary to repeat the same procedure until a satisfactory proposal has been developed. This process of continually returning to the beginning and repeating steps until satisfaction results is reminiscent of the looping technique used in certain phases of programming for the digital computer, where the program is repeated in successive steps until the desired information is received.

The fourteen steps in the actual formulation and implementation of a problem are to (1) determine a concern for which answers are not obvious; (2) ascertain whether or not the idea contains more than one basic problem; (3) delimit the subject to a topic that may be solved according to your background and training; (4) develop basic assumptions and/or hypotheses; (5) locate existing information relating to your topic; (6) ascertain what instruments, tools, or equipment will be needed and whether such items are readily available or may need to be devised expeditiously; (7) postulate tentative conclusions; (8) implement the plan and accumulate preliminary data; (9) reconstitute and revise the research plan in view of inaccuracies apparent as a result of the preceding steps; (10) accumulate and assimilate additional data; (11) interpret the data; (12) draw up conclusions, recommendations, and suggestions for additional research; (13) obtain an evaluation of the research from peers and associates; and (14) disseminate the results to the public.

In regard to the first point, *a concern for answers that are not obvious*, developing questions may seem to be redundant, but it is only through this kind of intellectual inquiry that it actually can be determined whether there is a solid basis for the proposed research. Answers to questions frequently are available from many sources, although you may not be aware of them. The need for a detailed study of a research concern may not be as critical as originally believed. If an instrumental music teacher would like to obtain background material on Hector Berlioz (1803–1869) to serve as motivation for introducing a high school orchestra to the composer's *King Lear Overture*, the teacher would hardly need to go beyond Jullien's biography of Berlioz, or Boult's *Berlioz's Life as Written by Himself in His Letters and Memoirs*. The attempt to locate some new or little-known facts of the composer's life, although it could be interesting, would hardly be worth the time and effort necessary to prepare for this orchestral rehearsal and might even be fruitless. If one's concern is with a specific aspect of Berlioz's life, then the research, although time-consuming, might result in a noteworthy contribution, such as Barzun's publication of some previously unknown Berlioz letters.[74]

After addressing the second point, *whether the idea contains more than one problem,* one might decide that an initial idea can be subdivided into several problems, each of which might constitute a topic in itself. "A history of music in the United States" obviously needs to be divided into several separate studies, or subproblems, before it is feasible to pursue. It has already been noted that it is very difficult to apply the techniques of solid research to proposals that are too broad in scope. Such an undertaking disperses one's energies in several directions. Figure 1.1 illustrates this process of delimitation.

Third, to *delimit the topic to your background and training* can be accomplished as a result of several delimitations. Using a title from figure 1.1, "The Development of Municipal Professional Symphony Orchestras in the State of Florida from Earliest Times up to 2000," is a subject for research that a student with appropriate background, training, and motivation could undertake. The focus of the title on municipal orchestras helps to confine the research to certain objectives and also enables a researcher to proceed with the research once the modus operandi has been established. The term "professional," as used in this illustration, might be defined differently for Florida than it would be for New York City, but the research could be just as valid in either instance, if the study were properly constituted and implemented.

After tentatively determining the feasibility of the topic and *developing basic assumptions and/or hypotheses,* the fourth step, consider whether *basic assumptions and/or hypotheses* are needed. (These terms will be clarified in greater detail in later chapters.) Furthermore, assumptions and hypotheses could serve as the core of a study.

The fifth of the fourteen steps, *knowledge of relevant information,* is a most important step. After various sources, both published and unpublished, have been examined, and it has been determined that the proposed research has been adequately investigated, either recast the problem or abandon it altogether. A paucity of information might suggest nascent topics for research, on the other hand, inadequate information may indicate the research is not worth doing. A wealth of data may enable one to concentrate on a specialized facet of a problem. Methodology will be governed to some extent by the kinds of data sought. An experimental project, which would have as its end result formulating and drawing conclusions to controlled ob-

Title	Delimitation
A History of Music in the United States	Title is too broad
A History of Instrumental Music in the United States	Delimited to instrumental music
A History of Instrumental Music in the Southern United States	Further delimited to one section of the United States
A History of Instrumental Music in the Southern United States from Earliest Times up to 1965	Additional chronological delimitation
The Development of Municipal Symphony Orchestras in the Southern United States from Earliest Times up to 1965	Slight change of title and further delimitation to specific form of instrumental ensemble
The Development of Municipal Professional Symphony Orchestras in the State of Florida from Earliest Times up to 1965	Delimitation to exclude amateur groups and to identify a specific state of the United States; title finally selected

Figure 1.1.   Delimitation of a Research Problem

servations, would necessitate the quest for a different kind of data than would a historical study, which likely would rely heavily on original documents or manuscripts found in archives. In either case, the data sought must be pertinent to the topic at hand.

Experimental, quasi-experimental, and descriptive research, in particular, usually make use of *tests, statistics, special equipment, interviews, or questionnaires.* In this sixth step, it may be necessary to devise and validate tests or to develop special equipment with the specific purposes of the research in mind; in others, standard validated tests or other instruments may be used. Almost without exception, investigators devise questionnaires to fit the needs of a particular study that is usually descriptive or qualitative. Unlike a validated test, a questionnaire rarely can be used by more than one researcher unless another researcher is investigating the same problem under comparable conditions. Standardized tests may be used to supplement those you have devised. Existing tests may be adapted—with permission, of course—for purposes of your research, or revise your methodology to use those tests in print.

The seventh step, *postulating of tentative conclusions,* enables one to anticipate the outcomes of the research. To paraphrase an old cliché, "if you do not know what you are looking for, how will you know when you find it?" Tentative conclusions essentially are postulated from hypotheses initially formulated.

In the eighth step, it is through the *implementation of the plan and accumulation of preliminary data* that the hypotheses testing can begin. You are then in a position to know whether and to what extent the research plan needs to be revised. If *revisions are necessary,* the ninth step, it is imperative to *accumulate and assimilate additional data,* the tenth step.

Mere accumulation of data, however, is not enough. The eleventh step calls for these data to be *interpreted in light of objectives of the study.* It may be of little practical value, for example, to find out that there are two hundred school-owned oboes in the public schools of a certain state. More important is determining whether or not these instruments are in good playing condition, how many of them are being used and by whom, and the proficiency level of the students playing them. It may be necessary to accumulate additional data to make logical and valid interpretations.

The significant twelfth step, *conclusions, recommendations, and suggestions for further study,* usually consists of grouping these data together in the final chapter of a research report. Final conclusions, although they may be similar to tentative conclusions identified earlier, are deduced after the data have been accumulated and interpreted. Recommendations and suggestions for additional research then follow in normal sequence after the conclusions have been drawn. Recommendations usually include topics that, as you reflect on the project, might either have been approached differently or pursued in greater depth. On the basis of these, suggestions are offered for the benefit of future researchers. The final chapter of a research report is vital to someone searching for a research idea, for it is here that suggestions for future research are proffered.

An evaluation of the research by peers and associates, the next to the last of the fourteen steps, can be most helpful to avoid redundancies that sometimes crop up in the creative efforts of researchers. You should welcome the opportunity to have an outside observer examine your completed project objectively and impartially. It is here that the outside members of a final oral commission can be helpful because they view the study from that of outside observers. Because of a natural preoccupation with one's research, it sometimes is difficult to be unbiased.

As a final point, a weakness common in music education has been the *dissemination of research results to the public.* Most doctoral dissertations contain an abstract of the study that is included in *Dissertation Abstracts International (DAI)*[75] or some other database, but only a small percentage of the musical public who might be able to use the results has access to them. *Master's Abstracts* also contain short excerpts of research completed by master's degree recipients. Most libraries have online access to *DAI* so this should make an investigator's search much easier. *The Journal of Research in Music Education (JRME)*, edited most recently by Cornelia Yarbrough, also is available online.

Research reported in *DAI*, as the name implies, consists of an abstract of 300–350 words. A companion to *DAI* is *Comprehensive Dissertation Index (CDI)*. Those appearing in the *Journal of Research in Music Education (JRME)* contain both an abstract and an article describing the research. Other publications featuring research in music education and music therapy include *Bulletin of Historical Research in Music Education, Journal of Music Therapy,* and *Journal of the International Association of Music for the Handicapped.* Most of these are online. Some state music educator associations also publish research journals, among them Colorado and Missouri.

THE LIBRARY AND OTHER RESOURCES

It hardly seems necessary to say that one of the most important repositories of information for a researcher is the library. Acquaint yourself with the general floor plan and holdings of the libraries you are planning to use. Most large libraries, as well as many smaller ones, now have their catalogs computerized so it is much easier and quicker to locate items instead of thumbing through the catalogs manually. Become familiar with the general and special collections, reference rooms, and facilities for the reproduction of items you are interested in for research purposes. Don't forget that members of the library staff stand ready to assist you.

Sources cataloged under the Library of Congress Classification include *L*, with subsets *LB*, *LC*, etc., for Education. *M* designates music scores, *ML* music literature, and *MT* music study and instruction. Fine arts sources are classified as *N*. Music entries in the Dewey Decimal System comprise the numbers *780* through *789*. Fine arts are classified beginning with *700*. In the Dewey Decimal System Education is spread among *100* Philosophy and Psychology and *300* Social Studies, to cite a few. Research with a historical bent in the Library of Congress Classification likely would be found under *C* History—Auxiliary Sciences and *D* History and Topography. Under the Dewey System *900* History, Geography, and Biography probably would be the proper place to look. If the author and/or title are known, most online services will show the call number and location of source (e.g., stacks, circulation, reserve desk). General collections include books, periodicals, government documents, and other publications, both recent and vintage.

Special collections consist of writings, diaries, programs, letters, MSS, and personal effects and artifacts of an individual or group. Here is an example. An investigator tracing the role of music in the life of Georgia-born poet-musician Sidney Lanier (1842–1881) might examine the Lanier holdings in the Lanier Room at Johns Hopkins University in Baltimore, Maryland. Since Lanier was incarcerated during the Civil War (also known as the War Between the States), records in the National Archives in Washington, D.C., might shed some light on Lanier's musical activities during the period 1860–1865. Uncataloged materials in special collections often are a lucrative source of data.

Reference rooms contain standard sources such as encyclopedias and dictionaries of all kinds. Finally, because some desired items have to be reproduced by some photographic process rather than copying them laboriously by hand, check out what technical processes are available, how much they cost, and how long it will take for duplication.

Listing of all resources to meet the needs of every graduate student is impossible and unnecessary. Print resources usually fall under one of two categories: print or literary (which include computerized printouts) and nonliterary. Under the former are items obtained from libraries, archives, and other repositories. Nonliterary sources include questionnaires, interviews (in person and via Internet), experiments, and observations, to name a few to be discussed in later chapters.

Potentially useful research sometimes remains unknown because the researchers either did not take time to write an interesting account of it or they believe that their responsibility to the academic world has been discharged once the research is completed. The final step in the research process for graduate students culminates in a degree; it deserves to be made more readily available to academia. Of course, there is *Dissertation Abstracts International (DAI)* and on a more restricted scale, *Master's Abstracts*; however, circulation of both is restricted to libraries.

You may ask, How about literary sources housed in other locations? Usually it is necessary to write, telephone, or send an e-mail to the archive, agency, or unit housing the desired materials. Before proceeding, however, you need to know if the items you are seeking are available for examination. Archives usually contain information necessary for graduate students and scholars' research. These usually involve a personal visit, as do private collections, which entail personal contacts with executors or family members. No rule holds for access to these sources, each must normally be worked out on an individual basis.

Any research depends to a certain degree on the utilization of bibliographic techniques. Some kinds of investigation require more extensive use of source materials than others. Historical research, aesthetic and philosophical inquiry, and qualitative research usually will rely more heavily on data from libraries and archives than will descriptive, quasi-experimental, and experimental research. It is in the library that a preliminary overview of the availability of desired information will enable one to determine the feasibility of a topic. It is the library, also, that houses many of the sources to be included in both the preliminary and final bibliographies. Yet it is paradoxical that graduate students embarking on the initial stages of thesis or dissertation writing often are unfamiliar with some of the most fundamental techniques of efficient library use.

THE INTERNET AND OTHER ELECTRONIC MEDIA

Due to the technology explosion, many sources needed are on the Internet. Although the Internet is an excellent way to obtain up-to-date information, McMillan and Schumacher state that many of the sources may not have been checked for accuracy or quality.[76]

The numerous data banks and guides do not obviate the necessity for one to do individual "hand searching." Most libraries, especially at large universities, as noted earlier, have computerized card catalogs. One at New York University, a private university, is called Bobcat. This system interfaces with other private and publicly supported universities in the metropolitan New York area. A state-supported system called Lincnet housed at North Carolina State University in Raleigh ties together the indexes in the sixteen campuses of the University of North Carolina system and other North Carolina colleges and universities. Also in North Carolina, NCLIVE, a statewide system, provides citizens of the state access to a "rich array of electronic information."

The Music Index Online is a subject-author guide to music periodical literature (1979–2002). *Music Index* also is available on CD-ROM (1979–2001). The *International Index to Music Periodicals (IIMP)*, full-text edition, covers more than 370 international music periodicals. *IIMP* also contains abstracts, but is available only to authorized users at subscribing institutions.

Most of the online computerized systems enable you to obtain, via computer printout, items housed in other libraries throughout the particular system to which you are connected. These online tools can save many minutes and hours of looking thus giving you more time to search for other items. Some databases provide abstracts in addition to bibliographic information. Among the databases useful for music and art students are *CDI (Comprehensive Dissertation Index)* from 1861 to date, with almost 700,000 citations from many disciplines, including music. *CDI* provides a subject, title, and author guide to doctoral dissertations accepted at universities in the United States and Canada, as well as some overseas. A companion is *DAI (Dissertation Abstracts International)*, which includes 300–350 word abstracts of dissertations accepted by institutions that subscribe to this computerized system. (*DAI* also is available in paper.) *DDM (Doctoral Dissertations in Musicology)* is another online source that may have some value to music education researchers. *RILM Ab-*

stracts (*Répertoire International de la Littérature Musicale*), from 1972 to date, contains about 23,000 entries. Covered in this catalog are historical musicology, ethnomusicology, instruments, voice, performance practice and notation, theory and analysis, music pedagogy, music liturgy, and interdisciplinary research on music and other fields related to music.

In an attempt to make music education research results more easily attainable and useful, *Update: The Application of Research in Music Education* is published online twice a year by the Music Educators National Conference. It is available to MENC members who use a password. The ERIC network contains reports of research in education abstracted from *RIE (Research in Education)*. These reports are abstracted from the sixteen clearinghouses scattered throughout universities in the United States. The clearinghouse for reading, English, and communications, for example, is housed at Indiana University in Bloomington.

Many professional journals and periodicals also are available online, for example, *Arts and Humanities Index, Black Music Journal, Computer Music Journal, The Journal of Women in Music, Psychology of Music,* and *Research Perspectives in Music Education.* Look also for e-books–full-text books on the Internet. One example is James W. Mann, *Aesthetics.*[77]

REFERENCE MATERIALS FOR MUSIC EDUCATION

Several sources already have been mentioned in the section on the Internet. Others that might be of value, especially for historical background, are *Yearbooks of the Music Educators National Conference (MENC,* and its predecessor the *Music Supervisors National Conference,* published annually from 1910 to 1940. These can be beneficial to researchers who want to review philosophical and curricular changes in music education. *Music Source Book [I],* published in 1947, *Music in American Education: Source Book Number Two,* 1955, and *Perspectives in Music Education: Source Book Three,* 1966, also can provide insights into music education practices during the periods listed.

One of the prime repositories for music education sources is the Music Education Historical Research Center and International Society for Music Education Archives, located at the Performing Arts Center Library on the campus of the University of Maryland in College Park.

A recent acquisition was archival documents from Karl J. Glenn, MENC president from 1990 to 1992. Also housed in this library is the American Bandmasters Collection.

Historical or aesthetic research may make it necessary to examine MSS, writings, and artifacts in libraries or archives, some of which are not open to the public. Suppose you were interested in reviewing compositions of New England composers Charles C. Perkins (1823–1886) or James C. D. Parker (1828–1916). A visit to the Harvard Musical Association in Boston would certainly be necessary if MSS and other items of Perkins and Parker were to be examined. For Moravian aficionados, the collections at Bethlehem, Pennsylvania, and Old Salem (Winston-Salem, N.C.) contain prime source material, both musical and literary.

Unlike public libraries, archives normally are open only by invitation. Researchers are granted the privilege to make visits for research purposes if they follow the protocol governing such matters: (1) ask permission to examine a certain collection or collections at a time convenient to the archivist, (2) state purpose and objective of the visit, and (3) obtain sponsorship from an institution of higher learning or recognized scholar in the field who is interested in your research. Authorities in the field and advisers usually can give practical advice relative to the repositories most likely to house the items you are seeking.

After your research topic has been delineated and approved, the next step in the research process is to develop and implement a research proposal (design or prospectus). These processes will be discussed in following chapters. You should be aware by now that the research plan is one of the most significant steps in the research process. It should not be taken too lightly; it even can be invigorating!

FOR REVIEW, DISCUSSION, AND IMPLEMENTATION

- Compare the definitions of the term "research." Which one is closest to your proposed research?
- Identify some of the most important sources for potential research projects.
- What is the meaning of these terms: pure research, applied research, qualitative research, quantitative research? List synonyms for each one, as appropriate.

- How can the "scientific method" and "reflective thinking" be of value to a researcher?
- Starting with a research idea, follow through with the fourteen steps listed above.
- Using a research idea you have in mind, search the Internet for specific information to determine the feasibility of what you would like to do.
- Although there are many valid electronic tools available to a researcher, why is it still necessary to use the library to obtain information for your research?

NOTES

1. Don Fabun, *The Dynamics of Change* (Englewood Cliffs, N.J.: Prentice-Hall, 1970), 5.

2. Robert C. Bogdan and Sara K. Biklen, *Qualitative Research for Education: An Introduction to Theory and Methods,* 3rd ed. (Boston: Allyn & Bacon, 1998), 51.

3. William Wiersma, *Research Methods in Education: An Introduction,* 7th ed. (Boston: Allyn & Bacon, 2000), 27.

4. Donald Ary, Lucy Cheser Jacobs, and Asghar Razavieh, *Introduction to Research in Education,* 5th ed. (Ft. Worth, Tex.: Harcourt Brace, 1996), 44.

5. Richard D. Altick and John J. Fenstermaker, *The Art of Literary Research,* 4th ed. (New York: Norton, 1993), 24.

6. Paul D. Leedy, *Practical Research Planning and Design,* 6th ed. (Upper Saddle River, N.J.: Merrill, 1997), 48–49. Written with Timothy J. Newby and Peggy A. Ermer.

7. Daniel J. Hittleman and Alan J. Simon, *Interpreting Educational Research: An Introduction for Consumers of Research,* 3rd ed. (Upper Saddle River, N.J.: Prentice-Hall, 2002), 2.

8. Bruce W. Tuckman, *Conducting Educational Research,* 5th ed. (Ft. Worth, Tex.: Harcourt Brace College, 1999), 4.

9. John W. Best and James V. Kahn, *Research in Education,* 9th ed. (Boston: Allyn and Bacon, 2003), 24.

10. James E. Mauch and Jack W. Birch, *Guide to Successful Thesis and Dissertation: A Handbook for Students and Faculty,* 3rd ed. (New York: Marcel Dekker, 1993), 65.

11. Anthony M. Graziano and Michael Raulin, *Research Methods: A Process of Inquiry,* 4th ed. (Boston: Allyn & Bacon, 2000), 1.

12. James H. McMillan and Sally Schumacher, *Research in Education: A Conceptual Introduction,* 5th ed. (New York: Longman, 2001), 9.

13. Thomas K. Crowl, *Fundamentals of Educational Research*, 2nd ed. (Madison, Wis.: Brown & Benchmark, 1996), 5.

14. Louis Cohen, Lawrence Manion, and Keith Morrison, *Research Methods in Education*, 5th ed. (London: Routledge Falmer, 2000), 73.

15. Clifford K. Madsen and Charles H. Madsen Jr., *Experimental Research in Music*, 3rd ed. (Raleigh, N.C.: Contemporary, 1997), 4.

16. Joyce P. Gall, M. D. Gall, and Walter R. Borg, *Applying Educational Research: A Practical Guide*, 4th ed. (New York: Longman, 1999), 469.

17. Arthur E. Clarke, "Jamaican Folk Psalms: Choral Settings of Selected Psalms Based on Jamaican Folk Melodies, Rhythms, and Harmonies, Suitable for Jamaican Students in Secondary Schools, Churches, and Music Festivals" (Ed.D. diss., New York University, 1988), UMI 8812527.

18. Leedy, 107.

19. Edward L. Rainbow and Hildegard C. Froehlich, *Research in Music Education: An Introduction to Systematic Inquiry*, 3rd ed. (New York: Schirmer, 1987), 56.

20. Richard M. Jaeger, ed., *Complementary Methods for Research in Education* (Washington, D.C.: American Educational Research Association, 1997), chap. 3.

21. Bogdan and Biklen, 23.

22. Bogdan and Biklen, 30.

23. *Master's Abstracts* have been published since 1951–1952. In the 2001 edition, Art and Music are listed beginning on p. 1070.

24. Nancy-Louise Howe, "Some Effects of Sequential Music Tasks on the Cognitive and Social Skills of Learning Disabled Adults," *Journal of the International Association of Music for the Handicapped*, Winter 1989, 3–14.

25. Beverly J. Jones and June K. McFee, "Research in the Arts and Aesthetics," in *Handbook of Research on Teaching*, 3rd ed. Ed. Merlin C. Witrock (New York: Macmillan, 1986), 911.

26. Jones and McFee, 912.

27. Paul L. Dressel, *College Teaching as a Profession: The Doctor of Arts Degree* (East Lansing: Michigan State University Press, 1982), 1.

28. Richard G. Hunan, "The Online Trombone Journal: A Case Study of Credibility, Accessibility, and Performance in Electronic Journal Publishing" (D.A. diss., Ball State University, 2001), DA 3002122.

29. James L. Fern Jr., "The Effectiveness of a Computer-Based Software Program of Teaching Jazz Improvisation" (D.M.A. diss., University of Southern California, 1995), DA 9617097.

30. Bryan W. DePoy, "An Annotated Bibliography of Original, Twentieth-Century Compositions for Trumpet and Concert Band Accompaniment" (Mus. Doc. diss., Florida State University, 1998), DA 9839761.

31. Kimberly Ann McCord, "Music Composition Using Music Technology for Elementary Children with Learning Disabilities: An Exploratory

Case Study," (D.M.E. diss., University of Northern Colorado, 1999), DA 9939767.

32. Susan W. Hines, "The Effects of Motoric and Non-Motoric Music Instruction on Reading and Mathematics Achievement of Learning Disabled Students in Kindergarten through Ninth Grade" (Ph.D. diss., University of North Carolina at Greensboro, 2000), DA 9974029.

33. Katherine Lois Hendry, "Burnout and Self-Reported Vocal Health among Music Teachers and Other Educators" (Ed.D. diss., Teachers College, Columbia University, 2001), DA 3014770.

34. Richard S. Repp, "The Internet, Auto Accompaniment Software, and Spectral Analysis in Undergraduate Voice Lessons" (Ph.D. diss., University of Illinois, 1994), DA 9953121.

35. Todd Silberman, "N. C. Could Get Virtual School," *News and Observer* (Raleigh, N.C.), January 9, 2002, IA.

36. Ronald C. Martella, Ronald Nelson, and Nancy E. Marchand-Martella, *Research Methods: Learning to Become a Critical Research Consumer* (Boston: Allyn & Bacon, 1999), 23.

37. John J. Dawson, "The Education Value of Vocal Music" (Ped.D. diss., New York University, 1895), UMI 7233518.

38. Elsie S. Hug, *Seventy-Five Years in Education: The Role of the School of Education, New York University, 1890–1965* (New York: New York University Press, 1965), 113.

39. Paul E. Koefod, *The Writing Requirements for Graduate Degrees* (Englewood Cliffs, N.J.: Prentice-Hall, 1964), 11.

40. John Grossman, "Gorillacillins," *Health Magazine,* September 1983, 34.

41. Herbert Mitgang, "Catalog Reflects Jefferson's World View," New York Times News Service, June 2, 1989.

42. See Bruce Catton, *The American Heritage Picture History of the Civil War* (New York: American Heritage/Bonanza Books, 1982), 203, 314–15; also see Jerry Korn, ed., *War on the Mississippi: Grant's Vicksburg Campaign* (Alexandria, Va.: Time-Life Books, 1985), 87.

43. Benny P. Ferguson, "The Bands of the Confederacy: An Examination of the Musical and Military Contributions of the Bands and Musicians of the Confederate States of America," (Ph.D. diss., North Texas State University, 1987), UMI 8723754.

44. Truman Lee Kelley, *Scientific Method* (New York: Macmillan, 1932), 1.

45. Gordon B. Davis and Clyde A. Parker, *Writing the Doctoral Dissertation: A Systematic Approach* (Woodbury, N.Y.: Barron's Educational Series, 1979), 41–43.

46. Tuckman, 28.

47. M. M. Chambers, "Selection, Definition, and Delimitation of a Doctoral Research Problem," *Phi Delta Kappan,* November 1960, 73.

48. Chambers, 73.

49. Koefod, 74.

50. Kelley, 4.

51. Jones and McFee, 911.

52. Cornelia Yarbrough, "The First 50 Years of the *Journal of Research in Music Education:* A Content Analysis," *Journal of Research in Music Education,* Winter 2002, 276–79.

53. Jacques Barzun and Henry F. Graff, *The Modern Researcher,* 5th ed. (Boston: Houghton Mifflin, 1992), 12–13.

54. Leedy, 94.

55. John C. Almack, *Research and Thesis Writing* (Boston: Houghton Mifflin, 1930), 57.

56. Fred M. Kerlinger, *Foundations of Behavioral Research,* 3rd ed. (Ft. Worth, Tex.: Holt, Rinehart, Winston, 1986), 10.

57. Emanuel J. Mason and William J. Bramble, *Research in Education and the Behavioral Sciences: Concepts and Methods* (Madison, Wis.: Brown & Benchmark, 1997), 32.

58. Thomas Munro, *Scientific Method in Aesthetics* (New York: Norton, 1928), 23.

59. Best and Kahn, 6.

60. Graziano and Raulin, 28.

61. Carter V. Good, *Essentials of Educational Research: Methodology and Design,* 2nd ed. (Englewood Cliffs, N.J.: Prentice-Hall, 1972), 25.

62. Herbert L. Searles, *Logic and Scientific Method,* 2nd ed. (New York: Ronald Press, 1956), 4–5.

63. Best and Kahn, 5.

64. Ary, Jacobs, Razavieh, 9.

65. Gall, Gall, and Borg, 64.

66. John Dewey, *How We Think* (Boston: Heath, 1933), 107.

67. Kelley, 24.

68. Tuckman, 75.

69. Charles D. Hopkins and Richard L. Antes, *Educational Research: A Structure for Inquiry,* 3rd ed. (Itasca, Ill.: Peacock, 1990), 21.

70. Carter V. Good and Douglas E. Scates, *Methods of Research* (New York: Appleton-Century-Crofts, 1934), 51.

71. Wiersma, 27.

72. Almack, 45.

73. Leedy, 46.

74. Jacques Barzun, *New Letters of Berlioz, 1830–1848* (New York: Columbia University Press, 1954).

75. Before 1952 *DAI* was known as *Microfilm Abstracts.*

76. McMillan and Schumacher, 148.

77. James W. Mann, *Aesthetics* (Armonk, N.Y.: Sharpe, 1998). An e-book.

SUPPLEMENTARY SOURCES

Altick, Richard D., and John J. Fenstermaker. *The Art of Literary Research*, chap. 2. 4th ed., New York: Norton, 1993.

Anderson, Gary. *Fundamentals of Educational Research*, chaps. 1, 3–4, 6. London: Falmer, 1990.

Ary, Donald, Lucy Cheser Jacobs, and Asgher Razavieh. *Introduction to Research in Education*, chaps. 1–3. 5th ed., Ft. Worth, Tex.: Harcourt Brace College, 1996.

Barzun, Jacques, and Henry F. Graff. *The Modern Researcher*, chap. 2. 5th ed. Boston: Houghton Mifflin, 1992.

Best, John W., and James V. Kahn. *Research in Education*, chaps. 1–2. 9th ed. Boston: Allyn & Bacon, 2003.

Bogdan, Robert, and Sara K. Biklen. *Qualitative Research in Education: An Introduction to Theory and Methods*, chaps. 1–2, 6–7. 3rd ed. Boston: Allyn & Bacon, 1998.

Carspecken, Phil F. *Critical Ethnology for Educational Research: A Theoretical and Practical Guide*, chaps. 1–2. New York: Routledge, 1996.

Cohen, Louis, Lawrence Manion, and Keith Morrison. *Research Methods in Education*, chaps. 1, 13. 5th ed. New York: Routledge Falmer, 2000.

Colwell, Richard, and Carol Richardson, eds. *The New Handbook of Research on Music Teaching and Learning*. New York: Oxford University Press, 2002.

Crowl, Thomas K. *Fundamentals of Educational Research*, chaps. 1–3. 2nd ed. Madison, Wis.: Brown & Benchmark, 1996.

Duckles, Vincent H., ed. *Music Reference and Research Materials: An Annotated Bibliography*. 5th ed. With Ira Reed and Michael A. Keller. New York: Schirmer Books, 1997.

Eisner, Elliot W. *The Enlightened Eye: Qualitative Inquiry and the Enhancement of Educational Practice*. New York: Macmillan, 1991.

Fraenkel, Jack R., and Norman E. Wallen. *How to Design and Evaluate Research in Education*, chaps. 1–2, 5. 2nd ed. New York: McGraw-Hill, 1993.

Gall, Joyce D., M. D. Gall, and Walter R. Borg. *Applying Educational Research: A Practical Guide*, chaps. 1–4. 4th ed. New York: Longman, 1999.

Gay, L. R. *Educational Research: Competencies for Analysis and Application*, chaps. 1–2. 4th ed. New York: Macmillan, 1992.

Gay, L. R., and Peter Airasian. *Educational Research: Competencies for Analysis and Application*, chaps. 1–2. 6th ed. Upper Saddle River, N.J.: Prentice-Hall, 2000.

Graziano, Anthony M., and Michael L. Raulin. *Research Methods: A Process of Inquiry*, chaps. 1–2. 4th ed. Boston: Allyn & Bacon, 2000.

Hittelman, Daniel R., and Alan J. Simon. *Interpreting Educational Research: An Introduction for Consumers of Research*, chaps. 1–4. 3rd ed. Upper Saddle River, N.J.: Prentice-Hall, 2002.

Hopkins, Charles D., and Richard L. Antes. *Educational Research: A Structure for Inquiry,* chaps. 1–3. 3rd ed. Itasca, Ill.: Peacock, 1990.

Johnson, Burke, and Larry Christensen. *Educational Research: Quantitative and Qualitative Approaches,* chaps. 1–2, 6. Boston: Allyn & Bacon, 2000.

Leedy, Paul D., with Timothy J. Newby and Peggy A. Ermer. *Practical Research Planning and Design,* chaps. 1, 3–4. 6th ed. Upper Saddle River, N.J.: Merrill, 1997.

Madsen, Clifford K., and Charles H. Madsen Jr. *Experimental Research in Music,* chaps. 1–2, 7–8. 3rd ed., Raleigh, N. C.: Contemporary, 1997.

Martella, Ronald C., Ronald Nelson, and Nancy Marchand-Martella. *Research Methods: Learning to Become a Critical Research Consumer,* chap. 1. Boston: Allyn & Bacon.

Mason, Emanuel J., and William J. Bramble. *Research in Education and the Behavioral Sciences: Concepts and Methods,* chaps. 1–3. Madison, Wis.: Brown & Benchmark, 1997.

McMillan, James H., and Sally Schumacher. *Research in Education: A Conceptual Introduction,* chaps. 3–5. 5th ed. New York: Macmillan, 2001.

Murray, Thomas R. *Conducting Educational Research: A Comparative View,* chaps. 2–4. Westport, Conn.: Bergin & Garvey, 1998.

Patton, Mildred L. *Understanding Research Methods,* pts. A and B. 2nd ed. Los Angeles: Pyrczak, 2000.

Preece, Roy P. *Starting Research: An Introduction to Academic Research and Dissertation Writing,* chaps. 1–3. London: Pinter, 1994.

Schloss, Patrick J., and Maurice A. Smith. *Conducting Research,* chaps. 1–2, 4. Upper Saddle River, N.J.: Prentice-Hall, 1999.

Slavin, Robert E. *Research Methods in Education,* chaps. 1, 5. 2nd ed. Boston: Allyn & Bacon, 1992.

Sprinthall, Richard C., Gregory T. Schmutte, and Les Sirois. *Understanding Educational Research,* chaps. 1–2. Englewood Cliffs, N.J.: Prentice-Hall, 1991.

Tuckman, Bruce W. *Conducting Educational Research,* chaps. 1, 23. 5th ed. Ft. Worth, Tex.: Harcourt Brace College, 1999.

Wallen, Norman E., and Jack R. Fraenkel. *Educational Research: A Guide to the Process.* 2nd ed. Mahwah, N.J.: Erlbaum, 2000. (An e-book.)

Wiersma, William. *Research Methods in Education,* chaps. 1–3. 7th ed. Boston: Allyn & Bacon, 2000.

Chapter 2

The Research Process

The initial step in formulating a research problem, according to Gay and Airisian, is to identify a topic of interest that is relevant to your field of expertise.[1] Concurring, Tuckman writes that the development and successful implementation of a research plan largely hinges on a viable and workable proposal, design, or prospectus.[2] For purposes of consistency, in this book, the written plan will be labeled *proposal*. Although there are deviations in research requirements from one institution to another, especially in format of the research proposal, many components of the research process are common. As mentioned in the previous chapter, most successful research depends on (1) logically choosing a topic, (2) formulating a research problem, (3) developing procedures to solve the problem, (4) successfully implementing these procedures, and (5) carefully interpreting the results. This five-step process cannot be emphasized too much.

There is a great deal of truth in the following aphorism: When the problem is clearly identified, the problem is half solved. All too often research novices are so impressed with a sophisticated statistical analysis, a research concept known as the Delphi technique, or collecting data via the Internet, that they become adamant on formulating a research problem to fit the methodology or statistical analysis of what they have perceived. Pursuing a research process in reverse order seldom results in a solid piece of research. Another problem sometimes encountered in graduate-level research is a proposal that is the result of a topic eventually proven to be unmanageable because the purpose of the research, from which the problem flows, has not been thought out carefully. There always are some students who begin collecting data before the research has been officially approved. Attempting to make data collected fit the proposal before it officially has been accepted is often disastrous.

In some institutions the term "thesis" refers to a written document for either a master's or a doctoral degree. In others, "thesis" is reserved for the master's degree, and a "dissertation" is only for some type of doctorate. Check carefully with your graduate office to find the distinction between these designations to make sure you are pursuing the correct degree track.

The importance of logical thinking and reflective reasoning, stressed in the first chapter, cannot be taken too lightly. Sometimes students who begin graduate study know very little about research. Obfuscatory writing, sometimes prevalent in the written work of music students who have perfected performance skills at the expense of liberal arts courses, can be diminished somewhat if careful logical and reflective thinking are followed.

Regardless of what the research proposal, guide, design, or prospectus is called, the purpose is the same, to indicate systematically in writing, the process the investigator proposes to use to procure, organize, and interpret data collected to provide answers for the research problem. A committee of four or five members usually is formed to assist you as progress is made toward the completion of your research plan. Committee approval of the research plan becomes an unofficial contract indicating that if procedures spelled out in the research plan are followed, the writing requirement will be fulfilled, assuming the completed research is approved by an examining committee, sometimes referred to as "the final oral." Some members of the examining committee likely will be from disciplines other than your own. Selection of committee members usually is determined by an adviser and/or graduate dean based on the focus of the research. For instance, if statistical analysis or testing is involved in your research, a faculty member from the psychology department probably would be included on your examining committee.

Selection of an inappropriate research problem, failure to specify appropriate procedures for collecting data, and intentionally bypassing suggestions from committee members can make the writing phase of your research less than pleasant. A researcher ought to be encouraged and confident of the successful completion of the research, not unduly discouraged.

After the research proposal officially has been approved, it becomes the "road map" for continuing the research. When verbs are changed from future to past, the proposal may serve as the actual first chapter of your dissertation. Cohen, Manion, and Morrison report that the research proposal is analogous to the architect's blueprint, which must be prepared and approved before construction on a building can begin. The clearer and more detailed the blueprint is, the more refined the finished product should be.[3]

Even after the proposal has officially been accepted, it should not be considered immutable. Occasionally changes in procedure will be required when the actual data collection proceeds. One would hope that these changes are not major, but minor, such as a slight change in title. Occasionally unforeseen circumstances will require major changes, such as adding another subproblem. If extensive changes are made after the proposal has officially been accepted, an addendum should be filed in the graduate office to reflect these changes so committee members will be apprised of any changes and/or additions. Minor changes normally do not require extensive emendations.

THE RESEARCH PROPOSAL

A research tyro was overheard asking this question: "If I know what I want to do and how to do it, why is it necessary for me to write a research proposal?" As if in reply, Behling reports that a proposal is a plan that enables one to better comprehend the time and resources necessary to complete the study.[4]

The research proposal (design, plan, prospectus) should be long enough to clearly indicate what is proposed and how it is to be carried out, but not so verbose that it appears to be the proposal and thesis or dissertation combined into one document. All necessary components of the proposal usually comprise no more than fifty double-spaced word-processed pages.

The traditional research proposal normally will include the following parts: title (or topic), problem statement, subproblems, definition of terms, delimitations, basic assumptions, basic hypotheses (if required), need or significance of the study, related literature, methodology or procedures for obtaining and treating data, preliminary

Title—scope of study, may include subtitle

Problem Statement—what you want to find out, or do; may include purpose

Subproblems—components of problem statement

Definitions—meanings of terms used

Delimitations—restrictions imposed by researcher or outside factors

Assumptions—"givens" accepted without verification

Hypotheses (if required)—positive or null statements to be tested

Significance or Need—why proposed study is needed

Related Literature and Sources—literary and nonliterary sources to be included

Methodology—how information will be obtained and tested

Bibliography—preliminary listing of literary and other sources

Personal Qualifications—education, experience, and skills of researcher

Appendix (if required)—items not part of main body of study

Figure 2.1.   Format for a Research Proposal

bibliography, personal qualifications, and appendix, if required. Each of these points is discussed in the following sections. Figure 2.1 identifies the sections normally found in a traditional research proposal. Adaptations can be made depending on policies of the university and predilections of your committee members. Slavin believes a good research proposal should eliminate as many extraneous, irrelevant statements as possible.[5]

Title

Rarely does one decide the final research title early in the research process. While the title is important in the process of writing the proposal, it usually is determined shortly before or after the research has been completed. The working title is a broad but accurate account of the scope of the research stated in a clear conceptual or cognitive form. The title finally chosen may reflect some elements of the procedures (e. g., survey, quasi-experimental, or meta-analysis). The writers of this text have reviewed research in which the title and the problem statement represent two entirely different entities. This can be frustrating, not only to the student's committees, but also to other researchers who review thesis and dissertation titles through various information retrieval systems. Readers may even order studies that seem to be pertinent to their proposed research and after receiving them realize that the titles are misleading.

Here is a hypothetical example of a title that is considerably different from the problem statement: (1) Title: Teaching General Music in the Classroom: A Comparative Study of Methods. (2) Problem Statement: The focus of this research is to review and compare textbook series published for grades 1–5 to teach music in elementary schools. In comparing the title and problem statement we observe several inferences, some valid and some not. The reference to "general music" in the title suggests the research will include elementary school classes in general, not music classes. On the other hand general music also is included in some middle and high schools, especially with the requirements of basic education courses for graduation in many states. The term "methods" in the title does not refer to ways of teaching, but to textbooks, and is limited to series published for five grade levels.

To reiterate, you should decide on the final version of your title *before* the problem statement is clear. A taxonomy, or flow chart, to the steps involved in the formulation of a research problem is seen in figure 2.2. In this taxonomy you proceed directly from the broad problem statement to the specific subproblems inductively and then to more specific questions. By the time this thought process has been completed, the research plan as well as specific items

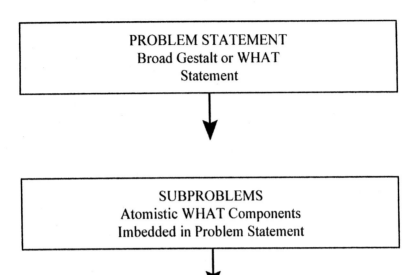

Figure 2.2.   Taxonomy for Formulating a Research Problem

needed to collect the data should be evident. Note that subproblems are embedded in the problem statement and research
questions relate to each subproblem. This inductive-deductive
process is necessary for the successful development and eventual
execution of a research plan.

For purposes of illustrating the reflective process, a hypothetical
statement follows, which will be developed into a title, problem statement, subproblems, basic assumptions, and basic hypotheses. All
these are components of research that involve critical thinking rather
than the actual presentation of information found in other parts of the
research proposal. The statement that follows will serve as the basis
for the development of a research proposal, referred to earlier:

*The nocturne, a character piece for piano, was introduced by John Field
(1782–1837). As applied to a somewhat melancholy or languid style, with*

an expressive melody over a broken-chord accompaniment, the term "nocturne" has been used by many composers, but perhaps the one who adapted the idea most successfully was Frédéric Chopin (1810–1849). (It is interesting that both Field and Chopin wrote eighteen nocturnes.) As a pianist you might want to examine the development of the nocturne to assist you in performing nocturnes by various composers.

Title

A title that might be derived from the statement above is: "The Nocturnes for Piano of John Field and Frédéric Chopin." Observe that a general title is not complete without the addition of a subtitle. When the subtitle is added, the focus of the research becomes clearer, as follows: "The nocturnes of John Field and Frédéric Chopin: A Stylistic Study to Aid in Their Performance."

Problem Statement

The term "purpose" often is used in research and frequently is synonymous to the problem statement. According to Miner and Miner, the purpose of the problem statement is to indicate the rationale for the research project and situation you want to change.[6] For purposes of illustration, the problem will identify *what* is to be found out, and the purpose will indicate *why* the research is being pursued. Sometimes the purpose and the problem statement can appear in the same sentence, causing readers to confuse the difference between the two. Behling refers to the problem statement as a "general research question," and the subproblems as "specific research questions."[7]

Since the statement of the problem should be a clearly worded indication of the focus of the research, it should be more specific than the title. The problem statement is a cognitive or conceptual statement of *what* you want to find out or do. It does not indicate *how* the information is to be obtained, and sometimes is referred to as the *gestalt,* or organismic representation of a problem.

Although many researchers prefer the declarative form, a problem statement also may be expressed in interrogatory form. Compare the hypothetical statements that follow with the title just noted:

1. The nocturnes of John Field and Frédéric Chopin are the same basically because of their designation as "nocturnes."

2. The nocturnes for piano of John Field are comparable musically to those of Frédéric Chopin.
3. The problem of this study is to compare stylistically the eighteen nocturnes for piano of John Field with those of Frédéric Chopin.
4. The purpose of this study is to compare stylistically the nocturnes of John Field with those of Frédéric Chopin as an aid to their performance.

Of these declarative statements, the clearest is the third because it encompasses the important items necessary for a clear understanding of what the researcher proposes to do (the problem) when compared with the original source material and title above. The first statement is not valid because it is an assumption rather than a problem statement; furthermore, it assumes all compositions designated as "nocturnes" are the same. Not valid, either, is the second statement because an indication of comparing the composers' nocturnes is not given in the original statement. The third statement, then, is the preferred one because it incorporates more of the information contained in the original statement. While valid, the fourth statement is not as complete as the third although the term "purpose" is used and "as an aid to their performance" is missing.

Recasting the third statement into interrogatory form might read: "Is there a stylistic difference between the eighteen nocturnes of John Field and the eighteen of Frédéric Chopin?" You must determine whether you prefer the interrogatory or the declarative form by writing and comparing the forms of the two statements.

During the course of collecting data it may prove desirable to make changes in the title as well as the problem statement, as noted previously. Still valid is Whitney's statement written several years ago, that an alteration of both research proposal (design) and title should result when it is evident that the research is proceeding differently than originally proposed.[8]

Subproblems

Subproblems, or "specific problems," either in declarative or interrogatory form, state the atomistic or more precise aspects of the problem statement. In other words, the statement of the problem is broken down deductively into more finite components. Subproblems, however, are not to be confused with subtitle. Subproblems are expressed in cognitive or conceptual terms, and like the statement of the problem, indicate *what* one plans to find out. Subproblems also are *what* statements (not *how*) and are derived from the whole or *gestalt*. Answers to these subproblems must be found in the research questions in order to resolve the main problem. Subproblems should be proffered in logical order because they indicate the direction the research will take. In many theses and dissertations each subproblem eventually becomes a separate chapter in the final document after all the data have been collected.

Using the hypothetical statement of the problem finally determined, examine each of these subproblems: (1) To compare the musical worth of the piano nocturnes of John Field and Frédéric Chopin; (2) To trace the antecedents of the nocturne up to the time of John Field; (3) What system of analysis may be derived to analyze the nocturnes? (4) To determine similarities and differences in the eighteen nocturnes for piano of John Field and Frédéric Chopin.

Of these four statements, three are in declarative form, beginning with an infinitive. The third, however, is in interrogatory form. The two ways of stating a subproblem should not be intermingled; the subproblems should be all declarative or all interrogatory. The first statement would be a valid subproblem although musical worth is not a concept being compared according to the original problem statement. The second would make a good initial subproblem because it is necessary to set the stage for any development that is to be traced, as would be true in this study. Referring to subproblem 2, it could be stated in interrogatory form as follows: "What are the antecedents of the nocturne up to the time of John Field?" The third statement, even though expressed here as a question, would be viable if it were expressed as an infinitive because of the need to adapt some existing approach to musical analysis or to devise another if this is an objective of the research. Restated as an infinitive, the third subproblem might read: "To adapt or develop a system to analyze the nocturnes." Finally, the fourth statement would be a valid concluding subproblem because the intent is to pull together information for all previous subproblems Still needed, though, is another subproblem to offer suggestions for performance based on data obtained from the previous subproblem (recall that in the third subproblem reference was made to "an aid to their performance"). Research questions also are *what* statements. They will evolve out of each subproblem in the methodology section.

Definition of Terms (Terminology)

Any terms used in the title, problem statement, subproblems, or throughout the research should be defined if they are ambiguous or technical. In addition, terminology used to connote a meaning different from that usually accepted should be clarified.[9] This would be true for such terms as *Gebrauchsmusik*, which might not be understood by any except the well-read musician, but also for seemingly well-known terms as "chorus," when a specific meaning is employed. This is not to suggest you have license to manipulate a definition to meet the purposes of a study or to use one that is not generally accepted by authorities in the field. The sole purpose of definitions is to bring about clarity. A well-balanced definitions section contains both direct quotations from the literature or other sources and paraphrased terms. Do not make the mistake of taking the easy way out and using only direct quotations for terms to be defined. It demonstrates greater intellectuality to intermingle direct quotations with paraphrased terms; also the reading is more interesting. Definitions may be conceptual—clearly and concisely indicating *what* the concept means—or operational—for instance, indicating what tool, instrument, or technique will be used to obtain the desired information. A case in point: a researcher provides a cognitive definition of "creativity" and then states that "creativity" will be operationalized by using an instrument such as the Torrance Tests of Creative Thinking (TTCT).[10] Moreover, your reader must not be offended by the inclusion of terms that are obvious, but you cannot assume all your readers are as familiar and as well versed in your subject as you are. It is this delicate balance for which you must constantly strive.

Referring again to the third hypothetical statement, study these definitions: *nocturne*—a musical piece suggesting night visions and dreams, sometimes called *Nachtstuck*—a piano composition in melancholy or pensive style, characterized by an expressive melody over a broken-chord accompaniment.[11] Other terms that might come into play are *style, texture, rhythmic complexity,* and *expressive markings.*

Of the two definitions of nocturne, the second is more indicative of what characterizes that term, and thus expresses its meaning more clearly; also, in the second example the definition is paraphrased, although the source is given. With definitions this is a desirable practice; for direct quotations citations are mandatory.

Delimitations

An open-ended research proposal rarely will result in the most expeditious accumulation and interpretation of data. In their understandable enthusiasm and zeal to make a contribution to knowledge, research tyros finding their study too broad frequently delimit it further than the subproblems require. At this point a distinction needs to be made between "limitations" and "delimitations." Limitations, report Best and Kahn, represent circumscriptions imposed on a researcher by external circumstances.[12] For example, certain documents may be unavailable because they have been destroyed by some catastrophe, are lost, or are inaccessible because they have been classified as confidential material. Delimitations are circumscriptions you place on the research so it will not "balloon" out of proportion. Delimitations are necessary to eliminate ambiguity and exclude certain inferred terms. Delimitations and limitations are both cognitive or *what* statements, and often include a rationale for their inclusion. Some factors that might determine the extent of a delimitation include time and money available, personal qualifications to conduct the research, and availability of special equipment or tools needed for the project.

One of the most important delimitations is time. This is not to imply that a topic should be delimited so much, ostensibly because of the pressure of time, that the proposal is virtually emasculated before the research has begun. Delimitations must be those that permit the research to be organized so that data can be collected as efficiently and effectively as possible. By contrast, there are very few occasions when it is necessary to expand a topic. Such a dilemma may suggest the proposed research is too insignificant to be implemented.

Delimitations may be *negative*—proscribing categories in which the research will not venture, thus giving a better idea of what is to be effected—or *positive*—succinctly and clearly circumscribing limits of the research from an affirmative standpoint. Positive delimitations normally are not found as frequently as those stated negatively because it is easy to confuse them with objectives of the research.

Consider these delimitations as they relate to the third hypothetical problem statement: (1) No attempt will be made to compare the editions of the nocturnes of John Field and Frédéric Chopin; (2) The moods pervading nocturnes are melancholy and dreamy; (3) The only system of analysis to be used in this study is the one devised by

Heinrich Schenker; (4) This research will be delimited to a stylistic comparison of the eighteen nocturnes for piano by John Field and Frédéric Chopin; and (5) No attempt will be made to compare the relative worth of the nocturnes of John Field and Frédéric Chopin.

The first of these delimitations is viable because the researcher does not intend to compare the various editions to ascertain if they correspond to what the composers intended in the original versions. This could be stated as a limitation as follows: "The first printed editions of the nocturnes of Field and Chopin will serve as the basis for comparison since the original manuscripts (MSS) are no longer available. You would need to be certain, of course, that the MSS are not available before this statement is made. The second delimitation is vague and would be better omitted because it is positive and more difficult to conceptualize, serving as a good example of the difficulty faced in providing a meaningful delimitation. Furthermore, only one format should be used; do not mix up positive and negative. Inaccurate is the third delimitation since the Schenkerian techniques have been modified by many individuals, including Felix Salzer and Adele Katz. The Schenkerian approach is more than a system for musical analysis. There are very few occasions when it is necessary to hew the line in strict fashion with only one approach; the complexity of many musical compositions requires that an analysis include aspects of different approaches. Expressed well is the fourth statement because only the eighteen nocturnes of Field and Chopin will be compared. The last delimitation is important because no attempt will be made to determine whether one composer's music is better than that of the other.

Basic Assumptions

Almost all research is predicated on certain principles or propositions for which no proof is necessary or possible. You are not expected to prove these assumptions, but a rationale for them should be given. Assumptions, report Best and Kahn, are statements that a researcher accepts as valid and that require no verification.[13] It is not always necessary to include basic assumptions unless they are needed. To fabricate false assumptions just to meet a criterion is pointless. When included, assumptions should be cognitive or conceptual statements relevant to the research.

Referring to the third hypothetical statement of the problem stated earlier, a decision must be made relative to these basic assumptions: (1) It is assumed that the nocturnes of Frédéric Chopin are more melancholy than those of John Field; (2) It is assumed that the first printed editions of the nocturnes of John Field and Frédéric Chopin represent the true intentions of the composers; (3) It is assumed that John Field was less proficient as a pianist than was Frédéric Chopin; and (4) It is assumed that a detailed analysis of the nocturnes of John Field and Frédéric Chopin will enable a pianist to perform them more effectively.

The first assumption is invalid because of the bias toward Chopin, suggesting that his troubled life caused him to write melancholy music. In addition, mood of the compositions being compared is not even under consideration in either the problem statement or the subproblems. Mood could be a subject for consideration by itself. Since there will be many occasions when it will be impossible to obtain original MSS for comparison with the first printed editions, the second assumption is very important. Furthermore, no indication is given that the first printed editions include changes that may have been made by the composers. Invalid and biased is the third statement because Field is not generally as well known as Chopin. Furthermore, performing ability of the composers is not a focus of the research nor even relevant to it. Such a study would be difficult to justify at best. The last assumption is valid and really serves as the focus of the research. By examining in detail the music of both composers, you should be able to better understand the works and thus perform them more efficiently and musically.

Basic Hypotheses

A hypothesis is a shrewd guess of the outcomes of a study. Unlike assumptions, hypotheses must be tested to determine their validity. Basic hypotheses, as is true with assumptions, are not necessary for all research projects. Rarely, if ever, do hypotheses appear in historical, or aesthetic–philosophical, research. If they are present they likely will appear after the research has been completed and hypotheses formulated to relate to data collected. By contrast, it is extremely difficult to locate experimental and descriptive research proposals that do not include hypothesis statements. Basic, also known as "working," hypotheses represent the best guess of results of the research setting. Setting forth the basic theory or rationale underlying the hypotheses prevents the appearance of false or "wild" hypotheses. Hypotheses remain tentative until the research is completed, when they either are confirmed or rejected.

There are various types of hypotheses, but two useful types for most music education research are as follows: *research*, also known as deductive, declarative, or positive; and *statistical, null,* or *negative.* Positive hypotheses may either be directional or nondirectional. In directional, some adjectives such as "more," "greater," or "less" would be used to indicate a direction; in nondirectional, "difference" is the most important distinction. A difference is expected in a nondirectional hypothesis, but no direction usually is stated when the hypothesis is formulated. Research hypotheses state that a difference is expected. The formula A>B can be used to test whether A indeed is greater than B. If it is, then the hypothesis is confirmed or sustained. If A does not prove to be greater than B (A<B), then the hypothesis is rejected.

The statistical hypothesis states that no difference may be expected between two or more variables when measured statistically. Although the procedure usually results in a direct testing of the hypothesis, it nonetheless is constructed with the expectation that it will be rejected. Rejection then results in the affirmation of the research hypothesis. Using the formula "$A \neq B$," the researcher hopes there will be a difference so the *null* hypothesis can be sustained. A *null* hypothesis is *not accepted,* meaning one fails to accept it. Does it seem pointless to state something negatively when it may appear easier to do so positively? Statistically, a *null* hypothesis usually is easier to handle because it is predicated on the Gaussian or bell-shaped curve (see chapter 6).

To reiterate, a hypothesis should be stated clearly and concisely. When so formulated, it is easier to test, thus fulfilling the purpose of the research more readily. To put it another way, a basic hypothesis is an unbiased statement of anticipated conclusions. Note that *hypothesis* is not synonymous with *conclusion.* After data have been accumulated, a conclusion might coincide with a hypothesis formulated in the beginning of the research proposal. Obviously any bias will tend to skew the data as well as conclusions reached.

Using the third hypothetical statement once more, determine which of the following statements represent valid hypotheses: (1) It is hypothesized that, since the term "nocturne" is used by both John Field and Frédéric Chopin, no technical difference between the nocturnes will be evident; (2) It is hypothesized that because of his national background the nocturnes of Frédéric Chopin will be more somber than those of John Field; (3) It is hypothesized that melancholy compositions are more highly developed structurally than are bright compositions; and (4) It is hypothesized that there will be no difference in the results irrespective of the system of analysis used.

The first hypothesis is invalid and not tenable because each composer writing under the rubric of "nocturne" obviously is going to express himself in his own way. Furthermore, there is no technical limitation implicit or explicit in the term "nocturne." "No difference" obviously designates this as a *null* hypothesis. The second hypothesis is invalid and untenable because national background and mood are not common elements. To state that the music of composers of any country is more or less melancholy is irrational and has no basis. Since the word "more" is used for this hypothesis, some specific direction is indicated, and the hypothesis would be labeled "directional." If the statement simply indicated that there was a "difference," it would be nondirectional, and the researcher would then have to determine through a comparison of variables whether the judgment would be "more" or "less." Research and null hypotheses should not be mixed in the same proposal. To put it another way, one hypothesis should not be stated positively and another one negatively in the same proposal. Emphasis in the third hypothesis is on mood and structure. There does not necessarily need to be a relationship between them, so this hypothesis would be very difficult to test. The focus in the final hypothesis is on the system of analysis used, which is a fallacy. One of the most important decisions to be made is whether any one system or approach for stylistic analysis will bring more valid results than any other. The upshot of this discussion is that none of the hypotheses above is valid and testable; all are false. Research of the type illustrated in the "nocturne" examples rarely requires hypotheses.

Need for the Study (or Significance)

Up to this point sections of the research proposal do not contain much narrative. The need, or significance, section sets forth why the proposed research is needed and how the results might be used. The task is to convince a committee that the proposed research will result is a significant contribution to literature in your field of study. Sometimes this section is called "Significance of the Study," but regardless of the designation, one must avoid on the one hand giving the impression that here at last is research that will resolve the most vexing problems in music education or the arts, and on the other hand an aura of apology. For instance, the use of such equivocal phraseology as "interest of the writer," "encouragement from the writer's peers," and the "writer's desire for musical growth," is not very persuasive. Such euphemisms are redundant, to say the least, and they indicate intellectual immaturity. To lend credibility to your assertions, use citations from the literature and from individuals who share the same convictions about the need for the research. These may be in the form of personal correspondence, e-mail messages, telephone interviews, or sections from completed theses or dissertations where the writers elucidate on further research needed. The more convincing the evidence for need is, the less likely a reviewing panel will say "so what?" Evidence must be based on critical thinking or obtained from the literature, as just noted. The presence or absence of corroborating and supporting declarations may or may not be sufficient affirmation that the research is needed. To be significant, a proposal must rest on its own merits, with or without the substantiation of others.

Sometimes a forthright, convincing account of the investigator's selection process will be included. Frequently referred to as "Incidence of the Problem," this information, if needed, should be included in the need or significance section. Formerly it might have been included as a separate subheading in a proposal but is rarely found there anymore.

Related Literature and/or Sources

One of the most important sections of a research proposal is a review of literature and/or sources. This review is important to (1) avoid duplication of efforts, unless the research is replicating a study already completed; (2) delimit the research; (3) determine what areas need further investigation; and (4) discover new approaches, methods, or insights into a problem.

The related literature or sources section contains a brief account of the research focus, listing some of the most important sources of pertinent information. In addition, concise accounts of other concepts that may be relevant, such as philosophical, psychological, or sociological implications, may be included. The importance of a thorough review of the literature cannot be stressed too much. Without a careful, exhaustive examination of the literature and/or sources needed, you will not know what has been researched and what remains to be done, as Phelps related in an article in a professional journal.[14]

It is necessary to present a brief account of the significant points found in each source as well as the relevance of each one to the proposed research. While it is necessary to include enough information on each source to give an adequate picture of relevance, verbosity must be avoided lest this section "balloon" out of proportion to the other sections. Information should be presented from both positive and negative points of view. Don't hesitate to point out items reviewed that have little or no relevance to the proposed research. On the contrary, some sources may have been omitted purposely so your reader needs to know why. This review of literature will be helpful when preparing bibliography for the completed research. Citations, when fitting, are included in the literature section, with appropriate corresponding acknowledgments, since they help to verify your familiarity with the literature and/or sources. A word of caution is in order: do not use excessive citations to make a case for the inclusion of related literature. Citations should be used sparingly because the emphasis in this section is on what each source is all about and the relevance of each item to the research. The onus is on you, the researcher, to determine what is pertinent and what is not.

Often it is necessary to list sources in addition to verbal accounts of related literature. Examples of sources are questionnaires, personal interviews, correspondence, e-mail messages, Internet information, diaries, musical compositions, among others. An account of various sources obviously cannot be included, but their relevance to the research must be stated; since they are important, their listing in the bibliography is needed. As must be evident by now, the related literature and/or sources section is written in narrative format when possible.

Methodology

Two parts normally comprise the methodology section: "Sources of Data" and "Treatment of Data." Sources identify *where* data will come from; treatment specifies *what* will be done with the data. The *where* and *what* must be indicated for each subproblem. Research questions, when required, will appear for the appropriate subproblems. Normally found in aesthetic, historical, and philosophical proposals, research questions also may be found in descriptive and experimental research. Research questions enable you to focus more clearly on *what* you want to find out.

To be included in the sources of information section, when appropriate for the proposal are (1) literature and other sources to be used; (2) kinds of data needed; (3) amounts of data needed; (4) when data need to be obtained if a time factor is significant; (5) instruments and their validity coefficients, and equipment or material to be used for data collection; and (6) personnel assisting with obtaining data, when required.

In the treatment of data section, the researcher specifies *what* will be done with the data received for each subproblem. Will answers to the research questions be presented in narrative form, in statistical tables, or some other manner? Research question answers are not complete until all data are received. Recall that the research paradigm in figure 2.2 consists of problem, subproblems, and research questions—the most significant of the three.

Here are some examples of research questions formulated from the hypothetical second "nocturne" subproblem (to trace the antecedents of the nocturne up to the time of John Field): (1) What are the antecedents of the nocturne?" (2) "Where did the nocturne originate?" (3) When it evolved was the nocturne written for instruments other than the piano?" (4) What induced Field to develop the nocturne form?" and (5) "What changes, if any, did Chopin make in the nocturne form?"

Questions to be posed on a questionnaire, in an interview, or statistics included in experimental designs also appear here. When a jury is being used, criteria for their selection must be specified.

Biographical and historical data, as an example, largely come from literary sources, so the information will be presented in "chronological, narrative form." Research involving an analysis of musical compositions should include a sample of a work that has been analyzed already. All references to appendix items appear in the appropriate place in the context. Procedures for handling questionnaire data, such as computer printouts, also are listed in the appendix. When historical data are presented, indicate how the authenticity and credibility of documents or statements are to be determined.

To reiterate, the sole purpose of the methodology section is to let your reader know where data come from and what will be done with them.

Bibliography

Known as "preliminary" or "tentative" bibliography, this section contains references to sources most important for your research. No attempt should be made in the proposal to incorporate all materials reviewed. Only the significant ones for your research should be listed. Additional references may be added as the research proceeds because the quest for data is an ongoing process right up to the final oral. Limits, of course, do need to be established. On occasion, at the final oral, you may be asked to include additional sources that final oral commission members believe should be added. All items appearing in footnotes (reference notes, or endnotes) also must appear in the bibliography. There are at least five ways to present bibliographic sources: (1) alphabetical by author's last name, irrespective of the kind of material; (2) author listing for primary and secondary sources; (3) identification by category of items (books, journals, unpublished documents, etc.); (4) division by cited and "other" references (interviews, e-mail messages, telephone interviews, etc.); and (5) alphabetical by last name according to category of items (historical, biographical, analytical, etc).

The easiest and simplest way is to present all bibliographical sources by last name, irrespective of kind of item, a format easy to read and follow. The reader looking for a certain kind of material (journal, article, dissertation, etc.) is at a disadvantage because it is necessary to read through the entire bibliography. Division into primary and secondary sources has the advantage of focusing on the most significant ones; namely, primary materials, which refer to firsthand or original accounts of information such as personal letters, e-mails (unless forwarded), or data reported at the conclusion of an experiment. Items not original with the one reporting them are identified as secondary. Although the writers presumably used many primary sources, their reporting makes them secondary. Often it is difficult to strike a clear difference between primary and secondary sources because such differentiation is not readily discernible without examining the contents. Based on the experience of the authors of this text, it is easier to list bibliographical sources by category: books, periodicals, unpublished documents, and others. List these alphabetically by author's last name and then the appropriate source. When no author, editor, or compiler is listed, the title of the item is included in the alphabetical listing.

If a more definitive bibliographical listing by category is preferred, then all items under each heading such as biographical, historical, and so on, would be given, irregardless of their designation as books, journals, or whatever. This procedure provides easy access to specific materials under a category but could be cumbersome if you were not sure what to look for.

Bibliographical entries are to be presented in standard format for bibliography. Include the most recent edition of a publication unless there is a valid reason to list an earlier edition. Not suggested is that older sources are less valuable; sometimes statements in older editions of the same work are in line with what you believe is most important.

Personal Qualifications

Your educational qualifications (degrees, courses taken) and professional and other experiences pertinent to your proposed research are listed. Include prior research and publications, although their inclusion is optional. The import of all sources listed is obvious; their purpose is to indicate preparation and background to pursue the research successfully. A reviewing panel sometimes has reservations about the ability of a student to carry out the project successfully because certain skills or techniques have not been spelled out explicitly. It is implicit that you either possess the skills necessary to the task, or you will obtain them.

Appendix

The appendix contains information to clarify or implement the proposed research. One or more appendixes (appendices) may be included. References to appendixes appear in appropriate sections of the text. Preliminary questionnaires, cover letters, and charts for musical analysis are typical of what usually is found in an appendix. Reference to these items will be included in both the research proposal as well as the final document.

To repeat, a research proposal serves a very important function. It is a plan, or blueprint, as it were, detailing what you plan to do. A well-organized, carefully prepared proposal can make the implementation of the research easier and interpretation of data less complicated and more meaningful. It is in the research proposal that the deductive process for implementation, illustrated in figure 2.2 earlier in this chapter, takes shape.

THE RESEARCH DOCUMENT

As noted earlier, the ultimate purpose of a thesis or dissertation is to present and interpret the findings of the research, which probably has been ongoing for several months. The writing style is narrative and should be as direct and objective as possible. Use of the third person (the researcher, one) is usually recommended rather than the first person (we, my). Occasionally the second person (you, yours) may result in writing that is less formal and rigid. Use of the second person needs to be approved by your adviser and/or committee. Mason and Bramble stress the use of third person because of its objectivity.[15] Using an infinitive (to report, to examine) also results in objective writing. Regardless of whether the third, second, or first person is used, the emphasis should be on writing that is clear and concise. The results obtained must be presented accurately and without prejudice.

When data from experimental research reveal a hypothesis that must be rejected when you anticipated it would be accepted, reasons *why* the hypothesis was rejected need to be stated. A rejected hypothesis may raise questions about the validity of sections of an investigator's research, or of previous research on which it is based. Format for the final document likely will vary from one institution to another, so suggestions from your adviser and committee should take priority. Results of completed research can conveniently be subsumed under three categories: *what was done, what was found out, and what the results mean.*

What Was Done

A discussion of what was done includes a prefatory section (title, abstract, copyright form, acknowledgments or dedication, table of contents, list of tables, list of figures). What to include in the prefatory section should be clarified by your graduate office. To be considered are numbering of pages, size of margins, software programs acceptable for preparing the final document, whether year only, or both month and year, will be stated for the completion date of the document. Clarify where Roman and Arabic numerals are to be used. Include the 300–350 word abstract, unless it is to be filed separately. Most abstracts eventually appear in *Dissertation Abstracts International (DAI)*. Some graduate schools require both paper and a CD version of a dissertation.

A release statement, signed by the degree recipient, absolves the institution of any litigation should it arise later. Signed release forms may be included with the research document, or filed separately in the graduate office. Verbs used in the proposal will be changed from future to past in the final document. (In the research proposal the researcher stated what was to be done and how it was to be carried out; in the final document the focus is on what actually was done or found out.) The writers of this textbook have discovered, on occasion, that the problem statement and/or subproblems in a proposal have been altered to conform to results of the completed research. In itself this may not be wrong, but it implies that some data have been "doctored" to make the proposal more nearly correspond to the results obtained. Certainly it is necessary sometimes to make modifications to the original proposal as the research proceeds. This can be handled easily by filing an addendum to the original proposal with the graduate office. Revisions, however, should not be made until it is deemed they are absolutely necessary. Related literature is the section of the proposal likely to need emendations; by then additional sources will have been incorporated in the final document.

Follow carefully suggestions for handling footnotes (notes), bibliography, and other items relating to your document. For example, the way to handle titles of musical works is clearly illustrated in *The Chicago Manual of Style 14th Edition.*[16]

What Was Found Out

The number of chapters to be included in the final document will be determined largely by the way data are presented and interpreted. Each subproblem may constitute a separate chapter, especially if the subproblems or research questions have been stated in interrogatory form in the proposal. Data from quantitative research usually can be included in a chapter for each subproblem. Data from qualitative, aesthetic, and philosophical studies often require more than one chapter for each subproblem. It is standard practice to include tables and figures in the chapter where reference to them is made. They are numbered consecutively throughout the document. If more than one table or figure is included in a chapter, numbering for them would look like this for the second chapter (as an example): Table 2.1, 2.2, 2.3, 2.4; Figure 2.5, 2.6, 2.7. A brief summary of results is often required at the end of each chapter in the final document.

What the Results Mean

Data presented without explications rarely are very useful. What significance can a reader draw from the data? Does interpretation of the results coincide with what was proposed? In defense of your research, you should be prepared to answer the questions, What difference, if any, do the results make? Can music and the other arts benefit from this research? The need or significance section is the logical place to question what benefits the research may have for the profession. Interpretation of the results also may impinge on related literature. As an example, refer back to the comparison of the Field and Chopin nocturnes. Conceivably the search could highlight previous research on the nocturne, using techniques described in the procedures section of the proposal. What if, in reviewing the Field and Chopin nocturnes, it was discovered they were more closely related to Chopin's mazurkas? This would necessitate further review of the mazurka in the recommendations for further research section.

A document's final chapter is eagerly scrutinized by fledgling researchers because it is here that everything comes together. In chapters where a summary is included it would be helpful to determine whether procedures for obtaining and treating data are clearly stated.

Sometimes conclusions are perplexing to a reader because a distinction between summary and conclusions or between conclusions and recommendations are less than clear. Posing the question again, What difference does it make? should enable your reader to more clearly understand the value of the research.

It is no understatement to point out to research tyros that recommendations for further research are like a shining light because (1) related topics requiring further investigation are identified and (2) priorities for additional research are spelled out. Recommendations may be predicated on conclusions that have confirmed hypotheses or rejected them.

The chapters that follow will guide you through procedures, techniques, and instruments to use for various methodologies embodied in qualitative, quantitative, historical, and aesthetic–philosophical formats. Based on the topic you want to investigate, decide which one, or ones, appear best for you to follow.

FOR REVIEW, DISCUSSION, AND IMPLEMENTATION

- Most successful research is based on what five steps?
- Compare the research proposal schema identified in figure 2.1 with the one recommended by your university. What components are the same? Which ones are different?
- What is the distinction between general research questions and specific research questions?
- Find out if your adviser and/or committee recommends the use of first-, second-, or third-person writing style for your proposal and dissertation.
- How does the research document differ from the research proposal?

NOTES

1. L. R. Gay and Peter Airasian, *Educational Research: Competencies for Analysis and Application*, 6th ed. (Upper Saddle River, N.J.: Prentice-Hall, 2000), 40.

2. Bruce W. Tuckman, *Conducting Educational Research*, 5th ed. (Ft. Worth, Tex.: Harcourt Brace College, 1999), 235.

3. Louis Cohen, Lawrence Manion, and Keith Morrison, *Research Methods in Education*, 5th ed. (London: Routledge Falmer, 2000), 73.

4. John W. Behling, *Guidelines for Preparing the Research Proposal* (Lanham, Md.: University Press of America, 1984), 2.

5. Robert E. Slavin, *Research Methods in Education*, 2nd ed. (Boston: Allyn & Bacon, 1992), 3.

6. Jeremy T. Miner and Lynn E. Miner, *Directory of Research Grants 2000, with a Guide to Proposal Planning and Writing* (Phoenix: Oryx, 2000), xxxv.

7. Behling, 33.

8. Frederick W. Whitney, *The Essentials of Research*, 3rd ed. (Englewood Cliffs, N.J.: Prentice-Hall, 1950), 123.

9. Utilitarian music composed for amateurs, characterized by simplicity of parts and length of movements.

10. E. Paul Torrance, *Torrance Tests of Creative Thinking (TTCT)* (Columbus, Ohio: Personnel/Xerox Center, 1966).

11. Don Michael Randel, comp., *Harvard Concise Dictionary of Music* (Cambridge: Harvard University Press, 1978), 337.

12. John W. Best and James V. Kahn, *Research in Education,* 9th ed. (Boston: Allyn & Bacon, 2003), 37.

13. Best and Kahn, 37.

14. Roger P. Phelps, "The Doctoral Dissertation: Boon or Bane?" *College Music Symposium,* Fall 1978, 83.

15. Emanuel J. Mason and William J. Bramble, *Research in Education and the Behavioral Sciences: Concepts and Methods* (Madison, Wis.: Brown & Benchmark, 1997), 425.

16. *Chicago Manual of Style,* 14th ed. (Chicago: University of Chicago Press, 1993). See sections 15.412–13; 16.199.

SUPPLEMENTARY SOURCES

Ary, Donald, Lucy Cheser Jacobs, and Asghar Razavieh. *Introduction to Research in Education,* chaps. 14–15. 5th ed. Ft. Worth, Tex.: Harcourt Brace College, 1996.

Behling, John. *Guidelines for Preparing the Research Proposal,* chaps. 1–2. Lanham, Md.: University Press of America, 1984.

Bogdan, Robert C., and Sara K. Biklen. *Qualitative Research in Education: An Introduction to Theory and Methods,* chaps. 2, 6. 3rd ed. Boston: Allyn & Bacon, 1998.

Chicago Manual of Style. 14th ed. Chicago: University of Chicago Press, 1993.

Cohen, Louis, Lawrence Manion, and Keith Morrison. *Research Methods in Education,* chap. 1. 5th ed. New York: Routledge Falmer, 2000.

Crowl, Thomas K. *Fundamentals of Educational Research,* chap. 16. 2nd ed. Madison, Wis.: Brown & Benchmark, 1996.

Fraenkel, Jack R., and Norman E. Wallen. *How to Design and Evaluate Research in Education,* chaps. 2, 19. 2nd ed. New York: McGraw-Hill, 1993.

Gelfand Harold, and Charles J. Walker. *Mastering APA Style.* Washington, D.C.: American Psychological Association, 1990.

Gibaldi, Joseph. *MLA Handbook for Writers of Research Papers.* 5th ed. New York: Modern Language Association, 1999.

Harnack, Andrew. *Writing Research Papers: A Student Guide for Use with Opposing Viewpoints.* 2nd ed. San Diego, Calif.: Greenhaven, 1998.

Irvine, Demar. *Writing about Music.* Ed. Reinhard G. Pauly. 3rd ed. Revised and enlarged by Mark A. Radice. Portland Ore.: Amadeus, 1999.

Leedy, Paul D., with Timothy J. Newby and Peggy A. Ermer. *Practical Research Planning and Design,* chaps. 5–6; appendix. 6th ed. Upper Saddle River, N.J.: Merrill.

Mason, Emanuel J., and William J. Bramble. *Research in Education and the Behavioral Sciences: Concepts and Methods,* chap. 15. Madison, Wis.: Brown & Benchmark, 1997.

Mauch, James E., and Jack W. Birch. *Guide to Successful Thesis and Dissertation: A Handbook for Students and Faculty.* 3rd ed. New York: Marcel Dekker, 1993.

Murray, Thomas R., and Dale L. Brubaker. *Avoiding Thesis and Dissertation Pitfalls: 61 Cases of Problems and Solutions.* Westport, Conn.: Bergin & Garvey, 2001.

Preece, Roy P. *Starting Research: An Introduction to Academic Research and Dissertation Writing,* chaps. 8–9. London: Pinter, 1994.

Publication Manual of the American Psychological Association. 5th ed. Washington, D.C.: American Psychological Association, 2001.

Roth, Audrey J. *The Research Paper: Process, Form, and Content.* 8th ed. Belmont, Calif.: Wadsworth, 1999.

Schloss, Patrick J., and Maureen A. Smith. *Conducting Research,* chaps. 15–16. Upper Saddle River, N.J.: Prentice-Hall, 1999.

Slade, Carol. *Form and Style: Research Papers, Reports, Theses.* 10th ed. Boston: Houghton Mifflin, 1997.

Slavin, Robert E. *Research Methods in Education,* chaps. 8, 11. 2nd ed. Boston: Allyn & Bacon, 1992.

Sprinthall, Richard, Gregory T. Schmutte, and Les Sirois. *Understanding Educational Research,* chap. 8. Englewood Cliffs, N.J.: Prentice-Hall, 1991.

Tuckman, Bruce W. *Conducting Educational Research,* chap. 12. 5th ed. Ft. Worth, Tex.: Harcourt Brace College, 1999.

Turabian, Kate L. *A Manual for Writers of Term Papers, Theses, and Dissertations.* 6th ed. Chicago: University of Chicago Press, 1996.

Wiersma, William. *Research Methods in Education,* chap. 15. 7th ed. Boston: Allyn & Bacon, 2000.

Chapter 3

Qualitative Research: Concepts and Techniques

Qualitative research is known by many names, including ethnographic, naturalistic, field study, interpretive, and postpositivistic. Most recently it has been termed bricolage and the qualitative researcher has been likened to a *bricoleur*.[1] (In French a *bricoleur* is literally a handyman or handywoman.) Qualitative researchers do not approach research problems with a preestablished method. Instead, they draw on multiple methods. In a sense, qualitative research methodology is like a handyman's tool box. As the researcher commences and moves through a research project, he or she selects and implements the appropriate method (or tool). In this way, qualitative researchers can be methodologically flexible and responsive to the actions and meanings of the person or group they are studying. In taking an eclectic methodological approach, qualitative researchers remain open to what a particular action or set of actions under study might mean. On the other hand, monolithic methods often narrowly define "how" (through the method's prescribed tasks) researchers should extrapolate meaning. In doing so, those more traditional methods delimit "what" those meanings can be.[2]

Unlike much scientific research, predictability is not a goal; prediction and control are released in qualitative research in favor of understanding for the sake of understanding. The focus of that desired understanding is to reveal participants' perceptions and views, not the researcher's. This represents a fundamental shift in the subject-object correlation as it is represented in traditional research. In a positivistic scientific method, for example, the researcher is the "subject" and as such (through the use of method) controls, dominates and delimits what the "object(s)" under study can signify. By way of contrast, qualitative research turns the traditional "subject-object" correlation upside down. In the field, participants are not "objects" but are "subjects," largely directing the development of the research through the information they provide. The researcher responds to (rather than controls and dominates) the information that participants provide. Flexibility in qualitative research includes modifying methods and questions as new information is presented through the participants' discourse and actions. In so doing, qualitative researchers inductively move toward the development of theory (from a preliminary set of questions and hunches). In contrast, quantitative researchers deductively work from theory to a hypothesized correlation in the object(s) under study.[3]

Methodology for qualitative research has its roots in ethnographic research designs developed by anthropologists and sociologists. Ethnographies are reports about cultural contexts or groups. They report, as comprehensively as possible, the totality of actions of the persons under study from the viewpoint of those participants. Assuming the viewpoint of the group being studied requires that the researcher empathize with that group. Ethnographic research is empirical and takes place in the setting under study; behavior by those under study is observed firsthand. Statements by participants are often taped, transcribed, and then studied critically in order to uncover patterns or themes that are congruent to the actual living context from which they were extrapolated. Consequently most of the date collection in qualitative research is performed during fieldwork.

Qualitative research utilizes two primary data-gathering tools for fieldwork: participant observation and interview. Both tools are marked by the centrality of the researcher as a data-gathering and data-analyzing instrument. In response to that centrality, the first topic covered in this chapter is a consideration of the uniquely explicit prominence of the researcher in much qualitative research. Next, an overview of some of the basic strategies involved in field research will be presented. This is followed by more detailed accounts of the research techniques involved in participant observation and interview. After collecting data in the field through observation and interview, the researcher must make sense of his or her notes. To that end, guidelines for analyzing data and drawing conclusions are presented in the next section of this chapter.

Accordingly, the following topics will be covered:

1. The researcher as instrument
2. Strategies for field research
3. Participant observation
4. Interview
5. Data analysis
6. Computer software and qualitative research
7. Creating a narrative report

THE RESEARCHER AS INSTRUMENT

Within qualitative research is a tradition whereby the principal research instrument is the researcher. It is unusual from the viewpoint of quantitative designs to think of the researcher as the primary instrument for data collection and analysis. Egon Guba and Yvonna Lincoln suggest several characteristics that qualitative researchers manifest in their role as primary instruments:[4]

1. Responsiveness
2. Adaptability
3. Holistic emphasis
4. Knowledge base expansion
5. Processual immediacy
6. Opportunities for clarification and summarization
7. Opportunity to explore atypical or idiosyncratic responses

Guba and Lincoln point out that the phenomenological character (see chapter 4 of this volume) of qualitative data gathering can be seen in the characteristic of responsiveness. *Responsiveness* is a mode of orientation toward data that is distinguished by the phenomenological stance of "letting an object show itself for its own sake." However, this is not the neutral phenomenological attitude espoused by Edmund Husserl (see chapter 4 in this text). Instead, qualitative researchers must interact with data. In studying a group of high school teachers, for instance, the qualitative researcher must not only respond to their signals, suggestions, and motives; he or she often provides prompts and suggestions to the group. The qualitative researcher interacts with the group in order to create an atmosphere in which the group can give its own account of its situation. Within this dynamic interaction with the group under study, the qualitative researcher does not seek to exert precise methodological controls.[5] Thus the demand for a neutral researcher, in Husserlian phenomenology and many conventional methods of educational research, is not followed. Responsiveness, more in keeping with a Heideggerian interpretive stance (see chapter 4 in this text), is based on interaction, not neutrality. As such, qualitative research is value laden, not value neutral.

Adaptability, the second characteristic, indicates the capability in the human instrument of adjusting spontaneously and creatively to different types of data. Guba and Lincoln note that, while conducting an unstructured interview, the researcher may uncover ancillary data that may be of considerable importance in understanding the person or group being interviewed. During such an interview, the researcher may register the aesthetic tastes of the respondent(s) by viewing their room(s), office(s), or general environment.[6] The researcher is not limited to the specific data collected in the interview; auxiliary data are limited only by the researcher's sensitivity to their presence and potential weight. Accordingly the researcher simultaneously must deal with the multiplicity of levels of direct data. Adaptability points to the multipurpose character of qualitative researchers. This quality is paramount. Much qualitative research does not begin with a specific hypothesis. Instead, one begins with research questions and hunches. Therefore one often enters the research process (1) with a methodology that is something like a tool box, (2) a chosen data site, and (3) a general sense of where that research may go. Adaptability is necessary in order for the researcher to investigate a field site until issues and patterns erupt and become concretized through the qualitative inquiry process.

The third characteristic of the qualitative researcher as primary instrument, *holistic emphasis*, is related to adaptability. The limit of testing constructs in the human instrument is measured by the inventiveness of both the researcher and the respondents.[7] Holistic emphasis points to the ability to see beyond a delimited topic to its overall context. Respondents in a study are interpreted from the standpoint that they are part of a world that provides a context that defines the meanings of their actions and lives. Traditionally educational researchers tend to dislocate these contextual and existential aspects of research entities from their overt purview because of the near impossibility of managing the inherently confounding variables in such data. Thus the traditional dislocation between the rich context of a site or group being studied and the purposes of methods in traditional research is an example of exerting some control over the data. However, in the qualitative researcher's responsive approach, if such data are collected in the field, then he or she must adapt the research design to that more holistic context. In this way, traditional control is replaced by openness. More directly observable data may help define and ground less conventional and somewhat existential areas inherent in the context of the field site. The interfacing of directly perceived and conceived data types can enrich the study, although the researcher may risk losing precision and control as he or she moves from directly observable entities to contextual concerns.

Guba and Lincoln also suggest that holistic emphasis points to the ethnographic demand for the researcher to understand statements and issues articulated by the respondents within their own frame of reference. However, they retreat from the requirement of some sociologists and anthropologists who have formulated ethnographic procedures that require the researcher to become a living part of the culture in which the research is being performed. Thus a qualitative researcher whose field site is in an inner-city high-crime area may not live there in order to achieve coherent qualitative research. Nevertheless, he or she must devote sufficient time to understand the context or "life world" of the educational setting. In so doing, more directly observable, specific day-to-day educational phenomena and actions can be enriched by understanding the often less overt holistic context of the field site.

Another quality is the ability to investigate subconscious experiences. That is what Guba and Lincoln term *knowledge base expansion*, the fourth characteristic they say qualitative researchers manifest. Discursive or propositional knowledge is usually defined as knowledge that can be articulated through speaking or in written language. Many writers, including chemist and noted philosopher Michael Polanyi, have explored a realm of knowledge that is prepropositional.[8] Anyone can recall an experience of knowing something intuitively without explicitly articulating that knowledge in language. Guba and Lincoln note that qualitative researchers must be open not only to their own "tacit knowledge" but also to the "tacit knowledge" base of the participants of their research. Tapping into and responding to this realm of knowledge may enable researchers to connect propositional data to the "life world" that helps to situate the holistic context of the field site.

Guba and Lincoln's fifth characteristic, *processual immediacy*, is the researcher's power to process data instantly as received, screen the data, and, as a result of that instantaneous distillation, be prepared to effect modification or variation in the direction of the investigation. Thus data analysis and collection are mutually dependent and depend to a large extent on the context and the practicalities of doing data analysis in the field.[9] Margot Ely and colleagues provide copious practical steps for formatting and keeping a log, the use of analytic memos, and ongoing data analysis.[10] In the field, Ely and colleagues suggest there are two ways for field researchers to make observational notes: (1) write notes directly into the text itself set off by the use of parentheses or (2) use marginalia.[11] In addition, participant observers may begin to categorize their observational notes in terms of (1) their methodology, (2) ethical issues, or (3) the clarification of earlier observations.[12] While Guba and Lincoln suggest that data analysis and modifications in method and focus are best made at a distance from the field site, given the relative flexibility in the human instrument, data collection processes and directions as well as analysis are often refined and modified in the field. While conventional questionnaires cannot be changed in midcollection, qualitative researchers often alter their inquiries based on clearly determined evaluations (albeit qualitative) that provide justification for such changes. This allows them to accommodate data that cast a new light on the overall database. Guba and Lincoln assert that the ability of the human instrument to redirect inquiry increases the credibility of qualitative research. The ability to process immediately and respond to data through adaptation to the database is a great strength of the qualitative researcher as primary instrument. While there is a clear connection between processual immediacy and adaptability, they remain distinct. As a result of the ability to process data instantaneously, one may choose to adapt the inquiry to new themes, issues, and patterns. Thus research focuses may change.

When performing an interview, the researcher has opportunities for *clarification and summarization*, Guba and Lincoln's sixth characteristic. When a respondent makes a statement, the interviewer can ask the interviewee to clarify or embellish. The purpose is to understand actions and meanings within the context of the field site from the vantage point of the participants in your research. In this way, during an open or unstructured interview, a qualitative researcher can examine and penetrate the meaning of a respondent's answers. Some interviews are spontaneous and others are systematically planned and performed. However, embellishment may not be so practical when utilizing written questionnaires that, by their construction, do not allow for any meaningful modification of the inquiry based on the responses received. Summarization, according to Guba and Lincoln, serves three purposes.[13] First, it allows researchers to check their data collection with the interviewee. Second, summarization is a way to "get the informant on record." The informant can choose to take issue with previously collected data or not. Of course, summarization does not guarantee that informants are being honest; it just increases the chance that they will more fully express and clarify their intent. This interview tactic can add credibility to the collected information. Finally information that has been neglected by the respondent or excluded by the researcher can be added.

Guba and Lincoln cite Lewis A. Dexter, who notes that standardized interviews and typical surveys handle atypical responses statistically.[14] There does not seem to be a way for standardized tests to *explore atypical or idiosyncratic* (sometimes termed "elite") *responses* effectively. Qualitative inquirers can obtain "inside" information more effectively than a test by placing themselves in positions that allow for the observation and/or interview of atypical, special, or "elite" respondents. Such data may be entrapped by the formula-like structure of a standardized instrument. The data collected from such individuals may significantly enlarge or alter the boundaries of the inquiry. With the strength of an inherent responsiveness to such deviations in the overall database (that written survey questionnaires may not have), the qualitative inquirer, through processual immediacy, can instantaneously modify the direction of the inquiry. Through such adaptation, researchers broaden the boundaries of their inquiries in a manner that will accommodate the goal of holistic richness in qualitative research.

STRATEGIES FOR FIELD RESEARCH

John Lofland and Lyn Lofland delineate several aspects of qualitative field research.[15] Many of those aspects, which in some cases define steps in the process, are summarized below. While the following section uses much of Lofland and Lofland's overall format, the discussion is not limited to their presentation. The steps are as follows:

1. Selection of a research topic
2. Selection of an appropriate field site
3. Gaining access to the field site
4. Getting along with the members of the group under study
5. Recording data
6. Confirming data
7. Analyzing data
8. Data presentation/the narrative

Often the *selection of a research topic* is based on the researcher's current or past concerns. These concerns may relate to their profession, social class, personal preferences, and so on. Starting the research process on the basis of where one is in one's life provides a genuinely personal and emotional commitment to the chosen topic. Chapter 1 in the current text provides many helpful procedures for selecting a research problem.

Once a research topic has been established, one must *select an appropriate field site*. If one were interested in doctoral programs in music education, the list of potential sites would tend to be limited to institutions that grant the doctorate in music education. Geographical and practical aspects of the site would be weighed. Familiar institutions (e.g., the researcher's alma mater) can be tempting. However, the overall criterion for the selection of a field site is the extent to which it will provide the richest and most meaningful data. Data collection in the field requires direct contact with the group under study. This points to the need to consider one's relationship with the setting. Will you be welcome? Can you gain the trust of the participants? Will you be able to maintain sufficient scholarly distance?

When the site has been selected, one must work on *gaining access*, the third step. According to Lofland and Lofland, researchers must decide whether to keep research activities secret or make their work known to the group. However, a covert field researcher presents ethical issues. Therefore, even though it can be a daunting task to gain access to the field site, ethically it is better to carry on overt rather than covert field study. In this instance, field researchers make their intentions known, secure cooperation, and in most cases acquire formal permission. Researchers must identify the decision makers or gatekeepers who grant or deny access to the field site. The presentation of oneself as a candidate for field research should balance knowledge about the importance of the field site with a self-portrait that conveys a desire to learn more about the setting. Marked by courtesy, one's style and delivery to gatekeepers can be an important element in the presentation of a request to gain access. Also important is that in qualitative research, the promise of anonymity is assumed. The researcher should assure the decision makers that the real names of persons, and possibly places, will be excluded from the final research report.

A thorough, written explanation of the proposed research should be submitted to the field site gatekeeper(s).[16] This could begin by placing your project into the context of similar projects and/or by articulating its theoretical tradition. The research goals should be delineated as well as its consequence and even, if appropriate, its urgency. The use of the field site and interview of human subjects should be clearly depicted. Most colleges and universities require a human subject review prior to the commencement of field research. Successful application to one's institutional human subjects review should also be communicated to the decision makers at the field site. The researcher should specify the form of the report and who the potential readership might be. Finally a current vita can be attached, with any other materials, to the field site request-for-access proposal.

Once you have gained entry into the field site, you must *maintain a positive relationship with the members of the group.* The field researcher treats every member as a potential consultant. The reception may be enthusiastic, but Oswald Werner and G. Mark Schoepfle warn field researchers to be wary of overly enthusiastic participants.[17] One can quickly become inundated with requests and responsibilities that may be beyond the scope of the designated research. Most often, according to Werner and Schoepfle, the immediate response by the group to the researcher is benign neglect. As time passes, the field worker's activities may make stronger commitments possible with group members. Of course, rejection by the group is also a possibility. In rare instances, a hostile group will cause the researcher to leave the site and require that he or she look for another site.

Many insights on how to get along with respondents are delineated at the beginning of the current chapter under the heading "The Researcher as Instrument." What is important to note is that relationships in the field are a dynamic affair in a continuous state of change. Lofland and Lofland subdivide that overall living dynamic into three tasks.[18] First, one must get along with oneself. Personal problems can arise as a result of being in a new environment, the feeling of isolation, the lack of privacy, the fear of disclosing certain reported information, dislike for the participants, or the temptation to lose one's critical distance and simply become part of the group. Second, a major part of the dynamic is, obviously, getting along with the subjects. Lofland and Lofland accent the need to engender a relationship of trust with respondents. The researcher should not cause participants to feel threatened. Third, qualitative field researchers must balance their knowledge of the setting between an appropriate investigator role and that of an inquiring student who wishes to learn as much as possible about the field site from the viewpoint and through the eyes of the participants. Researchers must decide whether to stay aloof during internal debates within the membership or to align themselves with one faction. Of course, aligning oneself with one faction could be dangerous. In educational contexts, Lofland and Lofland note that when factions develop, field workers usually align themselves with either teachers or students but not both simultaneously. However, it is better to remain somewhat aloof and not take sides or appear to be supportive of one faction over another. Some members of the group may attempt to exclude the researcher from certain aspects of the database. In these instances, the researcher may need to make use of "allies," who might be some of the gatekeepers who were approached during step three of this overall process. In addition, researchers must deal with ethical questions posed by their own conscience and by colleagues. Many questions can arise: (1) Is it ethical to use allies to gain entree? (2) Is it ethical to take sides with factions? and (3) Is it ethical to study people whose actions one hates or with whom one has developed strong emotional ties?

Recording data, the fifth step, is a process that occurs in concert with the next two steps: confirming data and analyzing data. The research proposal will guide many decisions on what data to record and what data to neglect. Nevertheless, reporting data can be rather open-ended in qualitative inquiries. Researchers must remain open to new hypotheses and modifications of direction. The chief sources of data are the words and actions of the group under study. Werner and Schoepfle give weight to the reflexive observations of the researcher's own internal states as another important source of recording data. To wit, they suggest that there are two broad types of observations: observations of the outside world and observations of one's inner world. In maintaining critical distance, the researcher's abstractive power can be brought to bear on the observation, recording, and ongoing analysis of the data. Werner and Schoepfle further recommend that the researcher keep two journals: one for outside data and one for introspective accounts.[19] On the other hand and as noted above, Ely and colleagues recommend the use of one log book that incorporates such reflexive observations in the margins or set off by parentheses.[20] Data are recorded by using handwritten notes, audio and video tapes, photographs, and in some cases documents. The log book should be duplicated immediately so that future modifications and deletions can be considered against the original, unedited version. At least one copy should be in chronological order. In the field, jotted notes and memory can be used to "fill in the cracks." When you have returned from the field, immediate review of log notes is strongly recommended in order to facilitate recall and understanding of written or taped data.

Confirming the data, the sixth step, occurs both in the field and in the act of rereading field notes. Confirmation is the degree to which the reported data clearly represent a given situation.

This establishes some measure of confirmation and credibility. Marion Lundy Dobbart suggests that qualitative researchers are more concerned with validity than replicability because there may be more than one valid account of any social situation.[21] While researchers may be able to agree on what actually occurred, they often disagree on the meaning of the underlying patterns in those happenings. Moreover, human situations are always changing. A second researcher returning a year later to replicate the study may discover a modified field site. In fact, the original study may have caused modifications in behavior. Validity can be enhanced when field researchers utilize several research methods. These include varieties of participant observation and interviewing that are presented later in this chapter.

Lofland and Lofland provide seven criteria (in the form of questions) by which the trustworthiness of the recorded data can be checked:[22]

1. Is the account built on direct perception or were the data gathered by secondhand or less direct means?

2. What was the spatial location of the researcher and is that a factor?
3. What is the impact of the social relationship of the researcher and the respondent on the possible validity of secondhand data? Might the respondent be intentionally distorting the information?
4. Is the researcher being self-serving? Has any information been ignored or omitted?
5. What is the history of errors and/or distortion in previous written field notes regarding researcher or participant information?
6. Is the recorded account internally consistent or are there contradictions?
7. Does the recorded account have external consistency with other reports of the same occurrences?

A more recent approach is represented by Laurel Richardson in the magnum opus of qualitative research, *Handbook of Qualitative Research* (2000).[23] Richardson promotes the act of writing as a "method of inquiry."[24] Qualitative research is meant to be read in its entirety. Richardson notes that distinctive from quantitative studies in which graphs and charts can be scanned, qualitative research must be read to understand its meaning.[25] "Writing up" one's field notes should not be a mere exercise that reads like a scientific report. Instead, qualitative researchers should study great literary styles in order to hone in on better writing skills. To that end, the use of metaphor and poetic style should be incorporated. Richardson opines that to the extent that qualitative researchers attempt to capture an informant's perception, they must narrate the informant's story. The use of poetic devices such as pauses and alliterations will better capture the informant's actual "talk."[26] In this way, the ethnographic constituents of qualitative research remain more closely tied to human conditions.

As described earlier in this chapter (as conceived by Guba and Lincoln), observing, note taking, confirmation, and data analysis are often simultaneous activities during field research. Data analysis actually goes hand in hand with data collection. Data is distilled or reduced almost immediately as it is collected. Thus analysis is always ongoing and continually helps the researcher to sculpt subsequent observation, data collection, and analysis. At a metacognitive level, the researcher is critically refining emerging themes. Data collection and analysis are intimately linked to the emerging quality of field research.

Lofland and Lofland's seventh step, *data analysis,* is thus not the conclusory step in a linear process, but part of a contrapuntal texture of multiple processes and strata interacting and informing each other. Clearly the log book is the central data collection tool. Ely and colleagues recommend numbering the lines and the pages.[27] Lofland and Lofland note that a chronological copy of field notes can act as the master file. A duplicate copy is then organized into categories of interest. In addition, a biographical cross-file can be composed for each of the participants. Events can also be categorized by type. Themes tend to develop as these events are connected. Studying cross-files can result in coding field notes in many different ways and under different categories. This process is closely related to the largely inductive strategies of the natural history method. In providing narrative analyses of the meaning of the field note descriptions, the researcher carefully uncovers linkages and patterns as well as relationships.[28]

Having provided an overview of the role of the researcher and general strategies in qualitative research, a more detailed account of techniques of data collection through observation and interview and data analysis is presented below.

PARTICIPANT OBSERVATION

A cardinal technique for data collection in qualitative research, participant observation is traditionally connected with field research.[29] Usually the researcher must dedicate a relatively long period of observation in a field setting.[30] Through participant observation, the researcher gains some level of membership as he or she is socialized in the field site group.[31] While in anthropology an observer's participation in the activities of a group of persons often requires learning their language and values, usually these requirements are adjusted in educational research. The need to "speak the language" tends to be met by qualitative educational researchers insofar as their field work tends to be in their own countries. Nevertheless, a researcher doing fieldwork in a distant part of the United States may have to learn indigenous habits of "talk." In the case of an ethnomusicological study of American Indian music, traditional ethnographic directives, including the assimilation of the native language, might have to be satisfied. But even in cases not so ethnographically distinct, matters of language and empathy remain important. For example, a study in jazz education might require understanding idiosyncratic "talk." In all field sites, qualitative researchers must remain sensitive to indigenous uses of language.

As participant observers, educational researchers engage in the activities of the group and then re-create those activities and interactions in field notes written during the activities as quickly as possible after their happening. Researchers try to draw from the group its sense of reality, its patterns, meanings, and issues. We collect stories, anecdotes, and myths in order to formulate the important concerns and meanings of the group.[32] At times, the articulation of themes and beliefs by the group might not be congruent with the observed behavior of its members.[33] Often the behavior of individuals in the group or the group as a whole is at odds with stated intentions and research goals. In some cases, participant observers become more actively involved with the group by informing that group about the discrepancies between its stated goals and behavior observed by the researcher. Responses to the observer's insights and possible modifications in behavior may become the subsequent focus of the research.

At times, field researchers perceive reasons to conceal their observer status. Observers may conclude that if they presented themselves as researches they will be rejected. However, as noted earlier, this presents ethical problems. Alternatively, an observer may conclude that their status as an observer will cause the group to behave differently from its usual habits. This reactive behavior modification might disallow an accurate reconstruction of the dynamics and activities of the field site. In these instances, the observer "infiltrates" the setting and becomes a member of the group.[34] Some researchers conceal their research purpose to be in a better position to build friendly trust so that members of the group more readily "open up."[35] However, many researchers (including the writer) reject concealed (covert) observation on ethical grounds as an invasion of privacy.[36] In addition, Raymond Gold notes that methodological problems arise because the researcher may lose scholarly perspective.[37] The concealed researcher may be reluctant to ask "too many" questions or taking on-the-spot notes for fear of being exposed. Finally the concealed observer cannot clarify and confirm earlier notes with informants for similar reasons.

There are various possible degrees of direct participation in the activities of the group. At one end of the spectrum, the researcher is involved completely. In studying high school orchestras, a field researcher might play in the violin section, eat lunch with the members, and interact with orchestra members before, during, and after rehearsals. At the other end of the spectrum, a field researcher minimizes participation with the group. Walter Borg and Meredith Gall refer to this type of observation as "nonparticipant."[38] While observing in the field, nonparticipant observers endeavor to achieve an impartial, neutral orientation by positioning themselves in unobtrusive places within the field site. Nonparticipant observation often entails minute-by-minute accounts of the activities of the group. Clearly one loses many of the creative and spontaneous strengths and qualities of the researcher as instrument (discussed earlier in this chapter) in nonparticipant observation.

J. P. Spradley distinguishes three types of field observation: descriptive, focused, and selective.[39] Descriptive observation is usually all that is possible in the early stages of a fieldwork project. One tries to capture "everything," clearly an impossible task. This is the case when the researcher must become oriented to a new field site and remain open to most forms of data. In so doing, researchers observe and describe in their log book virtually everything and anything. The most common problem with such open descriptive observations is that the researcher becomes mired in unessential details.

As the field researcher begins to distill and reduce data and moves to a metacognitive (abstract) level, Spradley's second type of field observation, focused observation, commences. The researcher becomes cognizant of patterns and issues that enable concentration on certain data while others are distilled. Focused observation accents the observation and report of types or categories of activities and the development of taxonomies and other semantic structures.

Finally, according to Spradley, selective observation requires a further sharpening of one's focus. Distinguished from focused observation, which tends to scrutinize types or categories of activities, selective observation concentrates on the "attributes" of those types of activities performed by the group. Instead of generating taxonomies, selective observation may provide folk or inveterate definitions of the structures that were identified in focused observation. Spradley also notes that all three observational stages are directed by the original proposal, the researcher's developing comprehension of the data site, and views expressed by the respondents. Indeed, the ongoing analysis of data (including the writing of analytical memos) should indicate gaps and additional questions for further exploration. These gaps and new questions tend to require new interviews of members of the group under study.

Goetz and LeCompte provide a framework that synthesizes observational matrices frequently used in field research.[40] Participant observers tend to watch and listen for answers to the following questions. Field researchers are not required to address all of them. Instead, Goetz and LeCompte provide this synthesis in order to delineate important areas of potential observational focus:

1. Who comprises the group or setting? What is their total number? How does one acquire membership? Are the characteristics of and types in the group relevant to the study?
2. What is occurring? What do the group members do and say to each other? What is the research problem or task?
   a. Are there repetitive or irregular behaviors? What resources are required in activities, and how are they disseminated? Are activities coordinated, categorized, taught, and justified? Are there different social contexts?
   b. What is the rapport between group members? How do they participate and interact? What is their connection? Are there evident differences in status and role within this interaction?
   c. What is the nature of the meaning and matter of their discussions? Are there common subjects? What stories or anecdotes are reportable? Are means of communication comprised of verbal and nonverbal languages? Are conversations rooted in beliefs? Do conversations follow formats? Do some people talk while others only listen?
3. Where is the group or setting? What are the physical contexts in that scenario? What natural resources are there? Are technologies created or utilized? How are space and physical objects allocated for use? What things are consumed? Are there any products that result from the activities of the group? Within the context of the group's usage, are there salient sights, sounds, smells, and feeling sensations?
4. When does the group meet and interact? What are the length and frequency of these meetings? What is (are) the group's position(s) on the use and distribution of time as well as the re-

lationship of the present within the context of the past and the future?

5. How are the elements identified above connected? Are there patterns of interaction? Is the perspective of those connections and patterns the researcher's or the group's? Is there stability? Is change possible and, if so, how is it handled? How does the group govern itself: through rules, norms or mores? Are there relationships with other groups or organizations?

6. Why is this group in existence? Why does it function as it does? Is that function and existence congruent with the group's history? Are there symbols, traditions, values, and cultural views that can be discovered in the group?

INTERVIEW

An interview with a member or members of the group may be structured or unstructured, or at some point in between.[41] In a strict sense, interviewing differs from observation: observation leans more heavily toward listening and seeing; in an interview, the researcher takes a more active role by prompting a participant with questions. As discussed earlier, however, observation is not always neutral. While demarcating lines might be easier to draw between nonparticipant ("neutral") observation and interviewing, in participant observation the researcher may take an active role in group activities by prompting, showing, manipulating, or otherwise intervening in the data-gathering process. In practice, therefore, participant observation overlaps with interviewing techniques; there are numerous degrees of active participation in observation. A similar spectrum of strategies is found in interviewing. Interviews can be in the form of highly structured surveys in which the researcher poses the same prepared questions to all participants. By way of contrast, unstructured (open-ended) interviews may have a list of areas of concern without a specified chronological order of formulated questions offering flexibility as new issues emerge in the field.[42] Spradley describes interviews in fieldwork as friendly conversations in which the researcher incrementally inserts new issues in order to acquire a fuller sense of the field site.[43] When such interviews take on the complexion of unstructured conversations with members of the group, it may be difficult to distinguish them from similar techniques of participant observation.

Preparing for the Interview

Werner and Schoepfle stress the importance of the preinterview or "contact" stage.[44] The early contact stage begins before the researcher arrives at the site of the interview. The selection of potential consultants may be ad hoc, opportunistic, based on the potential consultant's expertise or social standing, or according to a systematic plan.[45] Barbara Tymitz and Robert L. Wolf urge the researcher to contact personally each prospective consultant.[46] The introduction to the interview should be courteous and informative. Letters of introduction, friends, and colleagues can be used in order to urge potential consultants to agree to be interviewed. The researcher should acquire as much background information on the interviewee as possible. The entirety of this data should facilitate the formulation of preliminary questions and topics. Consultants should be informed in writing of the time, date, and place of the interview. An estimate of the time needed and a short description of the study are also helpful. A confirming telephone call or e-mail one day in advance of the scheduled interview is advised. Researchers should dress in accordance with the surroundings of the field site and interview.

Werner and Schoepfle warn interviewers to create a checklist of all of the items of equipment needed for the interview. Few occurrences are more disruptive than a malfunctioning tape recorder, lap top, and so on. To that end, a field researcher should have backup equipment and supportive related items such as batteries, wires, cables, and so on.

Before presenting several strategies that may be used in interviews, three types of interview will be discussed. According to Goetz and LeCompte, whether interviews are structured or unstructured, they generally fall into one of the following types: key informant interviewing, career or life histories, and surveys.[47]

Key Informant Interviewing

Key informants are members of the group who have special knowledge, status, or ability to communicate. One reason for interviewing a key informant is that he or she may have access to information otherwise denied to the researcher. If one were doing a study of choirs in junior high school settings, student members might be potential key informants. Students may have insights into perceptions of a field site that are considerably different from those of an adult music teacher or administrator. As Borg and Gall note, criteria for selecting students as key informants include whether they are (1) in leadership roles, (2) brighter than and more mature than other students, and (3) willing to be interviewed.[48] Goetz and LeCompte stress that care must be used in choosing students and in integrating their knowledge. While key informants may add valuable insights, they can also manipulate the researcher and confound otherwise developing patterns and meanings in the collected data.

Career or Life Histories

Career or life histories are interviews that encourage narrative accounts of the participant's professional or personal life. This type of interview is representative of the current interest in qualitative research in narrative methodologies.[49] The underlying logic is that overall observed actions can be better understood when a researcher can balance the intersubjective actions of the group with more private and biographic information specific to a particular subject, or participant.[50] For example, in studying chamber music instruction, a researcher could interview a chamber music teacher in order to elicit information that might provide a detailed account of their training, the development of their methods, modifications in their teaching practices, and other aspects of the working environment. Goetz and LeCompte note that career histories are more common than life histories in research concerning educational settings. Biographical career information that is collected from professionals may significantly impact on the researcher's understanding of the educational setting, its values, important issues, and practices.

Surveys

Survey instruments are used for highly structured interviews. Surveys are used when large amounts of data are needed from many respondents through a uniform and systematic instrument. In traditional educational research, surveys are used to collect quantitative data. In collecting numerical tabulations of some variable, the quantified results from a survey of a sampled population can be generalized to the entire group. In qualitative research, surveys are usually implemented subsequent to collecting data through less formal interviews and participant observations. When sufficient background information has been gathered, the survey instrument can be constructed and implemented by the researcher. Goetz and LeCompte (1984) explain three forms of surveys that are used in qualitative studies: confirmation instruments, participant-construct instruments, and projective devices.

Confirmation surveys assess the trustworthiness of earlier reports. These surveys are questionnaires that verify key informant and other kinds of data in terms of the entire group. Their purpose is to show the degree to which the group shares beliefs and behaviors. Confirmation surveys facilitate, and make manageable, investigations in which the group is comprised of a large number of members. In such a field site, it may be impossible to follow up with individual confirmation interviews. Goetz and LeCompte also note that the questionnaire in confirmation surveys provides easy storage of data for examination and possible replication of the study by other researchers. However, surveys in and of themselves lack the corroborational strength of observation. Participant observation is marked by direct, empirical data collection. When observation techniques, unstructured interviews, and surveys are used in concert, such triangulation of methods provides an eclectic ground that is most supportive of (1) capturing the holistic context while responding to details, (2) having defined directions yet being able to adapt to new issues and meanings, and (3) interfacing and thereby validating data that are gleaned through both formal and informal techniques.

Less structured than confirmation surveys, participant-construct surveys are used to understand how respondents structure their social and physical worlds, according to Goetz and LeCompte. Researchers attempt to determine a set of underlying structures that the group can agree on as important and real. Participants may be asked to delineate all of the members or entities that comprise a particular category of things. In studies in music education, one might ask participants to enumerate all types of repertoire performed by the group. Students in an elementary school band could be asked to compose two lists that specify what they and their teachers can do during rehearsals. Goetz and LeCompte note that in an analogous study carried out by LeCompte, a typology of children's thoughts concerning their roles and those of their teachers was developed.[51] The parameters of categories that respondents use to structure their world and the means they use to determine those categories are clarified through interviews. It is possible to formulate sociograms in which respondents arrange the names of other members of the group following any logical set of criteria. For example, respondents (teachers, students, administrators, etc.) may be asked to categorize students in a fifth grade band based on whether they take private lessons outside of school, whether they own their instruments, the level of their performance ability, their popularity, their dress, or their maturity.

Projective techniques are used when the researcher cannot observe the behavior of members of the group in actual situations involved in the study. This may be the case when eliciting information about home practice habits of junior high school orchestral players. In this instance, photographs, drawings, or games may be used to draw out opinions and reactions in order to determine patterns of behavior that are unobservable in the field site.[52] Goetz and LeCompte note that many researchers use ambiguous or indirect stimuli to acquire information about the respondent's values and self-image. These can be helpful in assessing the impact of different degrees of authority structures in classrooms on one's self-image. Projective techniques must be combined or triangulated with other techniques of field research in order to corroborate the meaning that respondents extrapolate from their environments.[53]

Performing an Interview

Fontana and Frey note that in structured interviews, interviewers ask preestablished questions with little room for embellishment.[54] In structured interviews, all interviewees are asked questions in the same sequence in as consistent a manner as possible. The interviewer must play the most neutral role possible. Fontana and Frey recount traditional guidelines for structured interviewing.[55]

1. Don't give long explanations regarding the study. Just give a standard introduction.
2. Don't deviate from the order of introduction and sequence of questions and keep the question wording consistent.
3. Don't suggest answers or debate answers. Do not expose personal viewpoints on the topics under questioning.
4. Don't interpret the meaning of a question. Just repeat the question if asked and simply provide clarifications that have been preestablished.

5. Don't improvise by adding new answer categories or by changing words.

In structured interviews, problems are defined by the researcher
in advance and the respondent is expected to answer in terms of
the interviewer's framework and research questions. This kind of
interview is closer to the end of a spectrum demarcated by the
questionnaire, with the unstructured interview at the opposite
end. The object of structured interviews is to gain largely representative or "typical" responses that will enrich the researcher's
frame of reference.

On the other hand, unstructured interviews are more open-
ended. Guba and Lincoln prefer the unstructured interview because it allows the respondent to shape the focus and direction of
the interview.[56] Key informant interviews tend to be unstructured
because the interviewee is usually in command of special knowledge. Giving a key informant as much license as possible may generate data of greater depth because the key informant probably
knows considerably more about the topic than the interviewer.
Thus unstructured interview questions should not limit the content
of the interview to the interviewer's knowledge base. In addition,
unstructured interviews are necessary when a researcher is suddenly confronted with unsolicited information. Spontaneous conversations between participants and the researcher are often in the
form of unstructured interviews.

Given the looser setting in an unstructured interview, the researcher can be more varied and informative in how he or she intro-
duces the project and one's role. Dexter advises that after introducing oneself, the researcher should briefly summarize the project
followed by a brief explanation of the interviewer's role.[57] The physical surroundings of the interview should support a feeling of ease.
Whenever possible, no other persons should be present unless this
has been discussed in advance or if the interview is unsolicited and
spontaneous and privacy is not possible. Guba and Lincoln stress
value-neutral behavior but also encourage gentle prompting by the
interviewer. The rhythm and ambience of the interview can resem-
ble an interesting conversation in which both conversants are actively involved and concerned. All writers on this subject concur
that of paramount importance is that the interviewer be sensitive to
the worldview of the interviewee.

Constructing interview questions is an activity of fundamental importance to the researcher. Clearly the nature of these questions will depend on the expertise, intelligence, and maturity as well as the social and professional status of interviewer and interviewee. Guba and Lincoln delineate ten useful types of questions that may be posed.[58]

1. Hypothetical questions start with a "what if" phrase.
2. Pose the ideal questions that prompt the consultant to respond to a hypothetical situation.
3. Devil's advocate questions confront the respondent with an opposing frame of reference or view.
4. Interpretive questions propose the meaning of events for response and consideration by the consultant.
5. Suggestive questions may elicit open-ended discussion.
6. Reason-why questions probe the respondent's explanation of an event.
7. Argument-type questions attempt to provoke the respondent to reveal information that might not be accessible without such provocation.
8. Source questions bring to light the grounds for information or supporting data and documents.
9. Qualified yes-no questions determine the earnestness of a respondent's feelings or beliefs concerning a particular issue or set of issues.
10. Filter questions require the respondent to create or modify categories, classes, types or kinds.

When an interviewer needs further information or more critical thinking about a particular response or issue, he or she may utilize different types of "probes."[59] According to Herbert J. Rubin, silence itself can be a useful probe.[60] Rubin notes that probes can provide reasons why certain reported actions took place. Guba and Lincoln list several kinds of probes:

1. Clarification probes require the interviewee to make a previous response less ambiguous.
2. Critical awareness probes ask the consultant to reflect on, evaluate, or exemplify an issue or an interpretation.
3. Amplification probes seek to draw further information.

4. Refocusing probes cause the respondent to draw new relation-
    ships or seek alternative answers.

Another aspect of questioning to consider while interviewing is
sequencing. Guba and Lincoln suggest three ways to sequence questions.[61] First, the funnel sequence orders questions from the general
to the specific. Questions must follow each other logically so that
there is coherence in the overall interview guide or list of questions.
Each question, building on information secured from previous answers, moves toward a narrowing of the topic. Starting with general
questions often helps to keep directions and concentrations in the interview open to different focuses. Second, the inverted funnel begins
with specificity and moves to more general issues. This sequence
type can encourage hesitant respondents to become more open to
subsequent broader questions.

Third, the quintamensional method starts with questions requiring "descriptive awareness" responses, then shifts to those eliciting
value judgments and the expression of personal feelings or attitudes
toward that issue or topic. For example, a question requiring a descriptive awareness response might be, "Did you know that even
though the repertoire requirement in the concerto competition was
open to all styles, the conductor preferred to select someone playing
a Mozart concerto?" That question could be followed by, "Did that
knowledge cause any resentment by competitors who prepared concerti by other composers and in other periods?" "Was anyone an-
gry?" "What did they say?" Then, in order to probe the personal in-
tensity of the respondent's part of this issue, "How do you feel about
this issue." "Do you think that the conductor should have delimited
the repertoire to Mozart concerti?" "Does the fact that the winner
happened to be the only person who prepared a Mozart concerto
have an impact on your feelings concerning the competition . . . the
winner . . . the conductor . . . the orchestra . . . the music program?"
As demonstrated in the previous sequence of questions, quintamensional method starts with questions that do not require emotionally
charged answers but ask for descriptive responses. However, those
descriptive responses open the door to a topic about which the researcher would like to probe the consultant's feeling. As one moves
the respondent in that direction, questions should intensify and
thereby elicit data that reveal the depth of the respondent's feelings
toward an issue. This could appear to be a "setup." That is, like an

attorney during a cross-examination, the interviewer using the quintamensional method as described above might appear to be baiting the participant. Therefore the researcher must strike an ethical balance between (1) probing in a way that situates the respondent's inner feelings as they bear on and possibly inform answers and (2) not becoming overly manipulative.

DATA ANALYSIS

Data analysis is a continuous process that happens during the activities of participant observations and interviews, the period immediately following each of these data-collection segments, and continues after fieldwork is completed. In each of these segments of the overall study, the analysis of data includes organizing, reducing, describing, prioritizing, and interpreting. (Note that some qualitative researchers distinguish the analysis of data from the interpretation of data.[62] In our view, such distinction is not necessary. Interpretation is understood as a mode of analysis.) In addition to it being a continuous process throughout and after fieldwork, data analysis is also an emerging process because the log book entries grow and emerge as the study progresses. Analysis includes dividing parts of the log book, as described below. However, deciding on which parts of the overall log book *are* constituent parts—meaningful segments of the log book—results from a continual dialectical relationship between those developing constituent parts with the entirety of the log book. This points to the hermeneutic aspects of data analysis and the circularity involved therein.

Simply put, hermeneutics is the field of interpretation theory. The concept of the hermeneutic circle is centuries old. German philosopher F. D. E. Schleiermacher (1768–1834), explains: "Every particular thing can be understood only through the intermediary of the whole, and thus every explanation of the particular already presupposes the comprehension of the whole."[63] Schleiermacher considered the exegesis or analysis of texts to be a heuristic part of the art of understanding. In addition to understanding the parts in relation to the whole, qualitative researchers attempt to understand the data through the eyes of the respondents and participants. Schleiermacher refers to this abstractive power as "divination."[64] True understanding of a text under study requires the qualitative researcher to reach back to the seminal moments of the conception of those words by the speaker or author.[65] In so doing, the qualitative researcher as data analyst re-creates the original (i.e., the respondent's intended) meaning of that segment of the log book text and places its meaning and potential priority in terms of understanding the log book in its entirety, an "entirety" that is ongoing and ever growing until the last words are written.

Data analysis can take the form of written thoughts regarding emerging questions, patterns, and themes. As one breaks the whole into constituent parts and then reassembles them, he or she can begin to understand those parts in terms of the whole.[66] Such analysis is part science and part art. Margot Ely, Ruth Vinz, Maryann Downing, and Margaret Anzul term the constituent elements of a log book "meaning units" or "thinking units."[67] In the many readings of a segment of data, researchers insert labels, often in the form of marginalia, that identify meaning units in a process termed coding.[68] The coded data are then categorized into "bins" and arranged into organized form, which can be an outline, according to Ely and colleagues (1997).[69] Data analysis can also entail the creation of key words in context lists. The researcher locates the uses of a particular word in the log book and considers its usage within the context of a number of words (e.g., twenty) before and after that word at issue.[70] Similarly "word counts" can help uncover patterns of ideas by tracing the similarities and differences in the use of specific words. According to Gery W. Ryan and H. Russell Bernard, word counts can be effected through analytical memos and can help in identifying noteworthy constructs and be of assistance when comparing across groups.[71]

Analytical memos build links between observational notes. These links may develop into patterns and themes that add a conceptual structure and logic to the data and to the meaning of the activities in the field site. This aids in planning each new observation and interview because it builds on what has been previously analyzed. In this regular review of observation notes and interview "write-ups," data analysis provides a reconsideration of data that might locate contradictions or conflicts regarding the perspectives of reality between the researcher and the group. Throughout this process, regular return to the original research proposal, from which the research may have diverged, is recommended.

Recurring ideas are often the basis of the formation of tentative categories. Categories can be clarified by comparing them to early thoughts that may have been written in the margins. As the researcher compares old categories to newer ones, she reconsiders the importance of previously notated themes. Often beginning with general themes that may have been extrapolated from the related literature, new themes can erupt as metaphors, word repetitions and shifts in content.[72] Another important device in the overall coding of data is the construction of codebooks, which are organized lists of codes.[73] Citing K. M. MacQueen and colleagues, Ryan and Bernard suggest that codebooks ought to include detailed descriptions of each code with examples thereof and the criteria that were used for inclusion and exclusion of codes.[74]

Robert C. Bogdan and Sari Knopp Biklen distinguish analysis performed in the field site from analysis that is performed after data collection is completed, day by day. They provide several helpful suggestions for executing the former.[75]

1. Plan future data-collection sessions and build new directives and issues based on insights developed from analyses of previous field notes.
2. Write many "observer's comments" on the field note pages in your ongoing data analysis. Begin grouping the meanings of recurring words, events, ideas, and topics.
3. Write self-memos about what has been learned thus far.
4. Check self-developing ideas and analytical insights on members of the group. Utilize the services of key informants for this purpose. However, do not defer to their opinions completely but balance them with your own personal insights.
5. Utilize metaphors and analogies. Try to raise actual events to higher levels of abstraction. Try to capture the spirit of the particular setting and happening.

In the final stages of data analysis, the researcher has left the field, and the line between analysis and interpretation blurs. The researcher must extrapolate and construct meanings. As the data analysis reaches its final stages, one should still review the original research proposal. It is important to understand new problems, questions, and directions in terms of the original plan. Some degree of divergence from the original proposal is to be expected in qualitative research. Similarly, like practicing scales on an instrument, one can never reread raw data as well as initial and intermediary analyses too much. The researcher should question data in a way that is similar to the manner in which respondents were questioned.[76] Underscored words, phrases, patterns, and events that have become "coding categories" provide a way of further sorting data.[77] These categories and analytical memos become the ground for further organization, abstraction, integration, and synthesis and can be placed in outline form. The overall process of locating patterns and regularities and placing them into categories is like putting together a jigsaw puzzle. The raw data are analogous to all of the pieces in a big pile, without form, pattern, or meaning. After sorting and filing, patterns begin to develop and a clearer picture of what the puzzle or field notes might represent and mean emerges. A critical point is that the data is being reduced through the analytic memos. Written summaries should accompany the creation of each new pattern or category in the developing puzzle. Justifications for fitting data together are derived both from the researcher's insights and from statements made by participants that have been recorded in field notes. Broad themes will begin to develop that run through all or significant portions of the data. Themes that begin by being pertinent to only one character may be discovered to also characterize other members of the group.

The late stage sorting and coding of data can be daunting. Bogdan and Bilken provide several "coding families" or types that can be helpful.[78]

1. Context codes contain very general data concerning the setting, topic, or subjects.
2. Definition of the situation codes clarify the manner in which subjects define a setting or issue. It is a place to file participants' world views. Data filed in this unit should answer questions such as, what is important to participants and what are their goals?
3. Participants' perspectives include data that shed light on the shared rules and norms of the subjects.
4. Participants' perspectives about other people uncover how subjects understand each other.
5. Process codes refer to words and phrases that cut across sequences of events or time. The researcher views persons, groups, or events over time and attempts to perceive change occurring within that sequence.

6. Activity codes signify regularly occurring types of activities.
7. Strategy codes refer to the means by which members accomplish objectives.
8. Relationship and social structure codes consist of patterns of behavior by members who are not officially defined as part of the organization. These might include friendships, romances, enemies, and cliques.
9. Methods codes separate data that bear on research procedures.

During later stages of data analysis, categories become building blocks or units for still larger categories. Goetz and LeCompte stress that broad categories or divisions must be congruent to the natural field site setting.[79] Categorization requires tasks that include comparing, contrasting, aggregating, and ordering.[80] This supports linking units to form larger categories. Bases for sorting items into categories include spatial, physico-temporal, conceptual, linguistic, or social relationships.

When analyzing similarities and differences in the developed categories, the researcher must articulate the manner in which each unit is used and identify their respective significance. Properties of each category are uncovered by delineating the ways in which all of a category's units are alike and different from units that constitute other large categories.[81] These properties then form the core of abstract definitions for each category. Some properties of units may be common to units that are in different categories. Searches for differences between units are accented in the later stages of analysis. These analyses provide further elaboration and qualification of the larger categories. On that basis, new categories can be formed and former categories abandoned. Thus new themes are discovered as previously identified themes are clarified, embellished, and even abandoned.

Many qualitative field researchers return to the field site after the final stages of data analysis. This rechecking of data analysis by returning to the field increases the credibility of data analysis. One may find that broad themes and meanings resonate (or not) with the worldview of the group and their living field site context. Discrepancies may materialize (or not). Insights that were developed away from the field site can be given a real or concrete perspective through which to reconsider their credibility.

COMPUTER SOFTWARE AND QUALITATIVE RESEARCH

A broad and ever-expanding number of software programs are available for qualitative data analysis. Eben A. Weitzman provides a helpful overview of the many uses of computer software for qualitative data analysis.[82]

1. Writing and transcribing field notes (broken out into separate uses in Weitzman)
2. Editing field notes
3. Coding by connecting words and tags to parts of the text or for audio and video
4. Systematic storing of the text
5. Locating parts of the text in quick searches
6. Linking data in order to create categories, clusters, and so on
7. Analytic memoing or commentary to be used for further data analysis
8. Analyzing content by instant enumeration of the use of words alone or in combination
9. Condensing data into various formats for review
10. Checking the trustworthiness of earlier insights by helping in the interpretation of displayed data
11. Testing hunches and aiding in the development of theory
12. Generating diagrams that represent findings
13. Aid in writing intermediary and final reports

Weitzman notes that qualitative data analysis software provides greater consistency, speed, representation, and consolidation than manual tactics.[83] For example, a manual search of every place where a word or code appears in a log book could miss some entries. A global software search thereof will consistently find all entries. Moreover, such software searches are completed instantaneously. Multiple searches can be completed in seconds. Furthermore, reformatting sorts, codes, and segments of the text can be done consistently and with great speed. In addition, available software can create graphs that represent a researcher's thinking providing convenient visualizations that can generate new thinking about the data and help form theoretical understanding. Weitzman notes that software can consolidate all manner of field notes, interview transcripts, codes, memos, categories, and graphs into one place and in numerous configurations. This greatly helps the researcher to manage a huge amount of data.

Finally, Weitzman lists five software types or categories based on their functions.[84]

1. Text retrievers support searches for words and phrases. Available software includes Sonar Professional and Text Collector.
2. Textbase managers are used to store and organize text in various ways and allow the researcher to retrieve it using numerous criteria. (Weitzman notes that textbase managers may be superior to text retrievers in search operations.) Available software includes askSam, Folio Views, and Textbase Alpha.
3. Code and retrieve programs enable researchers to connect category codes to segments of text and to retrieve and display the text according to that coding. Available software includes HyperQual2, Qualpro, and Data Collector.
4. Code-based theory building programs are like code and retrieve programs but do even more. Weitzman notes that these programs do not actually create theory for researchers. Instead, they enable researchers to represent connections between codes, create higher-order categories, and help formulate and check theoretical propositions. In addition, some of these programs support creation of links between all of the constituent parts of a text, photos, videos, and audios. Available software include AFTER, AQUAD, and QCA.
5. Conceptual network builders support the preparation and analysis of network displays. They can provide graphs that represent the relationships between concepts and can provide analysis of cognitive networks. Available software includes SemMet and Decision Explorer.

New voice recognition and multimedia software programs are being developed that may greatly reduce the need to write nearly as much in the field. Nevertheless, researchers must still conceive of their research purposes and significance, select and gain access to field sites, understand the strategies of participant observation and interview, command data analysis, and be able to formulate theoretical implications for the research. Thus computer software for qualitative research does not and will not replace the researcher as instrument. As Weitzman notes, software will provide consistency and

speed along with manageability of the data in ways that are not possible without such software. Numerous books and articles are available for a more in-depth presentation of software for qualitative research.[85]

CREATING A NARRATIVE REPORT

"Narrative" refers to any spoken or written exposition. In qualitative research it tends to be associated with writing in a story form.
Like a story, narrative reports in qualitative research recount sequences of events arranged in a temporal order. Narrative reports
appear to have a plot and draw the reader into its "story" through
the use of metaphor, analogy, amplifications, and rhetorical techniques. Denzin calls for narrative texts to move away from a visual
paradigm in recognition of the nature of how we learn and understand viscerally (in fieldwork) through feeling, hearing, tasting,
smelling, and touching, often in rather subjective ways.[86] Denzin
lobbies for narrative ethnographic reports to move away from styles
that present allegedly objective pictures of a static world. Instead,
Denzin notes that the world of the field site is ever changing and
must be approached by texts that capture the world's acoustic
"sound and feel" in a performance mode that captures these
"melodic, rhythmic, and acoustical" realities. He points to feminist
writings as particularly relevant insofar as such writings are often
"multiperspectival or multisensual."[87]

Denzin is also in favor of a shift in the style of narrative reports to
the style of journalists (e.g., Truman Capote and Norman Mailer)
who provide a usable storytelling paradigm from which ethnogra-
phers can learn.[88] The paradox is that these "new journalists" utilized ethnographic devices in their writing about portentous public
events.[89] Ethnographic qualitative researchers in education must re-
claim those techniques in their narrative storytelling reports. As
noted earlier in this chapter and echoing Denzin's call for a more literary and poetic narrative style, Richardson urges that researchers
"write up" their narrative reports as poems, using pauses, alliterations, and other rhythmic devices that capture the acoustic and natural flow of talk.[90]

It may be a wrenching experience for researchers to transcend
their research study sufficiently to remain close to the material and

yet think about narrative styles that will convey the significance and meaning of months of field research. Drawing conclusions in a final narrative report requires interpretation of the meaning of the data in contexts that can go beyond the immediacy of the data site and study. Old categories may be refurbished and new linkages may be constructed. The final narrative report (which may include graphs and can be triangulated with other methods presented in this text) is an opportunity to consider the strengths and weaknesses in the chosen methodology and to consider the impact of those strengths and weaknesses on the collection and analysis of data. Conclusions can include assessment of the appropriateness of the chosen methodology for the study and the application of that methodology to other related studies.

Moving beyond conventional writing style and as promoted by Denzin and Richardson, the researcher can use metaphor and simile in order to enrich the final story telling. While these linguistic tools are often used in aesthetic inquiry, some researchers may be reluctant to take such a projective leap in qualitative research. Nevertheless, the similarities between arts criticism and curriculum criticism have become a leitmotiv in works by many qualitative researchers, Elliott Eisner most prominent among them.[91] Language use in qualitative narrative reports must be capable of achieving resonance and confluence with the holistic reality of the data site. The projective power of metaphor and simile provides the linguistic thrust necessary to send one's narrative in an intersecting course with the meanings that emanate from human living contexts.

FOR REVIEW, DISCUSSION, AND IMPLEMENTATION

- Qualitative researchers do not approach research problems with a preestablished method. Where does the qualitative researcher begin? How do early research questions and hunches become clarified?
- What are examples of social structures in music educational settings?
- How can qualitative researchers be the primary research instrument and yet replace their role as the subject in the subject-object correlation? Discuss the ideas of openness and responsiveness.

- What is the nature of the constituent parts to the whole in field sites and in data analysis?
- How can researchers in the field sharpen their "tacit knowledge" abilities?
- In what ways do participant observation and interview strategies and techniques intersect? In what ways are they different?
- Is it ethical to "infiltrate" a field site as a concealed observer?
- How can qualitative researchers in the field balance relationships with participants marked by sufficient professional distance yet the creation of a warm, friendly, and interested rapport? Is such a balance a self-contradiction?
- What is the nature of discursive language as compared with poetic language as that bears on the narrative report? Can discursive language adequately capture the multiple levels of social and individual behavior and action in the field site? Is poetic language insufficiently precise to convey analysis and interpretation of the data?
- How can computer software aid in qualitative research? Are there dangers in using such software? What are the advantages?

NOTES

1. Norman K. Denzin and Yvonna S. Lincoln, eds., *Handbook of Qualitative Research*, 2nd ed. (Thousand Oaks, Calif.: Sage, 2000), 4–6.

2. For a discussion of the need to utilize multiple methods for research in music, see Lawrence Ferrara, *Philosophy and the Analysis of Music: Bridges to Musical Sound, Form, and Reference* (New York: Greenwood, 1991), 33–46.

3. See Ferrara, 44–46.

4. Egon G. Guba and Yvonna S. Lincoln, *Effective Evaluation* (San Francisco: Jossey-Bass, 1983), 128–52. Also see M. H. Agar, *The Professional Stranger: An Informal Introduction to Ethnography* (New York: Academic, 1980).

5. Guba and Lincoln, 130. Also see work in "action research" by Christine O'Hanlon, ed., *Professional Development through Action Research in Educational Settings* (Washington, D.C.: Falmer, 1996). For example, in O'Hanlon, see Anne Edwards, "Can Action Research Give Coherence to the School-based Learning of Experiences of Students?" 141–54.

6. Guba and Lincoln, 131.

7. Guba and Lincoln, 132. Also see L. Grossberg, *Bringing It All Back Home: Essays on Cultural Studies* (Durham, N.C.: Duke University Press, 1997).

8. Michael Polanyi, *The Tacit Dimension* (Garden City, N.Y.: Doubleday, 1967).

9. Guba and Lincoln, 136.

10. Margot Ely, with Margaret Anzul, Teri Friedman, Diane Garner, and Ann McCormick Steinmitz, *Doing Qualitative Research: Circles within Circles* (Philadelphia: Falmer, 1991), 69–91.

11. Ely et al. 1991, 74.

12. Ely et al. 1991, 74–75.

13. Guba and Lincoln, 137.

14. See Lewis A. Dexter, *Elite and Specialized Interviewing* (Evanston, Ill: Northwestern University Press, 1970), 6.

15. John Lofland and Lyn H. Lofland, *Analyzing Social Settings: A Guide to Qualitative Observation and Analysis* (Belmont, Calif.: Wadsworth, 1984).

16. Oswald Werner and G. Mark Schoepfle, *Systematic Fieldwork* (Newbury Park, Calif.: Sage, 1987), 1:198–99.

17. Werner and Schoepfle, 239.

18. Lofland and Lofland, chap. 4.

19. Werner and Schoepfle, 239.

20. Ely et al. 1991, 74.

21. Marion Lundy Dobbart, *Ethnographic Research, Theory and Application for Modern Schools and Society* (New York: Praeger, 1982), 259–66. Also see Denzin and Lincoln 2000, 6–7.

22. Lofland and Lofland, 54.

23. Laurel Richardson, "Writing: A Method of Inquiry," in Denzin and Lincoln 2000, 923–48.

24. Richardson, 923.

25. Richardson, 924.

26. Richardson, 933.

27. Ely et al., 74.

28. Judith Preissle Goetz and Margaret Diane LeCompte, *Ethnography and Qualitative Design in Educational Research* (New York: Academic, 1984), 164–207.

29. James P. Spradley and David W. McCurdy, eds., *The Cultural Experience: Ethnography in Complex Society* (Chicago: Science Research Associates, 1972).

30. Thomas A. Schwandt, *Dictionary of Qualitative Inquiry, Second Edition* (Thousand Oaks, Calif.: Sage Publications, Inc., 2001).

31 Schwandt, 186. Also see Rosalie H. Wax, *Doing Fieldwork: Warnings and Advice* (Chicago: University of Chicago Press, 1971).

32. Goetz and LeCompte, 110.

33. Goetz and LeCompte, 110.

34. Jack D. Douglas, *Investigative Social Research: Individualized and Team Field Research* (Beverly Hills, Calif.: Sage, 1976), 167–71.

35. Douglas, 172–74.

36. Kathleen T. Erikson, "A Comment on Disguised Observation in Sociology," *Social Problems* 14 (1967): 368.

37. Raymond L. Gold, "Roles in Sociological Field Observation," *Social Forces* 36 (1958): 217–223.

38. Walter R. Borg and Meredith D. Gall, *Educational Research,* 5th ed. (New York: Longman, 1989), 396–97.

39. James P. Spradley, *Participant Observation* (New York: Holt, Rinehart & Winston, 1980).

40. Goetz and LeCompte, 119–25.

41. Andrea Fontana and James H. Frey, "The Interview: From Structured Questions to Negotiated Text," in Denzin and Lincoln 2000, 645–46. Also see S. Kvale, *InterViews: An Introduction to Qualitative Research Interviewing* (Thousand Oaks, Calif.: Sage, 1996).

42. Schwandt, 135.

43. James P. Spradley, *The Ethnographic Interview* (New York: Holt, Rinehart & Winston, 1979).

44. Werner and Schoepfle, 291–92.

45. Werner and Schoepfle, 292.

46. Barbara Tymitz and Robert L. Wolf, *An Introduction to Judicial Evaluation and Natural Inquiry* (Washington, D.C.: Nero, 1977).

47. Goetz and LeCompte, 112–13.

48. Borg and Gall, 399.

49. For example, see Norman K. Denzin, *Interpretive Ethnography: Ethnographic Practices for the 21st Century* (Thousand Oaks, Calif.: Sage, 1997), 128–38; 231–49.

50. Schwandt, 17.

51. Goetz and LeCompte, 123.

52. Goetz and LeCompte, 123.

53. Goetz and LeCompte, 124.

54. Fontana and Frey, 649.

55. Fontana and Frey, 649–50.

56. Guba and Lincoln, 155–60.

57. Dexter as cited by Guba and Lincoln, 174.

58. Guba and Lincoln, 178.

59. Guba and Lincoln, 179.

60. Herbert J. Rubin, *Applied Social Research* (Columbus, Ohio: Merrill, 1983), 363.

61. Guba and Lincoln, 180–83.

62. Harry F. Wolcott, *Transforming Qualitative Data: Description, Analysis, and Interpretation* (Thousand Oaks, Calif.: Sage, 1994), 23.

63. F. D. E. Schleiermacher, *Hermeneutik,* ed. Heinz Kimmerle (Heidelberg, 1959), 90; cited in Tzvetan Todorov, *Theories of Symbol,* trans. Catherine Porter (Ithaca: Cornell University Press, 1977), 183.

64. Ferrara, 93–94.

65. See Hans-Georg Gadamer, *Truth and Method* (New York: Seabury, 1975), 164.

66. Schwandt, 6.

67. Margot Ely, Ruth Vinz, Maryann Downing, and Margaret Anzul, *On Writing Qualitative Research: Living by Words* (Washington, D.C.: Falmer, 1997), 162.

68. Ely et al. 1997, 162.

69. Ely et al. 1997, 162.

70. Gery W. Ryan and H. Russell Bernard, "Data Management and Analysis Methods," in Denzin and Lincoln 2000, 775.

71. Ryan and Bernard, 776–77.

72. Ryan and Bernard, 780.

73. Ryan and Bernard, 781.

74. Kathleen M. MacQueen, Eleanor McLellan, Kelly Kay, and Bobby Milstein, "Codebook Development for Team-based Qualitative Research," *Cultural Anthropology Methods Journal* 1 (1998): 2, 31–36; cited in Ryan and Bernard, 781.

75. Robert C. Bogdan and Sari Knopp Biklen, *Qualitative Research for Education* (Boston: Allyn & Bacon, 1982), 145–70.

76. Goetz and LeCompte, 191.

77. Bogdan and Biklen, 156.

78. Bogdan and Biklen, 157–62.

79. Goetz and LeCompte, 168.

80. Goetz and LeCompte, 169–71.

81. Goetz and LeCompte, 170.

82. Eben A. Weitzman, "Software and Qualitative Research," in Denzin and Lincoln 2000, 805–6.

83. Weitzman, 807.

84. Weitzman, 808–9.

85. For example, see Nigel G. Fielding and Raymond M. Lee, *Computer Analysis and Qualitative Research* (Thousand Oaks, Calif.: Sage, 1998); U. Kelle, "Theory Building in Qualitative Research and Computer Programs for the Management of Textual Data," *Sociological Research Online*, vol. 2 (available at www.socresonline.org.uk); and Eben A. Weitzman and Matthew B. Miles, *Computer Programs for Qualitative Data Analysis* (Thousand Oaks, Calif.: Sage, 1995).

86. Denzin 1997, 46.

87. Denzin 1997, 46, 64–75; 274–278. Also see Virginia L. Olesen, "Feminisms and Qualitative Research at and into the Millennium," in Denzin and Lincoln 2000, 215–55; Esther Madriz, "Focus Groups in Feminist Research," in Denzin and Lincoln 2000, 835–50.

88. Denzin 1997, 126–43.

89. Denzin 1997, 279.
90. Richardson, 933.
91. For example, see Elliott W. Eisner, *The Educational Imagination* (New York: Macmillan, 1979); Eisner, *The Enlightened Eye: Qualitative Inquiry and the Enchantment of Educational Practices* (New York: Macmillan, 1991).

SUPPLEMENTARY SOURCES

Brunner, Diane Duboise. *Inquiry and Reflection: Framing Narrative Practice in Education*. Albany: State University of New York Press, 1994.

Carspecken, P. F. *Critical Ethnography in Educational Research: A Theoretical and Practical Guide*. New York: Routledge, 1996.

Coffey, Amanda, and Paul Atkinson. *Making Sense of Qualitative Data*. Thousand Oaks, Calif.: Sage, 1996.

Colwell, Richard, and Carol Richardson. *The New Handbook of Research on Music Teaching and Learning*, chap. 61. Oxford: Oxford University Press, 2002.

Cortazzi, Martin. *Narrative Analysis*. Washington, D.C.: Falmer, 1993.

Creswell, John W. *Qualitative Inquiry and Research Design: Choosing among Five Traditions*. Thousand Oaks, Calif.: Sage, 1997.

Emerson, Robert M., Rachel I. Fretz, and Linda L. Shaw. *Writing Ethnographic Fieldnotes*. Chicago: University of Chicago Press, 1995.

Flick, Uwe. *An Introduction to Qualitative Research*. Thousand Oaks, Calif.: Sage, 1998.

Gubrium, Jaber F., and James A. Holstein. *The Active Interview*. Thousand Oaks, Calif.: Sage, 1995.

———. *The New Language of Qualitative Method*. Oxford: Oxford University Press, 1997.

Hatch, J. Amos, and Richard Wisniewski, eds. *Life History and Narrative*. London: Falmer, 1995.

Have, Paul T. *Doing Conversational Analysis: A Practical Guide*. Thousand Oaks, Calif.: Sage, 1999.

Janesick, Valerie J. "A Journal about Journal Writing as a Qualitative Research Technique." *Qualitative Inquiry* 5, no. 4 (1999).

LeCompte, Margaret D., and Judith Preissle, with Renata Tesch. *Ethnography and Qualitative Design in Educational Research*. 2nd ed. Orlando, Fla.: Academic, 1993.

Merriam, Sharan B. *Qualitative Research and Case Study Applications in Education*. San Francisco: Jossey-Bass, 1998.

Miles, Matthew B., and A. Michael Huberman. *Qualitative Data Analysis: An Expanded Sourcebook*. 2nd ed. Thousand Oaks, Calif.: Sage, 1994.

O'Hanlon, Christine., ed. *Professional Development through Action Research in Educational Settings*. Washington, D.C.: Falmer, 1996.

Strauss, Anselm, and Juliet Corbin. *Basics of Qualitative Research: Techniques and Procedures for Developing Grounded Theory.* 2nd ed. Thousand Oaks, Calif.: Sage, 1998.

Visweswaran, Kamala. *Fictions of Feminist Ethnography.* Minneapolis: University of Minnesota Press, 1994.

Wolcott, Harry F. *Writing up Qualitative Research.* Newbury Park, Calif.: Sage, 1990.

Chapter 4

Philosophical Inquiry: Concepts and Techniques

Aesthetics, logic, epistemology, ethics, and metaphysics are individual branches of philosophy. Aesthetics has been defined as the study of beauty, artistic tastes, attitudes, and standards; a philosophy of the arts; the study of art works; the study of aesthetic qualities; and the study of aesthetic experiences, to name only five broad approaches. On the other hand, *philosophical inquiry* is not a branch of philosophy but instead provides a methodology that, for the purposes of this text, can be used in research in music education. Philosophical inquiries can be directed to subject areas such as the analysis of musical compositions, the process of creating music (which would include both traditional compositional and improvisational processes), musical performances, and the meaning and inherent values of music education per se or some aspect thereof. Philosophical inquiry is used to interpret and critique extant concepts, beliefs, and theories that may contribute to the development of new theories and to ponder systematically activities as well as the assumptions that underlie those activities. Simply put, philosophical inquiry can facilitate theoretical research in music and music education.

Presenting a chapter on philosophical inquiry as a method for research in music education may appear to be an impossible task to many philosophers. Philosophy *is* inquiry, with as many kinds of inquiries as there are branches of philosophy. One could persuasively argue that the content of a particular philosophy is inextricably linked to its underlying method. A philosophical method provides a system for uncovering and articulating the meaning of that content. Furthermore, as historical epochs change, so do philosophical interests and contents. From such a standpoint, a methodological account of philosophical inquiry is possible only when presented as a history of philosophy. To that end, historical accounts are numerous and often require multivolume studies. Although this chapter expounds and clarifies several philosophical approaches that can inform research in music education, its scope does not include a comprehensive history of the subject. In addition, the treatment of this topic is selective: the approaches chosen for discussion are currently (overtly or covertly) influential and comprise a broad view of methodology and orientation in philosophy. Thereby, the aggregate presented below may enable researchers in music education to direct their research to many varieties of philosophical problems in the field.

Overall, this book attempts to locate the underlying methodological structures of conventional and nonconventional research designs. In traditional research (e.g., experimental, descriptive, and historical), underlying methods are readily definable and help to demarcate the parameters, ground rules, and tasks inherent in each of those designs. In these traditional methods, the method tends to be clearly separable from the content or object(s) of research. On the other hand, in philosophical inquiry (a nontraditional design), content is not easily separable from method. It is necessary to present methods used in philosophical inquiry in concert with their objects of inquiry, that is to say, with content. For that reason, although the focus of this chapter is methodology, some of the contextual meat must remain on the methodological bone. A methodological skeleton cleaned of content does not provide a readily understandable and transferable model.

An important part of this chapter on philosophical inquiry comprises a review of "realist" philosophies of science. Research in the humanities and education have for a long time appropriated research methodologies from research in science. As is the case in traditional research designs in music education, approaches to scientific research can be useful in philosophical inquiry. Accordingly, the protocols and underlying logic in current approaches to the philosophy of science (often written by scientist/philosophers) can provide a ground for philosophical inquiry in music education. It is important to note that traditional texts in philosophy that present methodological accounts of philosophy often deal mostly with logic.[1] While logic is an important research tool in philosophical inquiry, its primacy in the philosophy of science has been seriously challenged within that community. Although this chapter provides a basic account of the nature of logical structures in philosophical inquiry presented as basic rules of logic, in following the current literature in the philosophy of science, its purview will not be limited to that mode of thinking. Indeed, research in the social sciences over the last forty years has been largely defined by the "interpretive turn" (i.e., the use of hermeneutic or reflexive methods). Phenomenological methods have also been heavily used in research in the social sciences, the arts, and the arts in education. *It is the mission of this chapter to move beyond a narrow vision of research in music education and in the broadening thereof, to put forward an eclectic philosophical approach that incorporates insights from current realist philosophy of science as well as from hermeneutics and phenomenology.*

THE STATUS OF PHILOSOPHICAL INQUIRY

Philosophical inquiry is employed to study underlying principles and to build theory in any field. One could attempt to develop a comprehensive philosophy that unifies the entire field of music education or argue that such a unification is impossible. Philosophical inquiry could be used to clarify the nature of music and the inherent value of music education. Current practices can be studied in order to determine which ones should be retained, abandoned, or modified. Whether an approach to music education is called Suzuki, Kodaly, or Orff or more broadly "aesthetic"[2] or "praxial,"[3] each is directed by a philosophical ground. Sometimes philosophical bases and presuppositions are not systematically or clearly articulated. The clarification of underlying premises of an approach to music educational practice can impact greatly on practice insofar as all practice is theoretically informed. In other cases, extant theories in other fields (such as psychology and sociology) that have not been directly connected to music education can be reviewed and shown to be relevant and fruitful for theory and practice in music education. Similarly, one can examine the strengths and weaknesses of existing philosophical positions in music education in order to clarify and develop theory for the field.

In historical, descriptive, and experimental research designs, questions concerning the philosophical basis for such research activities are not so overt. However, if researchers wish to investigate the philosophical implications of historical, experimental, or descriptive methodologies, philosophical inquiry could be used. Many debates in research in music education concern the suitability and fashionability of empirical versus philosophical methods. When a researcher defends the adequacy of his or her methodology or attacks that of another approach, philosophical inquiry is often engaged.

Professionals who demand that research methods in music education must be empirically based miss the rich possibilities of the juxtaposition of philosophical with traditional research methods. The empirically grounded and often quantitatively reported results of experimental and descriptive studies can be enriched and embellished by philosophical accounts of the contexts and presuppositions of the same objects of research. In like fashion, philosophical research findings can be clarified, corroborated, and tightened by parallel research that generates results in seriational or statistical formats. This suggested interaction (sometimes called triangulation) of methods for research in music education is often debated at a philosophical level. Openness toward new and other research approaches will enhance an environment that might support systematic and broad interfacing of research data from divergent approaches.

In the recent magnum opus, *The New Handbook of Research on Music Teaching and Learning*, the last unit concerns research designs in music education. Research activities are characterized by Jack J. Heller and Edward J. P. O'Connor as systematic studies that provide solutions to posed problems based on empirical observation.[4] While historical, descriptive, and experimental methods are deemed acceptable research designs, philosophical inquiries do not constitute "research" according to Heller and O'Connor. A key reason for their dismissal of philosophical inquiry as a bona fide research design is the invariable criterion that they assign to all research if it is indeed research: to present "unbiased evidence."[5]

Heller and O'Conner's position—demanding that research, if it is research, must be empirically verifiable and based on "unbiased evidence"—is surprising because that "positivist" position has been largely abandoned in scientific and social science research. For example, the process of integrating "empirical" and "interpretive" dimensions of research in the philosophy of science, the human sciences, and the arts is now decades old. Unrelated but important to note, a landmark book, Thomas Kuhn's *The Structure of Scientific*

Revolutions, established the social and cultural status of scientific research and knowledge.[6] Dozens of major thinkers in a variety of fields of study over the last forty years have established that the allegedly "unbiased" and abstract purity in scientific research is a myth and is demonstrably false.[7] Furthermore, human actions, which constitute music education and are the objects of study in traditional and nontraditional research designs, are *meaningful.* Therefore research in music education must merge understanding of *meaningful* human actions with (traditional) causal explanation in order to generate insightful and useful results.

But most important is that insofar as research in music education should continue to look to science for its research models, Heller and O'Conner's research paradigm is not fully reflective of current research in science. While an entire chapter could be dedicated to this issue, suffice it to say that Heller and O'Conner's *philosophical* position—that proper research should be delimited and restricted to hypothetico-deductive and causal explanations based on empirical verifiability—has been all but abandoned in the social sciences, the arts, and the arts in education. Furthermore, the empirical verifiability principle has been deeply qualified in the theory and practice of *science.* To omit philosophical inquiry from the acceptable arsenal of research designs in music education would place the field in the unenviable position of being decades behind the ongoing intellectual tradition and wisdom in science and the social sciences. Heller's and O'Conner's position regarding what is and what is not *research* represents a *philosophical* approach termed "positivism" that has largely been deserted in the philosophy of science and the social sciences. In fact, current "realist" philosophy of science and the social sciences offers a firm and fruitful alternative to such positivistic constrictions. It is important to note that whether a researcher embraces (1) positivism or (2) a current realist approach, each choice has deep *philosophical* implications. In addition to theory building, philosophical inquiry is the mode of research in which researchers consider and engage such underlying presuppositions of their methods and activities.

Traditional research designs in music education are grounded in objectivism: research data are accepted as largely autonomous from researchers insofar as they are (allegedly) objectified through the use of experimental or descriptive methods. Furthermore, there is acceptance of the verifiability principle: a statement or research finding is only meaningful if it is empirically verifiable.[8] This philosophical position is often termed "positivist," and more specifically represents "logical positivism."[9] Broadly speaking, logical positivism maintains that through the use of scientific methods, a worldless "unbiased" subject (the researcher) can engage subject-free, natural objects. There is an attempt to see things as they really are, in fact, without idealization or speculation. From this perspective, research is thought to be capable of providing firm bases because research techniques are thought to be independent of the data being studied. Logical positivists believe that their definition of scientific method is the only acceptable approach to knowledge building. Therefore, a logical positivist approach in the social sciences or the arts would affirm that the methodology of the natural sciences can appropriately be utilized in the human sciences and arts research, retaining the level of objectivity achieved in the natural sciences. In such a view, metaphysical questions such as the nature of music and musical expression are relegated to the status of pseudo-questions or to the realm of the nonsensical.

Realists, for decades, have largely dispelled the rigid, empirical requirements of logical positivism for the philosophy of science.[10] If a researcher follows the positivistic demand of empirical verifiability, the parameters of his or her database are greatly restricted. Realists have discredited the positivistic view that theories which cannot be confirmed through observable evidence do not qualify as scientific theories. This relates to the realists' attack on the Humean view of causality that undergirds positivism. In traditional terms, "causality" refers to the relationship between A and B in which whenever A happens first, B succeeds as a result of A. Hume suggests that there is no element of necessity between these two (A and B) events. The only thing that a researcher can perceive is that B follows A; the researcher cannot successfully theorize that B necessarily must follow when A occurs (such a move would project human rationality on nature). Thus, for Hume and the positivists, a researcher's ontology (or what he or she accepts as real and therefore researchable) is limited to observable facts.

Current realists point out that in the practice of science, scientists regularly "conceive" what they cannot immediately "perceive," "observe," or "empirically verify" in order to explain and predict. Rom Harre, a scientist and noted philosopher of science, contends that while perception is at the heart of scientific research, so are conception and imagination.[11] Many scientific explanations are the result of conceiving (as in philosophical inquiry) without perceiving.

Harre maintains that there are at least three realms of scientific *research* and theory: the first realm is marked by ordinary perception in which what is known is based on observable and empirically verifiable facts,[12] in the second realm, perception may catch up with conception—there is a promise of technological development (e.g., with increasingly powerful microscopes, telescopes, or computers) through which researchers will eventually be able to "observe" and empirically verify what they only conceived (as in philosophical inquiry) as the probable explanation;[13] and in the third realm there are genuine theoretical acts of imagination (as in speculative modes of philosophical inquiry) that will never be directly perceived, for example, empirically observed or verified.[14]

Harre further substantiates the view that the positivist dictum, that research findings must be empirically verifiable, is unrealistic in relation to actual scientific research and practice. Rather than attempt to define theoretical language through observational terms, thereby reducing or discarding them, theoretical language is understood as the means by which observable entities can be explained in the first place. Realists understand that *there are no theory-free observations in the processes of scientific inquiry (or in research in music education). All methods, scientific or otherwise, are theory laden.* One cannot escape a theoretical position that supersedes or transcends what is immediately verifiable. While observation remains important in scientific inquiry (and certain approaches to research in music education), rationalism (which functions in what Harre called the second and third realms of scientific inquiry) is at the heart of much current scientific inquiry.

Further clarifying the relationship between theoretical and observable data, Mary B. Hesse notes that a positivistic view of the use of models in science is not in keeping with actual scientific practice.[15] Conceptual models in science are often in the form of analogical descriptions of unobservable data that have a causal relation to observable data. Theoretical conceptions often must be used to ground and explain observable or perceivable entities. Therefore, in positivism, the relegation of such models to the status of psychological aids is not in keeping with actual scientific practice. Finally, and as noted earlier, Hesse also holds that scientific theories are not always developed through the canons of logic. One could never limit the development of scientific theories to strict logic and argument. Rather, metaphor and simile are the core cognitive processes in scientific practice, as they can be in philosophical inquiry.

Thus researchers in music education utilizing traditional and non-traditional designs need not delimit the structure of their methods or the theories that inform them to the canons of logic or to the observable. In taking imaginative license they can be confident that they are emulating scientific research and theory building in the natural sciences. *A realist philosophy of science provides a much more fluid sense of scientific practice, method, and theory construction than in the positivistic vision. Why then should research in music education be delimited to a positivistic vision of research that is not representative of scientific inquiry?*

It should be obvious that research in the human sciences, history, and the arts is not as empirically verifiable as in the natural sciences. Studying music teaching and learning is not the same as studying molecules or chemical reactions. For example, in natural science, that real blood flows through a subject's veins need not be understood as a "relative" truth. Such a truth would be in Harre's first realm of perceivable (observable) data and therefore no one can seriously doubt that real blood actually flows. Truth, in the social sciences as well as in the arts, is not so definite. Research in music education does and should function in correlative ways to Harre's three "realms" of scientific research; in some cases perception may have to catch up (at some future time) to conception or it may never become observationally/empirically corroborated. Simply put and in accordance with a current realist philosophy in science, theories utilized in all modes of music education research cannot always be corroborated through observational means: the criterion of empirical verifiability of findings may not be a useful, realistic, or fruitful criterion for what is "research" in music education. If forms of philosophical inquiry are necessarily practiced in certain realms of scientific research (as Harre demonstrates), surely philosophical inquiry is a legitimate research design in research in music education.

PHILOSOPHICAL ISSUES IN LOGICAL POSITIVISM, RATIONALISM, POSTMODERNISM, AND REALISM: AN OVERVIEW AS THEY RELATE TO RESEARCH IN MUSIC EDUCATION

This section provides a context for the methodological issues inherent in philosophical inquiry as a research design for music education with brief overviews of logical positivism, rationalism, postmodernism, and realism. Within the area of postmodernism, two specific philosophical tools, phenomenology and hermeneutics, will be reviewed.

Logical Positivism

Logical positivism,[16] a school of thought, with roots in the nineteenth century, overtly blossomed in Vienna in the 1920s and 1930s and, with less fanfare, continued for at least two more decades. While the tenets of logical positivism—particularly its accounts of confirmation and verification—have been largely abandoned, some of the details of that theoretical position continue to serve, in some form or another, as criteria for the evaluation of educational research. True to its other name, "logical empiricism," logical positivism demands that research conform to the principle of "verifiability": a statement is meaningful if and only if it is, in principle, empirically (i.e., observationally) verifiable. Meaning is dichotomized into cognitive and emotive categories. When a statement can be verified by sense experience (i.e., through one of the senses), positive knowledge is obtained, and that knowledge can be said to be cognitive or rational. On the other hand, statements that deal with emotion or feeling are categorized as "metaphysical" (i.e., beyond or above the physical and consequently not empirically verifiable) and are judged to be meaningless. Metaphysical statements are not, in principle, empirically verifiable and hence there is no way to determine the truth or falsity of such statements through direct experience. For the logical positivist, scientific method of the strictest kind is the only source for pure knowledge about reality. Philosophical inquiry must therefore emulate this severe image of science through the use of logical and mathematical reasoning or be relegated to the status of mysticism.

According to logical positivists, philosophical language must be as precise and literal as language used in scientific inquiry. Logical positivists envisioned language becoming a form of calculus. Once formalized by philosophers, language would be neutral and pure. A neutral philosophical language could distinguish between real problems and pseudoproblems. It would distill metaphysical positions to reality or show that such positions were meaningless and inconsequential.

What logical positivists missed was that their own philosophy was equally rooted in a metaphysical position (which is the case in any philosophy and any research design). Logical positivists believed (or accepted on faith) that human rationality, as a human construction, facilitates only the observation of nature. It follows that for logical positivists, rationality or reasoning, in itself, reveals nothing. Appearance alone is "real" for logical positivists. There is no rationality in nature; rationality remains a human construct. Logical positivists concluded that the image of nature as a rational machine is the result of the incorrect projection of the model of human rationality onto nature. Thus theories based on logic and reasoning were viewed as instruments or means for the observation of nature in a systematic and rigorous manner. Human intelligence and rationality are merely neutral instruments for the observation of nature. The image of scientific inquiry was thus relegated to the administration of neutral techniques for the purpose of pure observation. Logic was used to provide order and system. There was no allowance for imagination or leaps of theoretical insight in this view of scientific inquiry. As sociologist Max Weber proclaimed, the image of the world as presented in *positivism* is that of an intellectual and bureaucratic "iron cage" filled with "sensualists without heart" and technicians without vision.[17]

Logic as a Tool in Philosophical Inquiry

In their discussions of the use of philosophical inquiry, some researchers in music have accented the rigorous methods, precise terminologies, and logic that have made science so successful in explaining, predicting, and thereby controlling the environment. Logic is the analysis of the structure of reasoning in the form of arguments. In formal logic, an argument is a set of sentences, one of which claims to be a conclusion that follows from the others. In the syllogism

A1) All Americans are human beings
A2) John is an American
A3) (Therefore) John is a human being

A3 is a conclusion that is based on statement A1 and A2. That is to say, from A1 and A2 one can deduce A3. One can also say that the conclusion (A3) and the premises (A1 and A2) are both *valid* and *true*. In formal logic, validity and truth function as two distinct terms. The argument

B1) All pianists have three feet
B2) John is a pianist
B3) John has three feet

is valid; the conclusion (B3) follows the premises (B1 and B2). However, the premise (B1) is obviously not true. Thus validity is an intrinsic characteristic, whereas truth must be corroborated through the explanation of the relationship between the argument and the real world (outside the syllogism) to which the argument points.

While *deduction* involves reasoning from a general truth to a particular instance, as one type of exercise in deduction, *induction* involves reasoning from a part of a whole to a general statement, from individual elements to universals. In logical terms, in *deduction* one infers the consequence from a conditional statement and its antecedent:

If X, then Y (conditional statement)
X is the case (the antecedent is the case)
Therefore Y (the consequent)

In *induction*, one infers a generalized antecedent from a conditional statement and its consequent:

If X, then Y (conditional statement with X as a generalization of Y)
Y is the case (the consequent)
Therefore X (the antecedent as a generalization)

It is clear that logic clearly reflects mathematical reasoning. Each statement or proposition is developed to support subsequent premises that culminate in a conclusion. However, as Abraham Kaplan notes, the process of scientific discovery (what he terms "logic-in-use") is quite different from the report of scientific findings (what he terms "reconstructed logic").[18] In science, the object under study cannot always be observed directly. Using laws of physics and rules of logical reasoning, scientists deduce conclusions that are not directly observable. At other times, scientists go beyond accepted modes of mathematical logic in order to extend or revamp established scientific theories. One example was Einstein's extension of physics with relativity theory. In such cases, scientists accept the tenets of rationalism.

Edward L. Rainbow and Hildegard C. Froehlich clarify the use of "scientific process" in philosophical inquiry and present useful rules for defining terms.[19] Milton Babbitt contends that analysis in music must be constituted of scientific language and scientific method in order for it to reach the status of meaningful discourse.[20] One of the best known methods of logic is Carl Hempel's deductive-nomological or D-N method.[21] The D-N method combines descriptive methods that list features that are immediately given to the senses by the object under scrutiny with explanations of the relationships between those features or events that comprise the object. The term "deductive" suggests that descriptive statements progress logically to explanations and finally to an ending or conclusive explanatory statement, termed the "explanandum." Thus deduction is based on logic. Garry Potter and Jose Lopez state that Hempel and Karl Popper's hypothetico-deductive descriptions of scientific explanation became the dominant approach to understanding science in the twentieth century.[22] Both Popper and Hempel were critical of logical positivism's reliance on confirmation and verification. However, Potter and Lopez also note that Popper and Hempel's stress on the importance of empiricism and their acceptance that prediction automatically follows explanation in science places them firmly within the positivist camp.[23]

Rationalism

Generally, rationalism in philosophy considers reason to be the cardinal source of knowledge, a priori to and independent of sense perceptions. Thus, unlike logical positivism, the process of abstract, rational thinking is believed to be able to uncover fundamental and possibly apodictic truths which are knowable without the "verification" that comes from the use of empirical/observable methods. For the rationalist, thought is a copy of independent reality. Language (in the form of propositions) is determined by thought and is simply a means of transmitting thoughts, which are independent of language. The truth of a proposition is therefore ascertained by its correspondence to thought, which (according to the rationalist), already conforms to reality. In Aristotle's rationalist (and realist) account, propositions are symbols for thoughts.[24] While propositions may be different among language users, thoughts about reality itself remain the same for all humans. Reality determines knowledge or thought, and language simply carries out the conformity of thought to reality in an impartial and independent manner. Accordingly for rationalists, one can use language and reason to step out of culture. For example, in modern-day "structuralism," this rationalist view contends that it is possible to transcend culture and understand "underlying structures" or "culturally invariant factors."

Ludwig Wittgenstein's early philosophical output provides an important source in rationalist philosophy. Often one reads about the "early" and "late" Wittgenstein because of his dramatic turn away from earlier positions in his later writings. The key book in his early period is *Tractatus Logico-Philosophicus* (often referred to as the *Tractatus*).[25] This work presents a rationalist account of propositional truth, stating that language is a picture of reality. Like a photograph, language is said to represent or mirror reality in a one-to-one correspondence. Thus reality is its presentation in language. One can readily see the substantive shift from an empiricist view, in which observation of the physical world must be the final place in which to decide truth, to the rationalist view in which one need only study language (which includes the languages of mathematics, physics, and geometry), not physical reality, to decide truth. Thus the requirement of empirical verification in the logical positivist brand of realism has been substituted with the requirement for reason as manifest in language.

If the rationalist account of propositional truth is to be successful, it must be demonstrated that the structures of propositions (linguistic premises) are isomorphic (i.e., picture copies) to the structures of the facts (in reality) to which they refer. The writings of the early Wittgenstein and those of Bertrand Russell during the same period ascribe to this "copy" theory of the relationship between language and reality.[26] In such a view, philosophical language must be distilled to the most simple and literal terms. This linguistic distillation allegedly purifies the propositions that constitute philosophical inquiry. Just as reality is built on simple objects, language must also be reduced to the most basic terms or "atoms." This position on the use of basic, literal, and precise philosophical language (which as noted above, is a position that happens to be shared by logical positivists) is referred to as "logical atomism." Thus language and thought, it is believed, can be analyzed through indivisible linguistic "atomic propositions" that have an exact isomorphic structure to the facts in the real world to which they refer.

Research in music education under the methodology of the early Wittgenstein and Russell's logical atomism would shift the study of conditions and ideas in the real world of music education to an analysis of statements about those conditions and ideas. As such, philosophical inquiry becomes a methodology for the clarification of language. Most current philosophies of science do not ascribe to logical atomism. In addition, and as noted above, scientific inquiry often goes beyond the confines of inductive and deductive reasoning. The primacy of logic and the requirement of strictly literal language in philosophical inquiry have been strongly contested and in many instances abandoned by philosophers of science during the last forty years. In fact, some support for that abandonment is from Wittgenstein's later work.[27]

The "late" Wittgenstein retains the "early" Wittgenstein notion that any form of knowledge must be understood in terms of language. However, the "late" Wittgenstein proffers that language is a form of human life that must be understood in some social context. Thus, at this "late" stage, Wittgenstein argues that language can (only) express a "coherent" view of the world but that view cannot be verified outside language. Within the philosophy of science around 1960, Wittgenstein's later work was used to understand the socially constructed nature of scientific knowledge. For example, the presence of implicit prejudices and professional biases in scientific theory and practice was powerfully demonstrated in Thomas Kuhn's watershed book on science.[28] Kuhn explains that practicing scientists rarely question the paradigmatic or metatheoretical structure that informs their work. Rather, they accept the underlying logic, rationality, and correctness of their "paradigm" and its methods in an a priori manner. It is only during "revolutionary" periods of science, as in the Einsteinian qualifications of Newtonian physics, that scientists question the overall scientific paradigm in which they are working.

Also along these lines and concurrent with Kuhn's work, Michael Polanyi uncovered scientific knowledge as "personal" to the scientist who is part of a scientific community.[29] The distinctive mark of the idea of the "personal" for Polanyi is scientists' commitment to being responsible for their belief in the reality of nature. Polanyi maintains that because understanding the rationality of nature (an antipositivistic position as noted above) is always mediated by an individual scientist (a Kantian notion as explained below in the section on realism) within a community of scientists (a Kuhnian insight), the rationality of nature cannot be independently verified.[30] Scientists develop knowledge through the theoretical presuppositions that mark the community of researchers of which they are a part. Scientists (and researchers in music education) do not work in an objectivist vacuum. Researchers interact with and adopt approaches to research. As Kuhn and Polanyi have demonstrated in scientific research, adoption of theoretical and methodological approaches (and their implementation) are not unbiased. Kuhn and Polanyi understood the intersubjective nature of scientific research but did not relegate science to a subjectivist or postmodernist position. Thus, while they astutely uncovered and clarified the social context in scientific research, it is important to note that they did not intend to compromise the achievement of knowledge and truth in science.

Postmodernism

Our time seems to be marked more by being "post" something than "in" something—postpositivist, postempiricist, poststructuralist, postmodernist, and even postphilosophic. Postmodernism understands scientific research as a process of social construction. However, the postmodernist insight into the "social nature of science" is much more *subjectively* structured than in Kuhn or Polanyi. For many postmodernists, knowledge in or out of science is not objective at all but is no more than what a research community in a given time and place socially accredits it to be. As such, knowledge is historically and culturally based. Eternal truths do not exist but are relative to a historical and cultural context. Furthermore, many postmodernist thinkers present theories that simply *deconstruct* traditional notions of objectivity and methodology for the sake of such a deconstruction; no alternative methodology is offered.[31] While deconstruction for the sake of deconstruction is a controversial and somewhat extreme outgrowth of postmodernism, in the foregoing section, the assumptions of postmodernists who maintain a "historical relativist" position will be reviewed more for their positive insights into the nature of language and knowledge in research.

Phenomenology as a Postmodernist Method

Edmund Husserl (1859–1938) introduced phenomenology as a foundation for the natural and human sciences. According to Husserl, phenomenology would provide a methodology based on the absolutely verifiable foundations of immediate, conscious experience.[32] Such an empirically based philosophical method would have the rigor of science and would concomitantly have the conceptual means to provide the foundation for all knowledge. In the phenomenologist's direct investigation of phenomena, belief in theories and constructive interpretations are suspended in favor of the immediacy of what is directly given to consciousness. In keeping with his Kantian roots, Husserl maintained that researchers can transcend their own biases and ascertain the essential and necessary characteristics of objects under study.

Husserl attempted to formulate a philosophical position that would undercut both the rationalist account of knowledge (with roots in Plato as noted above) and the idealist version (as represented by Hans-Georg Gadamer and Martin Heidegger and presented later in this chapter in the section on hermeneutics). Husserl concluded that the rationalist movement caused a bifurcation between the mind and phenomena under study with the idea of a realm of pure knowledge that is not accessible through the immediate experience of things but only through acts of reason. For the phenomenologist, the rationalist approach dislocates consciousness from phenomena because one must insert a theory or "form" (as in Plato) through and by which phenomena-at-hand can be understood. This separation of the mind from the world culminates in Descartes's famous "mind–body" split. While Husserl hoped to remain close to objects, he didn't want to retreat fully from rationalism. He endeavored to maintain sufficient distance from objects so that his phenomenology would not be accused of acute subjectivism, the fate of idealism, in his opinion. Idealism was considered too subjective because in its stipulation that phenomena cannot be experienced separately from consciousness, the idealist position tends to posit a disproportionate focus on the knower as the center of knowledge, rather than the more "objective" realm of pure knowledge. What is interesting is that throughout Husserl's long career, he seemed to oscillate between both movements, rationalism and idealism. However, he never successfully undercut either position. The result is a phenomenology that derives characteristics from both schools but that ultimately leans more in the direction of idealism and its inherent subjectivism, although Husserl and many Husserlians would disagree.

Husserl's early period of phenomenology (approximately from 1896 to 1905) is an attempt to overcome subjectivism or what was commonly referred to as "psychologism" in turn-of-the-century philosophical circles.[33] Husserl's response to psychologism took the form of his *Logical Investigations* (1900–1901), in which he demanded that researchers get "back to the things themselves" and out of the subjectivistic and psychologistic pitfalls of idealism. However, by 1913, his major work, *Ideas*, seems to fall into the very psychologism from which he tried to extricate philosophy in his earlier turn-of-the-century period. The focus of *Ideas* is consciousness, not things. In this book, Husserl presents his famous method of "phenomenological reduction."[34]

There are at least two types of phenomenological reduction. The first is called the *epoche* or transcendental reduction; the second, the *eidetic* reduction. In the *epoche* or transcendental reduction one must transcend ordinary perception and examine oneself perceiving. This act of abstraction is not difficult. Imagine playing in a baseball game and, during the game, thinking about the game and your perception of it. In the transcendental reduction one thinks about what one is perceiving at that instant. This shifts one's mode of orientation away from what Husserl calls the "natural attitude."[35] The natural attitude is marked by (1) a kind of animal faith in the fact that things are simply as they appear, requiring no special interest or description and (2) the habitual proclivity to be predisposed to things. This "natural" disinterest and prejudice toward things is suspended in the transcendental reduction. In the transcendental reduction, one turns inward toward consciousness and examines it. Distinguished from the psychological act of introspection, a researcher using this phenomenological technique engages their process of conscious activity in a realm or metacognitive place termed the "transcendental ego." It is to transcendental consciousness that Husserl wishes the researcher to move. This is not the transcendental realm of pure concepts, divorced from consciousness, as in Plato's rationalism. In Husserl's transcendental ego there is a subject who is very present. But all sense of "mine" is, according to Husserl, canceled. The world has not changed; instead, the natural orientation that makes it "my" world has been bracketed. Indeed, the operational term for the *epoche* is "bracketing." For Husserl, this act of phenomenological transcendence objectifies consciousness by putting one's own subjectivity in check. Through this act of abstraction, one can hold on to consciousness and yet not be mired in its subjective nature. In this transcendental place of abstraction from things and consciousness, a "pure" consciousness or ego engages objects so that objects can show themselves "purely." The result, Husserl notes, is unencumbered description and apodictic or certain knowledge. However, before engaging the notion of the alleged "purity" of phenomenological description, let's look at the second phenomenological reduction, the *eidetic* reduction.

The transcendental (or first phenomenological) reduction sets up a context in which one can perform the *eidetic* or second phenomenological reduction. Husserl uses *eidetic* from the Greek *eidos* to mean essence. During the *eidetic* reduction, one performs a kind of free imaginary variation that includes imagining the object under study with and then without certain of its characteristics.[36] Characteristics that can be suspended without destroying the object are considered ancillary and are bracketed out of subsequent variations. Properties of phenomena that cannot be suspended without destroying the object itself are considered necessary or essential to the work. These invariant properties constitute the essence or *eidos* of the object. Thus the *eidetic* reduction seeks to shed objects of all but their essential and defining structures. And because these essences were described by the transcendental ego, those descriptions are believed by Husserl to be "pure" and apodictically true.

It is clear that whether one calls the activity of the mind "consciousness" or "transcendental consciousness," one is still working within one's own mind. Can one ever completely and purely transcend and thereby overcome one's own subjectivity? Even with the precise methodologies of science and a database comprised of the natural world, such purity and certainty of knowledge is not always possible. In research in music education when the objects of inquiry are human actions, an act of pure transcendence becomes more fanciful. Nevertheless, one can agree that the power of abstraction allows researchers to transcend the immediacy of things. No matter what level of abstraction one can bring to the study of anything, and regardless of whether one is doing research in natural science or in music education, it is doubtful that the power of immediate and empirical perception of data will reach Husserl's promise of a status of analysis that can be characterized as *immaculate perception*, a position that I countervail and a term I present in an earlier work.[37]

Nevertheless, Husserl's phenomenological account of *time* is useful in music research. In 1905, Husserl provided an extensive description of *time* as experienced in consciousness.[38] Consciousness "intends" or directs its awareness toward things in time. The nature of temporality as it structures experience is different from simple chronological time. When viewing a sculptural work from moment to moment, one accepts that the work remains the same work; one does not question its cross-temporal identity. According to Husserl, this is because consciousness retains past images and expects that those images will continue to represent the same work of art. Husserl coins the terms "retention" and "protention" to name the respective acts of retaining and anticipating. Objects remain consistently the same in consciousness because (1) they actually remain physically the same in reality and (2) "protentions" are continuously being verified in consciousness as a result of congruence with past "retentions" concerning the same object.

Husserl utilizes the concepts of retention and protention to describe the inner flow of time that occurs when listening to a melody. He uses the metaphor of a comet traveling through space. The glistening tail of the comet represents past notes of the melody that have been retained in immediate memory. The present is represented by the head of the comet, and the trajectory or "projectory" of the comet is analogous to "protending" or predicting where the melody might lead or be developed. During any "now" instant or point in a melody, notes heard earlier are retained in consciousness while one anticipates further development and closure. Thus, for the Husserlian phenomenologist, the manner in which sound occurs in time is of great importance in music analysis. One does not hear a melody as successive, dislocated notes but as a whole melody that is being constituted by consciousness in time. As one progresses through a melody (or work), protentions (future notes or phrases) become less and less protensive, then become present as "now" points and finally recede into the past. Perhaps most important is that during this entire experience of musical time, one experiences a melody (and an entire work) as one enduring whole.

The acts of stepping back and abstracting from an ongoing research study, constituting it over real time as one considers actually where one is in the research process, where one has been and where one is going, is a phenomenological activity often termed "constitutive phenomenology."[39] This is more than simply checking specific steps in a research process against a dissertation proposal or research outline. It requires bringing an essentially subjective presence of the researcher into relief and yet, not allowing that subjective presence to dominate or color the study at hand. As the study progresses and a researcher considers the meaning and import of what has transpired, the *eidetic* reduction may support a description of the essential constituents of the research project.[40]

Even if one accepted Husserl's notion of pure perception in principle, in the practice of philosophical inquiry it would prove to be unattainable. That is the case because any research activity must ultimately be articulated to a readership in a language. Language forces consciousness out of its allegedly "pure" or transcendental ego status and into the role of mediator and transformer. At best, Husserl's phenomenology might allow a researcher to intuit phenomena purely. But the purity of that experience will be contaminated as soon as one translates it into language. Husserl's transcendental consciousness is ultimately trapped within itself. The knowledge it generates is not pure but, like knowledge generated in the natural sciences, is relative to one's method, the overall theoretical structure or paradigm that informs and grounds one's perception and methodology, the community of professionals to which one writes and subscribes, and ultimately, the limitations and interpretations that abide in the use of language.

Hermeneutic Inquiry in Postmodernism

Hermeneutics is defined as "the science of interpretation." The term is associated with fields as diverse as philosophy, theology, history, literary criticism, and jurisprudence. Many scholars know hermeneutics by its use in the interpretation or exegesis of biblical texts. For others it names an alternate movement in phenomenology marked by interpretation rather than (Husserlian) "pure" description. Nevertheless, in all cases hermeneutics names the activity and theory of interpretation. This grows from its etymology in the Greek messenger god, Hermes. Hermes interpreted and translated the language of the gods into a form that mortals could understand. Similarly, researchers interpret and translate meanings into a form accepted by their disciplines.[41]

According to Martin Heidegger, each of us begins our existence in the world, as a cultural and historical being.[42] From the horizon or context of one's world, one discovers and defines oneself. There is no transcendental realm in the world or in (Husserl's transcendental) consciousness to which one can move for pure or perfect knowledge. Knowledge will always be relative to one's world. Hence, while Husserl contends that the phenomenological reductions enable investigators to describe phenomena purely, Heidegger denigrates the very notion of a pure description of anything. Instead of description, Heidegger notes that investigations are always interpretations that are relative to one's historical and cultural world, termed the "onto-historical" world. Husserl's attempt to transcend cultural biases through transcendental consciousness is viewed by Heidegger as another footnote to Descartes's bifurcation (into subject and object) of nature.

Hans-Georg Gadamer, who was one of Heidegger's many famous students, concluded that researchers utilizing different modes of philosophical inquiry cannot suspend their biases or, more broadly, the horizons of their existence.[43] There are no universal truths that can enable researchers to cross cultures or historical epochs without the residue of their own biases. However, this does not produce a radical relativism in which every belief is as good as every other. Instead, historical relativists such as Gadamer maintain that knowledge generated by all research is always in terms of the accepted procedures of justification held by a particular culture, society, or professional community. The search for objectivity is replaced by an effort to establish intersubjective agreement, a consensus among cultures, or what Gadamer terms a "fusion of horizons." As Richard Rorty suggests, instead of seeking the creation of a pure form of discourse, one can only recognize that there is a plurality of discourses and that rigorous discourse itself is a key goal of philosophy.[44] According to such postmodernists, the best that one can achieve in research is "interpretive discourse," but never in an absolute way. Thus, while sharing some tenets with the "personal" and "communal" characteristics of science demonstrated by Kuhn and Polanyi, the postmodernist vision of the nature of knowledge and methodology is nevertheless, more extreme.

The abandonment of the Platonic quest for absolute philosophical truths by historical relativists is marked by Heidegger's view that truths must always be understood within the context of one's historical and cultural horizon.[45] Explicit knowledge in research is always understood in relationship to a background of a shared paradigm or disciplinary matrix. This was Kuhn's great insight concerning the relationship between scientific knowledge and scientific paradigms. Heidegger's analysis of the ground for shared beliefs and practices, which predates Kuhn's by more than three decades, goes much deeper. When one converses with another person, acquired social techniques come into play that remain in the background of such a conversation. Heidegger stresses that such inherited cultural practices cannot be made explicit in theories because these existential modes of human being (i.e., of being human) are so pervasive that one could never define them sufficiently to make them objects of explicit analysis.[46] One cannot transcend this primordial dimension of understanding. Heidegger contends that all knowledge gathered by traditional research methods in the natural and human sciences is ultimately circular. Verification of results takes place within the confines of the theory that structures that research project. While the social constructionists in science have demonstrated circularity by showing that research conclusions are dependent on the accepted practices, theoretical assumptions, and biases of their research community, Heidegger asserts that the entire theoretical activity of formulating and verifying hypotheses is parasitic on the background of cultural practices and the "life world" (*Lebenswelt*) that constitutes the overall ontology (reality) of any cultural people.

Within the postmodern historical relativist perspective, all research is understood as marked by historical preunderstanding. The temporal present is part of a stream of history that moves from the past into the future. One's historical tradition is the basis for preunderstanding anything. *Understanding* is the fundamental manner in which historical people engage their world. Researchers cannot fully suspend their tradition or its underlying biases. However, rather than cause a negative result in research, according to Hans-Georg Gadamer, such historical biases are necessary and are a positive force in research; without historical and cultural contexts and biases, research would be buoyless and incoherent.[47]

Gadamer opines that any sense of method based on the natural sciences is inappropriate for research in the human sciences, history, and the arts. Yet, there is another methodological avenue. *Rhetoric* provides a claim to truth that at once defends the probable, is based on ordinary reason, and is not limited to that which can be tested or observationally demonstrated.[48] Gadamer traces rhetoric from the Greeks and through the humanist tradition in order to provide a vehicle that will free researchers from the traditional conception of scientific method. He notes that rhetoric has been applied systematically for centuries in the fields of law and theology, using principles of authoritative example, precedent, and customary standards of evaluation and modes of speech. However, this philosophical orientation led to a style of writing and argument that was often densely esoteric and more literary than philosophical. Thus irony and the playful use of language replaced a belief in the verifiability of research-generated knowledge. Under this view, clarity and parsimony in scientific discourse would be (and was) replaced with ambiguity and abstruseness. As such, the historical relativism in postmodernist thinking is strongly aligned with the (interpretivist) hermeneutic tradition. In such a view, there is a vast and radical difference of kind between human actions and that of chemicals or atoms. Thus the methods of science that seek to develop knowledge about the natural world will never be reasonably usable for understanding human activities, such as music making, teaching, and theorizing.

The interpretivist tradition suggests that understanding the meaning of human actions is closer to understanding a language than understanding the structure of chemicals or machines. While that insight about the obvious dislocation between understanding chemicals or machines and understanding theory and practice in music education is obvious, the use of effusively dense and elusive language in research in music education may not offer the clearest route for understanding. Nevertheless, it is important to have an example of a hermeneutic account of the arts. To that end, we engage selected writings by Martin Heidegger.

A Hermeneutically Conceived View of Art

Heidegger provides a conception of art that can be useful for hermeneutic inquiry in music education.[49] He suggests that all works of art have two fundamental elements: "earth" and "world."[50] Earth represents the materials that constitute an artwork: the paint in a painting, the stone in a sculpture, the metal in an architectural work, the *sound-in-time* in music. Without materials, there would be no work of art. In his essay on the nature of art, Heidegger analyzes an ancient Greek temple. His description of the stone or earth in this temple does not report lines, balance, symmetry, or geometric shapes; earth must not be confused with artistic form. The earth of this temple is the "stoniness" of the stone and is more fundamental than form. Heidegger draws his concept of earth from the early Greek term *physis*. According to his interpretation, *physis* is not comparable to the modern version of physical, inanimate nature. For the pre-Socratic Greeks, the physical earth was described as that which is emerging and rising within itself.[51] From this perspective, the work materials of art are described as emerging and rising up through the work. Paint is not neatly dissected into shapes and forms in Heidegger's brand of hermeneutic inquiry but moves in the direction of a step back to the nature of work materials in artists' creative processes. During the creative process, the raw work materials are emerging and erupting with potential for the artist. That potential in the work materials to emerge and rise up remains in the finished artwork, according to Heidegger, although rarely do critics and researchers uncover this dynamic element in art. In fact, Heidegger maintains that the presence of an emerging and dynamic character of a work's materials is one prerequisite for something to be called art. This is to say, it is one of the essential and defining characteristics for art to be art. Accordingly, during research in music education, at one point one must uncover the very work materials that constitute the research site: the sounds in themselves, the dynamic movement of physical bodies, the nature of the room as such, and so forth. In this way and up to this point, Heidegger is clearly drawing from Husserl's descriptive phenomenological method.

Nevertheless, Heidegger is no strict Husserlian. It is in the second essential constituent in art according to Heidegger, the "world," that Heidegger's hermeneutic approach is realized. By world, Heidegger means the onto-historical world of the composer or creator of an artwork; the cultural world that surrounds and informs every aspect of the research setting under study. If the world were only that of nature, one could simply call it "the world." Because humankind brings meaning to the physical world, the world is marked by significance and meaning. The onto-historical world is the cultural and historical reality that contextualizes persons who make up that world. The onto-historical world is not some physical entity. It is the ideational space in and through which people live and relate. That ideational context or "ontology" is ever changing. As events unfold in history, they often have a great impact on the manner in which people define and understand themselves. For example, the French and American Revolutions and the two World Wars are events that dramatically changed their respective ontological settings for Western culture. Heidegger's insight is that in manipulating work materials (the earth), composers set into their artistic creations a glimpse of their onto-historical world. Similarly, every research setting is colored and informed by the ontological world in which it exists. Thus, for Heidegger, research into music contexts and works can disclose the most profound realities about humanity.

As in his depiction of "earth" (the artwork's fundamental materials such as the *sound-in-time* in the case of music, the paint and canvas in a painting, and the stone in a stone sculpture), Heidegger describes the world as a dynamic happening that occurs in works of art. His statement, the world "worlds," conveys the inner energy and synergy in art in which the world of the composer erupts through the earth as a dynamic event. The world is characterized as an "openness" and a "spaciousness"; it is not a physical entity. Unlike the physical earth, the world of the composer as set into the work of art is ideational. Thus Heidegger's use of "world" in art refers to the setting in the artwork of a sense of the onto-historical context that surrounds the composer and is in the spirit, mind, value system, and meaning of that historical and cultural people. According to Heidegger, without grounding in art, as that onto-historical world changes, it is lost. Thus artworks "hold open" the "openness" of the world of the composer. Art "makes space for" the onto-historical world and thereby preserves it in the physicality of the work's earth.

While the earth sustains and makes durable the world, the world is responsible for opening up the earth and letting it be an earth, that is, material that can be experienced as emerging and "rising up." As a result of the onto-historical world set into the earth materials, those materials "come forth for the very first time."[52] Thus there is a marriage of earth and world in works of art in which the earth (in music, the sound-in-time) provides durability and sustenance for the ideational and finite onto-historical world whereas the world provides an openness that allows the earth to come forth as an emerging material. The earth grounds the world and the world juts up through the earth, with each carrying the other further than each alone could have gone. In Heidegger's opinion, it is this dynamic interaction between these seemingly opposite elements that causes a work of art to *be* a work of art.

According to Heidegger, the coming together of the ideational world and the physical earth is marked by a "strife" instigated by the work of art and preserved by the viewer/listener. It is in that strife that each element, the earth and the world, moves beyond its isolated potential. Ordinary materials (such as paint, stones, and even sounds) have the proclivity to close to inspection because they "disappear into usefulness" when persons engage them in the ordinary utilitarian or what Husserl calls "natural" ways. In ordinary experiences, we tend to use up ordinary materials, as in the paint that is used to paint a room or the stone that is used to fill a hole. In addition, we tend to be unpreoccupied by ordinary sounds in the environment or in the background music on an elevator or in a building lobby. However, in the experience of art, we can engage and realize the nature of an artwork's materials or "earth."

Similarly, the "world" of meaning and significance that mark any historical people is not confined to some physical space but remains in the ideas (that is, in the ideational realm) of that people. Yet, that onto-logical or ideational world is "set into" or "brought to a stand" in an artwork's materials or earth. Held in the "earth" materials of an artwork, the onto-historical world of the composer is not allowed largely to disappear (as the world of Mozart no longer exists actually today). A profound glimpse of the "world" of the composer is made "durable" and preserved in the artwork.

Given Heidegger's conception of art, both elements are radically altered in the work. The earth is forced to "open" by the openness that characterizes the world and the world is forced into the physically confining space of the work materials or earth. This causes a "strife" that is never brought to closure but that lives in the work and generates its dynamic character. Thus, for Heidegger, the nature of art is that it is a "happening," an active and propelling event in which the earth and the world struggle against the imposition of each on the other. Consequently, the term "art" in this usage changes from the name of a static category or a collection of a certain type of physical objects to the underlying dynamic process unleashed by the strife between earth and world. Similarly, research contexts in which music teaching, learning, and making are studied are sites in which music "happens." Thus, in addition to formal and historical analyses, research in music education can also engage and uncover the essential constituents of the sound-in-time ("earth") and the onto-historical world of musical works as they are created and performed.

However, according to Heidegger, for art to "happen," it must be appreciated. A painting hanging in a darkened museum or music used to stay awake in a car are not works of art under Heidegger's conception. The strife between the earth and the world is possible only if an appreciating person allows that strife to show itself. A hermeneutic inquiry would enable a researcher to engage this level of significance in music education. Such a method would not stop at formal, historical, or quantifiable elements but would step back to a report of the earth understood as the "sound-in-time" as it erupts into the world of the composer. In so doing, a researcher stands in the "openness" of the work and thereby preserves the world in which it was created.[53] However, a researcher's interpretation of the world of the composer is relative to his or her own cultural and historical world. Researchers keep their feet in the Western cultural world of the early twenty-first century as they remain open to other, earlier onto-historical worlds and cultures. This act of "preserving" the musical work of art by listeners is judged by Heidegger to be as essential as that of the composer. Without composers there cannot be musical works. But art cannot "happen" unless it is "preserved" in a way that allows both its earth and world to be experienced in their dynamic strife. This Heideggerian conception of art as a dynamic happening signals the importance of the *making and experiencing* of music in music education.

The narrative style of hermeneutic inquiry exemplified by Heidegger's account of art immediately above is obviously poetic and thickly constructed. Insofar as works of art are metaphorical, their significance is not limited to sound or syntax but radiates outward into musical reference. Indeed, onto-historical power is substantiated by the referential meanings that grow from a work. Insofar as music, at one level, functions as a symbol, researchers look through the music to its referential messages. Given this metaphorical nature of music, analyses of referential levels of musical meaning must also have the power to project. A purely literal language style cannot adequately respond to referential meanings because it lacks the projective power of metaphorical or poetic language. Just as a musical work's referential meanings project meanings outward an ideational space, hermeneutic inquiry sometimes radiates out beyond the confines of literal language. In the dual projections of the musical work and the analysis, both may intersect. That intersection is the principal criterion for evaluating referential analyses. That is, an analysis of referential meaning in music is successful to the degree to which it intersects with the work's projective (i.e., referential or metaphorical) meanings. One cannot stipulate that analyses of referential meanings are correct or incorrect with the precision acquired by the use of formal systems. The most positive assessment that one could direct to analyses of referential meanings in music is that the analyses are expressive of and congruent to those meanings.

Postmodernism and the Experiment

Postmodernism also asserts that scientific experiments are dislocated from the world or reality that they are supposed to be representing. Essentially, they find that experiments artificially create environments that purportedly represent the real world but do not include the world, in fact. Rom Harre explains that this postmodernist position disclaims "the principle of transparency" in science: that experiments represent dimensions of the natural world as it really is.[54] It follows in classical science that when describing the finding in an experiment the experimental procedure or apparatus may be omitted when describing the natural world because it is believed that the natural world is actually present in the experiment.[55] Thus the experiment is transparent to nature. Postmodernism rejects the principle of transparency in science. For example, according to Bruno Latour, the experimental environment is a "closed system" that is forever shut off from the natural world.[56] Latour joins Andrew Pickering (and not unlike Polanyi) in concluding that knowledge developed by scientific experiments is a function of the social power of the community of professional scientists that ascribe to that experimental modality.[57] Thus the postmodern critique of the experiment is that nature or the world is not properly represented in scientific experiments.[58] Insofar as nature does not pass through the artificial and unnatural environment of the scientific experiment, the principle of transparency is rebuffed. Similarly, Richard Rorty opines that insofar as hypotheses and facts are presented in propositional form, research in the natural sciences does not connect to the natural world.[59] Rorty notes that to the extent that experiments must be interpreted, they are discursive. As an entirely discursive activity, scientific truth has more to do with the human mind than with nature.

The realist version of science offers a better route and understanding of scientific experiments than the postmodernist viewpoint that was just reviewed. In addition, a realist philosophy of science better connects the experiment to the real world. However, first it is necessary to construct a brief overview of the roots of realism.

The Roots of Realism

Since the time of Socrates, philosophies have attempted to transcend culture by developing ahistorical and universal definitions, criteria, and theories. The thrust of realism is that through acts of reason, one can uncover pure concepts, theories, or structures that are not spoiled by the subject's biases, the subject's less defined but important cultural prejudices, or even the temporal nature of the subject's knowledge. This philosophical orientation, which dovetails with rationalism, is committed to the possibility of pure concepts and theories which provide knowledge that is above culture and therefore is forever certain and unchanging. Universal truths, by definition, exist independently of human perceptions and constitute objective reality. On the other hand and according to a realist view, humans abstract or formalize those objective truths through sense data (i.e., data empirically collected through the human senses), and thereby provide the foundations of the knowledge of reality.

Realism can be traced to Plato's desire to discover universals ("forms" or "essences") that are independent of perception and are unchanging and eternal. In Plato's work *The Republic* and specifically in the section "The Allegory of the Cave," humankind is metaphorically presented as living in a cave of ignorance. Outside the cave is the light and the basis of knowledge, that is, universal truths and essences. With its back to the cave opening, humankind is chained by leg and neck from childhood and can see only what is in front of them, the dark, inner wall. That wall exclusively presents the "shadows" of the "ideas" or "forms" that pass by the opening of the cave from the bright outside. The pursuit of the philosopher-king of *The Republic* is to turn people around toward the light outside the cave, characterized by universal forms. The allegory clarifies the responsibility of the philosopher-king and any person who wishes to gain "real" knowledge. It also provides a classical example of "rationalism," the hope that through acts of reason one can transcend one's community and culture and reach pure and unbiased knowledge.

According to Heidegger (whose philosophy is not representative of realism), at this momentous point in the history of the Western intellectual tradition, Plato caused a dramatic shift for philosophical inquiry.[60] The things outside that pass by the cave opening are not physical things but the "forms" (i.e., essences or ideas) of actual things. In Plato's view, knowledge requires that the "form" or idea of a thing be understood first, before understanding a concrete and immediate instance of that idea. Accordingly from a Platonist position, if one wants to understand and evaluate a particular musical composition, performance thereof, or an instance of music teaching, one must first have a conception of the pure "form" of each. Thus between the subject and the object is inserted a concept through which a specific object is understood. Based on this Platonist approach, before evaluating a music program, one must first have a concept or "idea" of a music program through which the program under study can be measured, described, or understood.

In the seventeenth century, Rene Descartes further separated the mind from objects with his famous dictum, "I think, therefore I am." Like Plato, Descartes sought to discover universal principles. Through his method of systematic doubt, Descartes bifurcates the mind from its own body.[61] He separates the inner world of consciousness from the outer world of objects (including one's own body as part of the outer world). With this separation of perception from what is perceived, an important basis for scientific methodology is established. In classic realist fashion, scientific methodology is placed between researchers and the objects of their research in order to control the subject (i.e., the researcher) and free the object(s) of research for pure, empirical inspection. With Descartes, philosophy was placed on the "secure path of science." With the strength of scientific methodology, and specifically by coupling philosophy with mathematics and logic, philosophy could claim to provide apodictic or certain knowledge. Scientific axioms transposed into philosophical directives control the researcher's cultural, historical, and personal biases when pondering philosophical issues, just as the scientist places his or her biases in abeyance during experiments. After all, the Newtonian image of the world was that of a perfectly running clock.[62] According to the conventional wisdom of the eighteenth and nineteenth centuries, eventually science would catch up with and explain every element of this wonderful machine called the universe. By the end of the nineteenth century, the same wisdom suggested that the human sciences would share this methodological control over the nature of human knowledge and actions.

The archetypal figure, Immanuel Kant (1724–1804), presents a realist position that is much less rigid than the extreme position of logical positivism discussed earlier in this chapter. The main difference is that in logical positivism, the researcher as subject is absent from inquiry; only the method and the object of research overtly remain. In Kant's form of realism, the researcher plays an active part in philosophical and scientific inquiry. Like Plato, Kant was committed to the possibility of pure reason. And like Descartes, Kant hoped to provide universal criteria for knowledge of universal principles; to that end, he remained committed to the development of "transcendental reason." Philosophy was to be the judicature that would assess all fundamental claims. Yet, unlike Plato and Descartes, Kant placed an inquirer's consciousness overtly at the center of all knowledge gathering.[63] Kant rejected David Hume's rigid realist model of mind as a passive response mechanism that comprehends things in themselves as they exist, separate from consciousness.[64] A philosophical rationale for the twentieth-century stimulus-response behaviorist model of mind, Hume's premise was that a researcher discovers knowledge as a passive reactor to information given by autonomous, external objects. In such a view, there is no "knower" (no researcher), only the "known."[65] Contrary to that view, according to Kant, external objects must be mediated by concepts that have been formulated by a knowing subject: objects "conform to the conditions of one's knowledge." While this places the subject at the center of knowledge gathering activities, Kant believed that through a transcendental method based on pure reason (note his Platonic roots), one constitutes the objects of observation in a purely formal manner, thereby saving objectivity. Thus for Kant, the human mind, as a proactive (not reactive as in Hume) mediator of experience, is capable of transcending its ordinary subjectivism and securing pure knowledge.

Current Realist Philosophy

The following account suggests that if researchers in music education wish to emulate current practices in the philosophy of science and the social sciences, they must look to the current literature for models. While there are many "varieties of realism" (see Harre 1986) in the philosophy of science, what most current philosophies of science hold in common is a convincing argument against positivism's rigid account of the nature of scientific theory and practice centered in empirical verification and the symmetry between explanation and prediction. That is to say, contemporary philosophy of science and the social sciences have largely abandoned the requirement of empirical verification for all scientific knowledge and the notion that explanation begets prediction.

Harre's article (1998) regarding the scientific experiment cited above provides an example of current realist philosophy of science. Harre's philosophical inquiry into the nature of the scientific experiment places the reader in the core of realism and provides a middle ground between the excesses of the positivist (at one end) and postmodernist (at the other end) approaches. In Harre's realist view, there is no question that in scientific experiments, nature is "domesticated."[66] This is necessary because in the experiment we seek to manipulate a piece of the natural world. However, contrary to the postmodernist critique of the scientific experiment and its alleged substantial disconnection from the natural world, Harre points out that although nature as such is not studied in an experiment, what is studied is still a piece of nature, albeit fragmented from its natural environment. In this realist vision, the experiment remains a part of the world. Harre does not deny that the experimental apparatus represents an artificial environment that is not identical to or captures the full richness of the natural world. However, he softens that distinction with the analogy that the experimental laboratory is like a farm, not an "art gallery" or a "zoo."[67] He suggests that an art gallery provides a representation of nature and a zoo is not entirely "wild." On the other hand, analogous to a traditional farm where animals are not entirely wild yet are not completely controlled, Harre believes that while science domesticates portions of the natural world for study, it does not so wholly change their nature as the postmodernists claim. Experiments are not, as Rorty retorts, just statements about nature, but are a part of nature. Thus Harre does not wholly embrace the principle of transparency. He accepts that in its domesticated form, natural objects that are under study are not exactly functioning in the way in which they function in nature (or the "wild"). Nevertheless, scientific experiments do provide researchers with a portal to the natural world.

Lopez and Potter note that scientific experiments are constituted of creating "constant conjunctures of events."[68] When such events are *invariant* or never changing, causality is inferred. Thus in Humean terms, when B always is preceded by A, it is true that A causes B.[69] However, it is important to note that the causal relationship between A and B is only verified in the *experimental environment* (not in nature), each time the experiment is repeated. Scientists then generalize that finding and raise it to the status of a universal invariance (i.e., a scientific law). Thus empirically viewed invariance in a subset of experimental events is generalized to all events as a law of nature. However, realist philosophy recognizes that *understanding* the meaning of human activities in the social sciences and the arts is not possible through the empirical observation and subsequent explanation of *invariant conjunctures of events*. The meaning of objects of study in research in music education exists whether we understand those meanings or not. Lopez and Potter note that meaning in social life is extant just as is molecular structure.[70] Realism maintains that there can be objective answers to questions of meaning in music education. Researchers can rationally ascertain which explanation of the meaning of a particular music educational activity is more correct or incorrect. Explanation is merged with the interpretive or reflexive powers of the researcher, undoing the narrow vision of the positivist research agenda. Nevertheless, research in music education can provide prediction along with explanation in some cases. Thus realist philosophy in science and the social sciences seeks to be more inclusive than positivism while retaining the main tenets of science as it is actually practiced, and theory building in science as it actually occurs.

Realism concurs with postmodernist claims that the human elements in music education are not necessarily responsive to scientific explanation. Similarly, realism suggests that music educational contexts are much more like a language than a chemical reaction or a mechanized machine. Realism accepts (1) the social and aesthetic centeredness of research in music education and (2) that theory is presented in language which is socially constructed. Nonetheless, realism supports the "scientific" study of the social sciences and, by extension in this chapter, music education. However, this is not the pure scientific research as conceived in positivism. The creation of knowledge remains a social process that is language dependent.[71] Thus the idea of apodictic and pure unbiased evidence in research is not possible.

While the experimental environment is a closed system (as cited in Harre above), nature is an open system. Experiments must exclude the confounding variables that naturally occur in nature. This points to the fact that what is being empirically "proven" in the experiment doesn't necessarily occur precisely that way in nature. Does this sound like postmodernism? Yes it does. But realism leaves postmodernism behind when it establishes that unlike a positivist vision of science which is "event" centered (as in the conjuncture of invariant events), realism is "thing" centered. Things in a realist approach may be powers, forces, or various relations that have "tendencies" to interact in specific ways with other entities in the natural world.[72]

Human beings are complex "things" in the real world. In Kant's transcendental sense, realism accepts that while our understanding of human activities (such as research in music education) is fallible, things remain potentially what they are in the world irrespective of human experiment, explanation, and understanding. Thus the thing-in-itself is out there in the world whether humans interact with it or understand it or not. Furthermore, realism accepts that there may be certain things for which scientific experimentation is not possible. It does not inextricably tie scientific explanation to prediction, as in positivism and it does not require that there be a single method.[73] Instead, realism recognizes that scientists select methods that are appropriate to the things under study. This attitude suggests an eclectic approach to research in music education.

CONCLUSION

In order to be responsive to what is being studied in research in music education, researchers must be open to applying appropriate methods. The realist view of philosophy is clearly a mainstream view in philosophy of science and the social sciences and will help to clarify many of the philosophical issues in music education as it is incorporated into that field. In addition, phenomenological and hermeneutic approaches to philosophical inquiry are recommended insofar as researchers in music education, like researchers in science, *must* function in ways that correlate to Harre's three "realms" of scientific research. Thus in many cases in music educational research, perception (empirical verification) may have to catch up (at some future time) to conception or may never become observationally/empirically corroborated.

The use of any method automatically places conditions on what the object of research can mean. Methods prescribe the tasks that researchers perform. Each method delimits what can be known about a research object based on the nature of its tasks. Researchers follow the protocols of a selected method to ensure that research is systematic, logical, corroborable, understandable to a shared community of professional colleagues, and objective and unbiased to some degree. Traditional methods in research are placed between researchers and their databases in order to control both the integrity of the data and the researcher. The method not only controls for the potential inconsistency of data collection and treatment but also helps to avoid unacceptable levels of subjectivity in research. Research is considered objective when a method controls bias and prejudice. However, that same method prescribes what the research object can mean. While the researcher presents the appearance of objective distance from the data, the method subjugates the data because data can only mean and show what the prescribed task of one's method allows data to mean and show. In transferring the subjective role from the researcher to his or her method, the impact on the data is not less subjective or dominating. Thus, in one sense, "objectivity" is not achieved through the use of traditional, "objectifying" research designs. That is to say, the idea of "objectivity" should be for the *object*, not the *subject*. To be objective means to protect the object from dominance of any kind. In focusing on the dangers that result from a researcher's subjectivity, traditional research designs have not registered a parallel subjectivism in their methods.[74]

An appropriate level of objectivity is achievable via a responsive approach to the nature and fullness of the database. For example, Heidegger suggests that truth (and for our purposes, truth in research) must be understood as "freedom."[75] In order to understand the truth about some object of research that object must be given the freedom to show itself. Objectivity marks research in which analytical tasks engender freedom for research entities to show themselves in any mode of appearance and meaning. Methods of research from this standpoint would have to respond to what research entities can and might mean. In such a paradigm, the tasks of research focus on the needs and questions posed by research entities. As a result, methods might be more fluid and flexible, with a less prescriptive role than is common in established methods. This is not to suggest that established and traditional methods are automatically dislocated from research entities. Certainly in the construction and development of such methods there is a response to the nature of research entities that, in turn, makes methods appropriate to data. The point made here is that research methods most often appropriate and thereby delimit what research entities can mean without a consideration of the potential of meanings that can be generated from those same entities. That is, as is the case in scientific experiments, researchers in music education "domesticate" their data by placing them in research settings.

In the current literature of the philosophy of science, research practices in the natural sciences are described as a blending of the use of perception (observation) and conception (theory development), logical reasoning and imaginative vision. Clearly, as one moves out of the natural sciences and into the domains of human social, behavioral, historical, and artistic activities, research can more readily leave the confines of the observable (Harre's first realm of scientific activity) based on perception (and the empirical verification of "conjunctures of events") to research and theory building that is based on conception and in which empirical verification is not possible or even appropriate. This orientation in research in music education supports interaction between traditional and nontraditional methods. Rather than produce chaos, researchers can be responsive to the rich fullness of research entities.

Responsiveness is a form of appreciation. Appreciation does not mean liking or disliking. Instead, it names a mode of inquiry that balances questions through the use of one's method with questions that grow more directly from the research entity. This oscillation between subject and object roles is rooted in a dialogical method in which the researcher remains rigorous and directed yet also follows the lead of the research entity. Researchers utilizing philosophical inquiry remain grounded in logical reasoning but, as in the classical dialects of Plato, also remain open to where the dialogue might proceed. As in a conversation during which neither party knows explicitly where the conversation will end, researchers in music education can also remain open to questions posed by one's database as they develop in the research. The delimitation of what *is* research in music education to activities that must list explicit hypotheses followed by an explanation of the research "events" is not only too narrow for music education, it does not properly represent the full nature of research in science.

It is significant to note that the constitution of explanations and conclusions that are presented in quantitative form in experimental and some descriptive research in music education is exceedingly foreign in substance to the original composition of the data. That is to say, the database in music educational research sites, which is constituted of human beings performing, composing, teaching, or learning music, is radically transformed into a mathematical formulation through some traditional research designs. On the other hand, in philosophical inquiry there are no clear safety controls over the data. Yet, that does not mean that philosophical inquiry is more precarious. After all, in experimental design, the researcher as "knower" is left "tacit" in favor of a method and the "known" (data).[76] In philosophical inquiry the researcher "holds on" to the data in a way that must be responsive to its constitution, and thus "control" (through the transformation of the human and artistic constituents of the object of study) is traded for the real ongoing presence of the researcher and the researcher's responsiveness to the database. During his or her "conversation" with data, the data site and participants under study, a researcher utilizing philosophical inquiry remains open to what data *might* mean. And in so doing, he or she is always and only "on the way" to conclusions.

FOR REVIEW, DISCUSSION, AND IMPLEMENTATION

- Why is philosophical inquiry considered a nontraditional research design in music education? How is philosophical inquiry similar to and different from traditional research designs in music education?
- What is the basis for Heller and O'Conner's conclusion that philosophical inquiry is not "research" as they define it? Provide a rationale for an alternate opinion.
- How can methods and models of research currently used in science and the social sciences be helpful to research in music education?

- What is the logical positivist position concerning research? Is this a useful approach for music education?
- What are some of the distinctions between realism and logical positivism?
- What is meant by the term "rationalism"?
- How does the "early" Wittgenstein relate to and yet differ from the "late" Wittgenstein?
- Is phenomenology a useful tool for research in music education? What are the two phenomenological reductions?
- How does Husserl's phenomenological method differ from a hermeneutic approach to research?
- What is realism's understanding of the nature of the scientific experiment, as expounded by Harre? How is that different from a postmodernist approach to the scientific experiment? How does this relate to research in music education?

NOTES

1. See Thomas Spencer Bayes, *An Essay on the New Analytical Logical Forms* (New York: Lenox Hill, 1971); Nino B. Cocchiarella, *Logical Studies in Early Analytical Philosophy* (Columbus, Ohio: Ohio State University Press, 1987); Anthony Flew, *Logic and Language* (Garden City, N.Y.: Anchor, 1965); Bas C. van Fraassen, *Formal Semantics and Logic* (New York: Macmillan, 1971); Max Hocutt, *The Elements of Logical Analysis and Inference* (Cambridge, Mass.: Winthrop, 1979); P. F. Strawson, *Philosophical Logic* (London: Oxford University Press, 1967); and Anna Teresa Tymieniecka, *Contributions to Logic and Methodology in Honor of J. M. Bochenski* (Amsterdam: North Holland, 1965).

2. For example, see Bennett Reimer, *A Philosophy of Music Education* (Englewood Cliffs, N.J.: Prentice-Hall, 1970).

3. For example, see David J. Elliott, *Music Matters: A New Philosophy of Music Education* (New York: Oxford University Press, 1995).

4. Jack J. Heller and Edward J. P. O'Connor, "Maintaining Quality in Research and Reporting," in *The New Handbook of Research on Music Teaching and Learning*, ed. Richard Colwell and Carol Richardson (New York: Oxford University Press, 2002), 1089.

5. Heller and O'Connor, 1091.

6. Thomas S. Kuhn, *The Structure of Scientific Revolutions* (Chicago: University of Chicago Press, 1962).

7. For example, see Jose Lopez and Garry Potter, eds., *After Postmodernism: An Introduction to Critical Realism* (New York: Athlone, 2001), 4.

8. For example, read Heller and O'Conner, 1089–92.

9. An excellent source is A. J. Ayer, *Logical Positivism* (New York: Free Press, 1959). Also see Ayer, *Language, Truth, and Logic* (New York: Dover, 1946); and Ernest Nagel, *The Structure of Science* (London: Routledge & Kegan Paul, 1961).

10. See D. Bohm, *Causality and Chance in Modern Physics* (London: Routledge & Kegan Paul, 1957); Rom Harre, *The Principles of Scientific Thinking* (London: Macmillan, 1970); Rom Harre, *Varieties of Realism: A Rationale for the Natural Sciences* (London: Basil Blackwell, 1986); Mary B. Hesse, *Models and Analogies in Science* (London: Sheed & Ward, 1963); G. Maxwell, "The Ontological Status of Theoretical Entities," in *Minnesota Studies in the Philosophy of Science*, vol. 3, ed. H. Feigl and G. Maxwell (Minneapolis: University of Minnesota Press, 1956); and J. J. C. Smart, *Between Science and Philosophy* (New York: Random House, 1968).

11. Harre, *Varieties of Realism*, 177–90, 237–42.

12. Harre, *Varieties of Realism*, 145–90.

13. Harre, *Varieties of Realism*, 191–236.

14. Harre, *Varieties of Realism*, 237–316.

15. Hesse, *Models and Analogies in Science*, 162–65.

16. An excellent source is Ayer, *Logical Positivism*; also see Ernest Nagel, *The Structure of Science* (London: Routledge & Kegan Paul, 1961).

17. Max Weber, *The Protestant Ethic and the Spirit of Capitalism*, trans. Talcott Parsons (New York: Scribner's, 1958), esp. chap. 5.

18. Abraham Kaplan, *The Conduct of Inquiry* (San Francisco: Chandler, 1964).

19. Edward L. Rainbow and Hildegard C. Froelich, *Research in Music Education: An Introduction to Systematic Inquiry* (New York: Schirmer, 1987), 128–61.

20. Milton Babbitt, "Past and Present Concepts," in *Perspectives on Contemporary Music Theory*, ed. Benjamin Boretz and Edward Cone (New York: Norton, 1972), 3–9.

21. Carl Hempel, *Aspects of Scientific Explanation and Other Essays in the Philosophy of Science* (New York: Free Press, 1965).

22. Lopez and Potter, 6–7.

23. See Karl R. Popper's discussion of the "falsification" of theories in *The Logic of Scientific Discovery* (New York: Harper & Row, 1968). However, Popper's idea of "falsification" is viewed by many philosophers of science as another instance of absolutism or the quest for certainty. In this sense, falsification replaces verifiability as a purported primary purpose of science. Along these lines, Marjorie Grene characterizes Popper's theory of "falsification" as an attempt to provide "absolute error" in place of "absolute proof." Marjorie Grene, *The Knower and the Known* (Berkeley: University of California Press, 1974), chap. 1.

24. Aristotle, *De Interpretatione*, in *The Basic Works of Aristotle*, trans. E. M. Edghill, ed. R. McKeon (New York: Random House, 1941), 5–7.

25. Ludwig Wittgenstein, *Tractatus Logico-Philosophicus*, trans. G. E. M. Anscombe (Oxford: Basil Blackwell, 1963), 4.

26. For example, see Bertrand Russell, introduction to Wittgenstein, *Tractatus Logico-Philosophicus*, p. ix.

27. Ludwig Wittgenstein, *Philosophical Investigations* (London: Basil Blackwell, 1953). Also see Ludwig Wittgenstein, *The Blue and Brown Books* (Oxford: Basil Blackwell, 1958).

28. Thomas S. Kuhn, *The Structure of Scientific Revolutions* (Chicago: University of Chicago Press, 1962).

29. Michael Polanyi, *Personal Knowledge* (Chicago: University of Chicago Press, 1958).

30. Polanyi, *Personal Knowledge*, 15–17.

31. For examples, see Jacques Derrida, *Deconstruction and Philosophy*, ed. John Sallis (Chicago: University of Chicago Press, 1987).

32. Edmund Husserl, *Logical Investigations*, trans. J. N. Findlay, 2 vols. (1900–1901; New York: Humanities Press, 1970). Although Husserl's phenomenological method was not conceived as postmodernist, it has been appropriated by postmodernism as an analytical tool.

33. Psychologism is a position in which all operations of thought and reason are reduced to psychological laws. In such a position, the mind is the ultimate center for knowledge.

34. Edmund Husserl, *Ideas: General Introduction to Pure Phenomenology*, trans. Ted E. Klein and William E. Pohl (1913; The Hague: Martinus Nijhoff, 1980).

35. Husserl, *Ideas*, 91–100.

36. Husserl, *Ideas*, 45–71, 181–84, 285–88.

37. Lawrence Ferrara, *Philosophy and the Analysis of Music: Bridges to Musical Sound, Form, and Reference* (London: Greenwood, 1991), 79.

38. Edmund Husserl, *Phenomenology of Internal Time-Consciousness*, ed. Martin Heidegger, trans. James S. Churchill (1905; Bloomington: Indiana University Press, 1964).

39. Herbert Spiegelberg, *The Phenomenological Movement: A Historical Introduction*, 3rd ed. (The Hague: Martinus Nijhoff, 1982), 708.

40. For a fuller discussion of Husserl's phenomenology and its use in music analysis, see Ferrara, *Philosophy and the Analysis of Music*, chapters 3, 6, and as implemented in the analysis of a composition by Bela Bartok in chapter 8. In addition, see Lawrence Ferrara and Betsy Behnke, "Phenomenology and Music," in *Encyclopedia of Phenomenology*, ed. Lester Embree (The Netherlands: Kluwer, 1997), 467–73; and Lawrence Ferrara, "Phenomenology as a Tool for Musical Analysis," *Musical Quarterly* 70 (1984): 355–73.

41. Ferrara 1991, 90.

42. Heidegger, *Being and Time*, trans. John Macquarrie and Edward Robinson (1927; New York: Harper & Row), 1962.

43. Hans-Georg Gadamer, *Truth and Method* (New York: The Seabury Press, 1975), 235–74.

44. Richard Rorty, *Objectivity, Relativism, and Truth: Philosophical Papers*, vol. 1 (Cambridge: Cambridge University Press, 1994). Also see Rorty, *Philosophy and the Mirror of Nature* (Oxford: Blackwell, 1979), 315–16.

45. While this is a theme throughout Heidegger's corpus, the most seminal presentation of it is found in *Being and Time*.

46. Heidegger, *Being and Time*, 122.

47. Hans-Georg Gadamer, *Philosophical Hermeneutics*, trans. and ed. David E. Linge (Berkeley: University of California Press, 1976), p. 9.

48. Gadamer, *Philosophical Hermeneutics*, 18–44, esp. 21–26.

49. This Heideggerian conception of art is not presented as a secure definition of art. Instead, it is being presented for heuristic reasons; it will enable us to locate and discuss certain essential constituents of art. It is not the intention of this researcher to enter the philosophical quagmire and imbroglio as to whether "art" or "music" or terms such as the "aesthetic" are definable in some closed form.

50. The presentation of Heidegger's conception of art herein is based on Martin Heidegger, "On the Origin of the Work of Art," in *Poetry, Language, Thought*, trans. Albert Hofstadter (New York: Harper & Row, 1971), 17–87.

51. Heidegger, "On the Origin of the Work of Art," 42.

52. Heidegger, "On the Origin of the Work of Art," 46.

53. Heidegger, "On the Origin of the Work of Art," 65–66.

54. Rom Harre, "Recovering the Experiment," *Philosophy* 73 (1998): 353–77.

55. Harre 1998, 355.

56. Bruno Latour, *Science in Action* (Milton Keynes: Open University Press, 1987).

57. Andrew Pickering, *Constructing Quarks: A Social History of Particle Physics* (Edinburgh: Edinburgh University Press, 1984).

58. Harre 1998, 360.

59. Rorty, *Philosophy and the Mirror of Nature*.

60. Martin Heidegger, "Plato's Doctrine of Truth," in *Philosophy in the Twentieth Century*, vol. 3, trans. John Barlow, ed. William Barrett and Henry D. Aiken (New York: Random House, 1962).

61. Rene Descartes, "Meditations" (1641), in *Discourse on Method and Meditations*, Rene Descartes, trans. Lawrence J. Lafleur (New York: Bobbs-Merrill, 1966), 118–43.

62. Karl R. Popper, "Of Clouds and Clocks," in *Objective Knowledge* (Oxford: Clarendon, 1979), 206–51.

63. Immanuel Kant, *The Critique of Pure Reason*, trans. J. M. D. Meikeljohn (New York: Everyman's Library, 1964).

64. David Hume, *Treatise of Human Nature* (New York: Everyman's Library, 1975).

65. Cf. Marjorie Greene, *The Knower and the Known* (Berkeley: University of California Press, 1974), particularly the introduction; and John Dewey and Arthur F. Bentley, *Knowing and the Known* (Boston: Beacon, 1949).

66. Harre 1998, 366.

67. Harre 1998, 368.

68. Lopez and Potter, 10.

69. Lopez and Potter, 11.

70. Lopez and Potter, 13.

71. Lopez and Potter, 9. Also see Roger G. Newton, *The Truth of Science: Physical Theories and Reality* (Cambridge: Harvard University Press, 2001), esp. chap. 2, "Science as a Social Construct?"

72. Lopez and Potter, 11. Also see Charles Varela, "Determinism and the Recovery of Human Agency: The Embodying of Persons," *Journal for the Theory of Social Behavior* 29, no. 4 1996: 385–402; Charles Varela and Rom Harre, "Conflicting Varieties of Realism: Causal Powers and the Problems of Social Structure," *Journal for the Theory of Social Behavior* 26, no. 3 1999: 314–25.

73. Lopez and Potter, 13.

74. For a fuller discussion, see Ferrara, 38–46.

75. Martin Heidegger, "On the Essence of Truth," in *Existence and Being*, trans. R. F. C. Hull and Alan Crick, ed. Werner Brock (Chicago: Regnery, 1949), 303.

76. For example, see Michael Polanyi, *The Tacit Dimension* (Garden City, N.Y.: Anchor, 1966).

SUPPLEMENTARY SOURCES

Adorno, Theodore W. *Aesthetic Theory.* Trans. by Hullot-Kentor. Minneapolis: University of Minnesota Press, 1997.

Alston, William. *A Realist Conception of Truth.* Ithaca: Cornell University Press, 1996.

Ballantine, Christopher. *Music and Its Social Meanings.* New York: Gordon & Breach, 1984.

Bartholomew, Douglas Roy. "A Phenomenology of Music: Themes Concerning the Musical Object and Implications for Teaching and Learning." Ph.D. diss., Case Western Reserve University, 1985.

Bernstein, Richard J. *Beyond Objectivism and Relativism: Science, Hermeneutics, and Praxis,* 1–49. Philadelphia: University of Pennsylvania Press, 1983.

Bhaskar, Roy. *A Realist Theory of Science.* 2nd ed. Brighton, U.K.: Harvestor, 1978.

Budd, Malcolm. *Music and the Emotions: The Philosophical Theories.* London: Routledge & Kegan Paul, 1985.

Clifton, Thomas. *Music as Heard: A Study in Applied Phenomenology*. New Haven: Yale University Press, 1983.

Colwell, Richard, and Carol Richardson, eds. *The New Handbook of Research on Music Teaching and Learning*. Oxford: Oxford University Press, 2002.

Dewey, John. *Logic: The Theory of Inquiry*. New York: Holt, 1938.

Elliott, David, "Music as Knowledge." *Journal of Aesthetic Education*, Fall 1991, 21–40.

———. *Music Matters: A New Philosophy of Music Education*. New York: Oxford University Press, 1995.

Feibelman, James K. *The Revival of Realism*. New York: Holt, 1938.

Fiske, Harold E. *Music and Mind: Philosophical Essays on the Cognition and Meaning of Music*. Lewiston, N.Y.: Mellen, 1990.

Gorovitz, Samuel, Merrill Hintikka, Donald Provence, and Ron G. Williams. *Philosophical Analysis: An Introduction to Its Language and Techniques*. 3rd ed. New York: Random House, 1979.

Harre, Rom. *Laws of Nature*. London: Duckworth, 1993.

———. *The Philosophies of Science*. 2nd ed. Oxford: Oxford University Press, 1985.

———. *Varieties of Realism: A Rationale for the Natural Sciences*. London: Basil Blackwell, 1986.

Ihde, Don. *Listening and Voice: A Phenomenology of Sound*. Athens: Ohio University Press, 1976.

Ingarden, Roman. *The Work of Music and the Problem of Its Identity*. Trans. Adam Czerniawski. Ed. Jean Harrell. Berkeley: University of California Press, 1986.

Kim, Paul Sung-Il. "Olivier Messiaen's *Catalogue D'Oiseaux* for Solo Piano: A Phenomenological and Style Analysis." Ph.D. diss., New York University, 1989.

Kivy, Peter. *The Corded Shell: Reflections on Musical Expression*. Princeton: Princeton University Press, 1980.

———. *Music Alone: Philosophical Reflections on the Purely Musical Experience*. Ithaca: Cornell University Press, 1990.

Langer, Susanne K. *Feeling and Form: A Theory of Art Developed from Philosophy in a New Key*. New York: Scribner's, 1953.

———. *Philosophy in a New Key: A Study in the Symbolism of Reason, Rite, and Art*. 3rd ed. Cambridge: Harvard University Press, 1957. Originally published in 1942.

———. *Problems of Art*. New York: Scribner's, 1957.

Langer, Susanne K., ed. *Reflections on Art: A Source Book of Writings by Artists, Critics, and Philosophers*. New York: Oxford University Press, 1961.

Levinson, Jerrold. *Music, Art, and Metaphysics*. Ithaca: Cornell University Press, 1990.

Margolis, Joseph. *Pragmaticism without Foundations: Reconciling Realism and Relativism.* Oxford: Basil Blackwell, 1986.

Mueller, Renate. "Perspectives from the Sociology of Music." In *The New Handbook of Research on Music Teaching and Learning,* ed. Richard Colwell and Carol Richardson. Oxford: Oxford University Press, 2002.

Ricoeur, Paul. *Hermeneutics and the Human Sciences.* Ed. and trans. John B. Thompson. New York: Cambridge University Press, 1981.

Schwadron, Abraham A. "On Relativism and Music Education." *Journal of Research in Music Education,* Fall 1965, 131–35.

———. "Philosophy and Aesthetics in Music Education: A Critique of the Research." *Bulletin of the Council for Research in Music Education,* Summer 1983, 11–32.

Chapter 5

Nonexperimental Research: Concepts and Techniques

Opinions vary among researchers regarding what concepts and techniques should be classified as descriptive, nonexperimental, qualitative, or quantitative. Best and Kahn report that qualitative research usually is nonquantitative and thus signifies a negative connotation because it does not utilize experimental research methodologies.[1] They state that descriptive research, in contrast to experimental, involves no manipulation of variables because the researcher reports on events or happenings as they occur or have already happened.[2]

Leedy is among those researchers who regard concepts and methods identified as descriptive, ethnological, and grounded theory, among others, as qualitative. Moreover, the designation "quantitative nonexperimental" is used by Leedy to identify some concepts, techniques, and methods that usually fall under "descriptive," "qualitative," or some other designation.[3] He puts the difference between "qualitative" and "quantitative" this way: qualitative data are *verbal*; quantitative are *numerical*.[4] Patten writes that quantitative research involves deductive techniques, while qualitative researchers focus on inductive processes.[5] Tuckman posits that "quantitative" or experimental research involves a systematic, objective measurement of variables, unlike research in which investigators rely on their own judgment.[6] Some techniques for gathering and treating data identified as "descriptive," "ethnographic," "naturalistic," or "field study" are considered to be "qualitative" as Ferrara notes in chapter 3 of this book. It should be apparent by now that the labeling of research concepts or tools is less important than the actual collection and interpretation of the data.

In several research textbooks written before the late 1980s, "descriptive" was identified as a method of research along with "aesthetic inquiry," "experimental," "historical," and "philosophical." The meaning of "descriptive," however, in research texts published since the 1990s is stated clearly by Gall, Gall, and Borg as the collection and "analysis of quantitative data in order to develop a precise description of a sample's behavior or personal characteristics."[7] Even more specific are Mason and Bramble, who aver that "quantitative research uses measurement, statistical principles, and models" to quantify the phenomenon being studied.[8]

Descriptive studies simply present characteristics of a sample with no attempt to show causal relationships among variables, write Freed, Ryan, and Hess. On the other hand, experimental research is designed to ascertain if a causal relationship exists between independent and dependent variables.[9] Mertens asserts that "qualitative" research consists of two types: discovering causal (or correlational) relationships and descriptive studies that use "quantitative" data to describe phenomena.[10] Adams and Schvaneveldt believe "descriptive research," whether it is defined as a method or process, usually concentrates on events that already have taken place or those in the process of being studied. The investigator then may vary methods of observation and description but cannot change actual events in a situation.[11]

The "quantitative" method has rarely been associated with history as a valid approach to acquire complete knowledge, or a close approximation to it, such as the asymptotic approach to truth. Aydelotte, Bogue, and Fogel point out that research by Kramer and Lepper on U. S. Congressional elections utilized statistics (clearly a quantitative procedure) to show that the "presidential effect" is carried over into congressional elections.[12] Leedy and Ormrod write that quantitative researchers look for explanations and predictions that may be generalized to other persons and places. Continuing, they report "quantitative studies represent the mainstream approach to research," and carefully structured guidelines exist for conducting these studies.[13] Martella, Nelson, and Martella contrast "quantitative" and "qualitative" research by stating that a natural setting is the source for qualitative research. While quantitative researchers conduct research in artificial settings, or under artificial contexts, qualitative researchers are "concerned with the 'real world' of 'big picture' questions."[14]

There is little agreement among educational researchers as to precisely what differentiates qualitative from quantitative research. To establish consistency, some concepts, techniques, or methods classified as descriptive, qualitative, ethnographic, field studies, or others will be identified as nonexperimental in this chapter, emphasizing the *verbal* account of the phenomena investigated, where inductive procedures are used.

NONEXPERIMENTAL CONCEPTS

Ethnology, interviews, and field observations have been covered extensively by Ferrara in chapter 3, so they will not be included in this chapter, except as passing mention of them may be necessary. For the purposes of consistency, as already noted, the term referred to as "qualitative research" will be included under the rubric "nonexperimental research."

There are two types of "qualitative" (nonexperimental) research according to Mertens: (1) research aimed at discovering if causal relationships exist and (2) descriptive studies that use "quantitative data to describe a phenomenon."[15]

Grounded Theory Research

The concept of grounded theory research begins with broad questions that are flexible enough to examine a phenomenon in depth.[16] In grounded theory research data are collected in the field rather than from research literature.[17] To be more explicit, Denzin and Lincoln state that grounded theory is an approach for developing a theory that is "grounded" in data systematically gathered and analyzed.[18]

Jeanette Young, for her doctoral research, used interviews of middle school music educators in order to identify values and beliefs that support teaching strategies for growth and learning. She then designated a grounded theory based on her findings.[19]

Concept-Input-Process-Product

Developed by Daniel Stufflebeam and associates in 1971, CIPP is a procedure to assist educators in evaluating and assessing instructional and noninstructional programs. As the evaluators work with the teachers they determine what types of information are needed for each phase of the evaluation. The information is synthesized to make it possible for decision making. Although essentially nonexperimental, CIPP makes use of some quantitative evaluation procedures.[20] The view of Mason and Bramble is that CIPP consists of six major components: (1) focusing on the evaluation, (2) collecting the data, (3) organizing the data, (4) doing a data analysis, (5) presenting the information, and (6) applying the results of the evaluation.[21]

Critical Theory

The focus of critical theory is on determining the "power relationships" in various cultures. Because of its unique coverage it is able to assist persons to "escape the many forms of oppression" that are believed to operate within various cultures. Since it is based on sociological principles, critical theory, as originally developed, is especially appropriate for cultures in certain European and Latin American countries. The assumption of critical theory is that there is oppression with many faces. Language obviously is central to the function of subjectivity (consciously or unconsciously). The relationship between signifier (researcher) and signified (subject) often is mediated by social relations based on capitalistic production and consumption by the public. Critical theory is based on power relations that are socially and historically constituted. "Mainstream research practices are unwittingly implicated in the reproduction" of the systems where class, race, and gender oppression are involved. This sociologically oriented concept, however, usually does not subscribe to a unified, formal methodology found in many disciplines.[22]

Survey Studies

The survey, a procedure for collecting data of various kinds, is a special kind of research used widely in various educational settings.[23] According to Sapsford, surveys involve systematic observation or systematic interviewing.[24] The questions asked usually lead to the answers desired. There are various kinds of surveys, among them social and public opinion, the ones most widely used.[25] Best and Kahn remark a survey is an important kind of research that must not be confused with just routinely obtaining and tabulating figures.[26] Leedy states that the descriptive survey is used to obtain information by some type of observation. He lists characteristics of a descriptive survey as follows: (1) the principal means of collecting data in a descriptive survey is observation; (2) populations for a descriptive survey must be chosen carefully, clearly defined, and delimited to a parameter discrete to the population; (3) data for descriptive surveys are subject to bias; and (4) accurate conclusions can be teased out of data organized and presented systematically.[27] Written questionnaires and personal interviews, commonly used to obtain survey data, can be computerized to save time and money instead of sending a mailed questionnaire or by interviewing subjects (Ss) in person.

Knop, for his doctoral research, focused on the internalization and generation of tempo by replicating the movements of walking. Nonmusic majors were observed walking, performing the LHM (lateral heel movement test), and performing various length notes and a major scale on the soprano recorder. Knop concluded that walking can be effective in the internalization and generation of tempo by instrumental performers.[28]

Social surveys became a common practice to collect data in the latter half of the twentieth century. One of the most important social surveys was conducted in the late 1930s by Swedish sociologist Gunnar Myrdal. He analyzed the social, political, and economic life of African Americans in the United States.[29]

Public opinion surveys have been widely used to obtain information, especially on controversial topics, by well-organized special interest groups. Topics run the gamut from abortion to academic achievement in the public schools, from the outcome of national and state elections to religion in the schools.[30]

Researchers are advised by Tuckman to consider the ethical aspects of their research. He says that because of tension often experienced by subjects being examined, researchers must be careful to avoid asking embarrassing questions or exhibiting behavior that could negatively affect the lives of the participants. To deal with the situation, the U.S. government, in 1991, promulgated a Code of Federal Regulations for the Protection of Human Subjects.[31]

Case Studies

A case study may profile a person or a group for a relatively short period of time. Best and Kahn write that a case study is a way of "organizing social data for the purpose of reviewing social settings."[32] Case study data may be obtained by many means: (1) observation by a researcher and/or team members; (2) interviews with subjects, teachers, and others; (3) questionnaires, opinionnaires, tests, and interviews; and (4) data obtained from newspapers, radio, television, the Internet, courts, clinics, government agencies, and others.[33] Huff, in a doctoral study, used the case study approach to concentrate on a single choral program during the preparation for and performance at a commercial music festival. Data were obtained through observation of rehearsals and performances, and interviews with choral directors, students and parents, and festival staff and adjudicators.[34]

Longitudinal Studies

Longitudinal studies, also known as "developmental," are concerned with growth over a period of time. Hakim writes that researchers take one sample or one group and collect data from them over a long period of time.[35] There are three kinds of longitudinal designs that enable a researcher to study different samples of student behavior: (1) *trend* study, which, as an example, could be used by music educators to assess the musical achievement of eighth grade band students compared with the performance of the same students as sixth graders; (2) *cohort* studies, in which the assessment of the eighth grade band students is compared to the same students who were tested in the sixth grade; and (3) a *panel* study, in which the same students are evaluated at various times to minimize selection bias. All types of longitudinal designs are susceptible to historical bias, or experience.[36]

Developmental Studies

Developmental studies primarily deal with behavior variables that can differentiate among children at various levels of age, growth, or maturation. Developmental research may be either longitudinal or cross-sectional, reports Gay.[37]

Cross-Sectional Studies

Cross-sectional research is used more extensively than longitudinal or developmental research because it is not as expensive or time-consuming. Cross-sectional studies are used to compare different subjects (Ss) of the same age or level of development. As an example, you might like to determine the musical achievement of all sixth grade students in a school system each year. Cross-sectional research normally involves a greater number of Ss and tease out fewer variables than do longitudinal or developmental studies.

Action Research

The focus of action research is to find solutions to problems in a local setting. Gall, Gall, and Borg state that action research is a systematic investigation conducted by practitioners who use scientific techniques to improve the performance of their students.[38] A broader definition is offered by Bogdan and Biklen with these words: "Action research is the systematic collection of information that is designed to bring about social change."[39] Cohen, Manion, and Morrison stress that action research is a sociological tool to effect change and improvement at the local level.[40]

The basis for action research is the immediate application of the results to a local situation. Best and Kahn lament that many researchers disparagingly refer to action research as simply "application of common sense or good management." Action research, however, does apply the "scientific method" to real-life problems and is a better indicator of the subjective judgments commonly used by some teachers.[41]

Causal-Comparative Studies

Also known as ex post facto research, causal-comparative research examines effects between variables in a nonexperimental situation, according to Wiersma.[42] In a rather obvious example, an instrumental music teacher realizes that thirty-eight girls and only two boys play flute; and that thirty-eight boys and two girls play trumpet. If reasons for the imputed imbalance can be determined, steps might be taken to ensure a more equitable enrollment by gender, if the director believes this to be important. Gay writes that in causal-comparative research an attempt is made to determine the meaning or causes that currently exist for the phenomenon being studied.[43]

Since causal-comparative research involves studying past events, you should be aware that all necessary information may not be available. Best and Kahn state that since it is difficult to know what variables were controlled, this leads to a post hoc fallacy, which is a conclusion drawn because two events occurred at the same time. If two variables are related to one another, then one of these factors must have caused the other.[44]

The Delphi Technique

Although not used as frequently as it was a few years ago, concepts of the technique still are utilized. Developed by the RAND Corporation to predict future defense needs, the Delphi technique has been used on occasion by educational researchers to identify problems, establish priorities, and provide for solutions to problems. It also has been used in conjunction with workshops. Used in this context, the workshop leader sends out a list of priorities or objectives. Recipients of the list prioritize the items and send them back to the workshop leader. A revised list, or questionnaire, is then sent back to each workshop participant. Further refining may result in a third mailing to participants until priorities or objectives are generally agreed on. These repeated procedures obviously take much time, especially if mail responses are expected. The time factor can be greatly shortened by using e-mail or the Internet. A positive factor in favor of the Delphi technique is that a consensus exists by the time the process has been completed.

Fritz, in a doctoral study, examined the insights of music educators turned school administrators relative to the state of music in the United States. Data were collected by employing the Delphi technique. The premise was that school administrators trained in music were in an excellent position to evaluate the status of music in the public schools. Fritz found that ex-music teachers continued to have useful insights into music after moving to administration.[45]

Ex Post Facto Research

Although some researchers consider ex post facto research to be quantitative or experimental, Cohen, Manion, and Morrison point out that ex post facto research is a procedure or method to "tease out" antecedents or events that have happened and thus cannot be replicated or manipulated by the investigator.[46] Experiments are not conducted to manipulate variables, but the independent and dependent variables are operative under natural conditions.[47] Ex post facto designs sometimes are confused with experimental and/or correlational research because many similarities exist in both designs. Like experimental research, ex post facto research compares cause and effect relationships on dependent variables.[48] Literally meaning "after the fact," this procedure is quasi-experimental in scope because experimental procedures are simulated and cause and effect are determined after they actually have taken place, thereby introducing a certain amount of subjectivity in the research. A serious weakness of ex post facto research is the difficulty in controlling the independent variable because it must be reconstructed after the circumstance has occurred. Yet, because such variables as personality, music or other aptitude, home background, and parental control are not manipulable, ex post facto research is important for certain kinds of information.

Pilot Study

Before a full-scale investigation can be launched, you should conduct a pilot study to determine whether or not the intervention hypothesized between independent and dependent variables will materialize in a situation comparable to the one proposed for the actual research. Sproul states that the purpose of a pilot study is a trial run conducted prior to investing time and money in the actual research project. Serving many purposes, a pilot study may include (1) sampling method; (2) research design; (3) data collection method; (4) instrument validity, reliability, ease of use and results yielded; and (5) data analysis.[49] If you propose to use 400 Ss in your research, for example, 40 Ss probably would be sufficient for a pilot study. Samples for the pilot and the research should come from comparable populations, but the pilot sample must not be included in the actual research. As noted already, the pilot is conducted like the research project, but with a smaller sample. Sproul cautions that although results of the pilot will not be included in the actual research, all the usual steps of the research process will be followed.[50] Tuckman recommends running a pilot test in conjunction with a questionnaire. In this way you can ascertain whether or not questionnaire results are comparable to the desired measurement and discrimination desired.[51]

Sampling

Since it is not possible to examine the characteristics of an entire population, it is necessary to use a procedure known as sampling. Wiersma writes that a sample is a "subset of the population to which the researcher intends to generalize the results."[52] Sampling sometimes is included under experimental or quantitative research, but the difficulty of control is so significant that it seems best to include it under qualitative, descriptive, or nonexperimental. Sapsford identifies sampling techniques as a qualitative procedure. He writes that sampling is identifying a group comparable to the one being investigated, so that valid generalizations can be made from the population "on the basis of the sample."[53] Best and Kahn state it this way: a sample is a "small proportion of a population selected for observation and analysis."[54]

In determining the specific nature of a sample, three factors stand out: (1) definition of the population, (2) location of the population, and (3) initiation of the representative sample. Here is an example. In defining the population you might restrict your study to teachers of wind instruments in public and/or private schools. Ask yourself several questions. Will the research be delimited to woodwinds only, or will brass also be included? Will it be necessary to ascertain who these teachers are and where they are located? What is the educational and performance background of the teachers? Does the sample include both private and public school woodwind teachers? It should be apparent that the procedure for defining a sample is similar to that of delimiting a research problem, discussed at length in the first chapter of this book.

Common types of sampling are random, systematic, stratified, and cluster. A random sample is unbiased, which means everyone in the population has an equal chance of being selected. Best and Kahn caution that a random sample does not necessarily mean that it is an identical representation of the population, and sampling errors that may appear can be minimized by using inferential statistical procedures.[55] A random sample may be drawn by using a table of random numbers found in research textbooks, or *SPSS (Statistical Package for the Social Sciences)* for Windows 6.0.[56] The tables usually consist of five or more numbers generated by a computer. Some computer programs have a range from 1 to 1,000 numbers. Microsoft Word, for example, has a built-in function that "automatically generates a new random number each time the application is calculated."[57]

Systematic sampling. The process in which the selection of the "first sample number determines the entire sample."[58] Every ninth person from a list is selected. If you need to draw a sample of 500 from a list containing 100,000 names, select the first number randomly, then every thousandth (nth) will be selected until a sample of 500 is obtained.[59]

Stratified sampling. The procedure by which a population is divided into two or more subpopulations. All subpopulations are represented and sample members from each subpopulation are drawn at random. A comparison is then made between various subgroups or subpopulations.[60]

Cluster sampling. The procedure that is used when selecting individual members of a population is impractical or too expensive; groups or "clusters" of members from a large population are selected.[61] Cluster sampling deals with groups that occur naturally. Suppose you wanted to study characteristics of high school juniors who play the oboe when lists from which junior high school oboists could be selected are not available. A school district in a certain state could be divided into "clusters," or areas, say twenty-four. After numbering each area, you would draw at random the schools to be sampled in each of the twenty-four areas. The junior oboe players would be chosen from the selected schools on the premise that every school has some junior oboe players, as risky as this may seem! Cluster sampling is likely to introduce an element of bias because the size of the subsets may not be equal.[62]

NONEXPERIMENTAL RESEARCH TOOLS

Questionnaire

One of the most widely used tools of nonexperimental research is the questionnaire. Unfortunately it also has been misused and abused, with the result that investigators and recipients alike often tend to regard the questionnaire as an anathema. Adams and Schvaneveldt state that a questionnaire is a device for obtaining "the answers or reactions to printed (prearranged) questions presented in a specific order."[63] Wiersma posits that in constructing a questionnaire much time and effort goes into its construction as well as developing ways to encourage respondents to complete the questionnaire.[64]

Questionnaires are of two forms: closed and open-ended. The closed form, also known as structured or restricted, is easy to administer through the mail, or using a computer. It is facile in response and easy to score by hand or by computer. The closed form questionnaire calls for "short, check-mark responses."[65] Because of its rigid construction, however, respondents may feel frustrated because they are not able to express their answers in the manner they wish. This weakness can be overcome to some extent by providing an opportunity for an alternative answer to what otherwise might be an unacceptable forced-choice answer,

There are three factors to consider in the construction of a questionnaire, says Tuckman: (1) the possibility that the instructions section has a question that might cause some respondents to view themselves in a better light than is the case, (2) the possibility that respondents may anticipate answers desired of them, and (3) the possibility that a question may ask for information about respondents that they may not know.[66]

Answers to the closed or restricted questionnaire may be in the form of (1) checking a yes or no answer, (2) underlining the correct response, (3) ranking items (1, 2, 3, 4) according to their correctness or validity, and (4) inserting specific data in a blank or space provided. An example of each of these four forms follows.

1. *Directions.* Check the correct answer.
   The section leader in each of your senior high school major performing groups (orchestra, band, etc.) is required to study his/her instrument privately. Yes _____ No ____.
2. *Directions.* Underline the correct response.
   Extra chorus rehearsals, when needed, are scheduled (a) before school, (b) during lunch hours, (c) after school, (d) other _____.
   If (d) is your answer, please specify the time rehearsals are scheduled _____.
3. *Directions.* Circle the correct answer.
   How would you rate the attitude of your principal toward music?

1	2	3	4	5
enthusiastic	sympathetic	impartial	tolerant	antagonistic

4. *Directions.* Insert the correct answer in the blank provided.
How many full-time instrumental teachers are employed in your school system? _____

The open-ended questionnaire, also called free response or unrestricted, enables respondents to reply in their own words, thus permitting them not only to be more candid, but also to give reasons for their responses. Greater effort is required of the respondent in replying to an open-ended questionnaire, meaning returns often tend to be meager. Sometimes the open-ended form is difficult to interpret, tabulate, or summarize.[67]

In constructing a questionnaire several factors need to be kept in mind: (1) Only seek information that cannot readily be obtained elsewhere. A questionnaire should not be used when data can be obtained easily from a dictionary, encyclopedia, the Internet, or elsewhere. (2) Instructions for completing the questionnaire should be clear and concise so they may be understood by the recipient. Terms that have a specific connotation should be defined carefully. (3) Questions should be phrased clearly and in unambiguous terms. When a respondent has to spend unnecessary time trying to determine the intended meaning, validity of the response is diminished. (4) The questionnaire should be brief and to the point, yet long enough to obtain the desired information. Unusually long questionnaires, if answered and returned at all, are likely to be completed rather hurriedly or with some desired information lacking. To reduce what may seem to be an excessive number of questions, several similar items may be incorporated into one or more questions. (5) The order in which questions are placed should be logical, proceeding from those that are simple and general to those that are more complex and specific. (6) Controversial questions and those that might be disconcerting to a respondent should be avoided. (7) Format of the questionnaire should be psychologically conducive to a response on the part of the recipient. A poorly reproduced questionnaire, one that contains print too small to read easily, or one in which items are too close together, will rarely elicit many responses.[68]

Prior to sending out the questionnaire it should be pretested either with a small group or with friends and colleagues. In this way questions that seem perfectly clear to the researcher may appear as ambiguous to those reviewing contents of the proposed questionnaire. Another way to pretest a questionnaire is to pilot-test the contents with a small group similar to those who will participate in the study.[69]

A cover letter should accompany the final version of the questionnaire in which you candidly state the purpose of the research, its relevance to your field (music education or other), its sponsorship (your university), and date by which the questionnaire is to be returned. Don't forget to enclose a self-addressed, stamped envelope, unless the respondent is to reply on the Internet.

The cover letter should preferably be three paragraphs long, but complete enough to impress on the recipient the importance of a reply. If answers are to be treated anonymously, the respondent should be so informed. Ethically you must retain integrity when questionnaires are returned and tabulated. If an anonymous questionnaire is sent out you should use a coding system, assigning consecutive numbers to questionnaires. Keep a record for you to identify who "001, 002, 003, 004" are in case follow-up is necessary. Sponsorship may be indicated in the body of the cover letter itself, or in the form of an attachment to it. Do not assume that enrollment in your university automatically entitled you to receive carte blanche endorsement of everything you send out.

A follow-up timetable for return of questionnaires is important so that they may be received at least a few days before, or after, the deadline for receiving them. Two or more follow-ups may be necessary. Follow-up may include one or more of the following: postal card reminding the recipient that questionnaire has not been returned yet, a personal letter courteously reminding the recipient of the importance of a response, telephone call to the recipient, or e-mail, if researcher has the recipient's e-mail address. The larger the percentage of returns, the more confidence you can place on the responses. A minimum acceptable response figure is 50 percent; one should strive for 70 percent or more. Certain times of the year are more hectic than others, so this could slow down response time. It is unreasonable to expect a quick response time at the beginning or end of a semester, for example.

The anonymous letter in figure 5.1 is based on a communication received in conjunction with, or in place of, a formal questionnaire. It is indicative of an omnibus or so-called shotgun approach, which must be avoided at all costs in a covering letter or in a questionnaire.

As soon as questionnaires are returned, the tabulation of information can begin, either with a paper tally, or in a computer database.

Dear Sir or Madam:
I am doing research for my doctoral dissertation. Please send me a bibliographical list of textbooks used in all your courses that doctoral students take at your institution. I know you understand the importance of this information to the success of my doctoral project. Thank you for your assistance.

Yours Sincerely,

Figure 5.1. Omnibus Request for Information

It is a good practice to date each questionnaire as it is received in case it is necessary to recheck later on.

Opinionnaire

Answers to questions may be obtained by using a questionnaire or an opinionnaire. In the former, facts are requested; in the latter, opinions are sought. The opinionnaire sometimes is known as an attitude scale. Answers received on an opinionnaire must be accepted at face value because objective measures to verify validity of answers do not exist. What people believe and how they feel is their attitude. Best and Kahn report that it is difficult to "describe and measure attitude."[70] For this reason the opinionnaire is not used as widely by researchers as are other instruments included in this chapter. In an opinionnaire, respondents are asked to indicate their agreement or disagreement with certain statements by circling their responses on a five-point scale (agree strongly, agree, agree with reservations, disagree, disagree strongly).

Rating Scale

A rating scale, or checklist, is used to record judgments on behaviors that are observed. Although there are several forms of rating scales, one developed by Rensis Likert is widely used. In the Likert-type scale all intervals are assumed to be equal, and may have three, four, five, or more points, as shown in figure 5.2.

Most rating scales are designed to provide for an odd number of judgments, in other words, five, seven, nine, rather than four, six, or

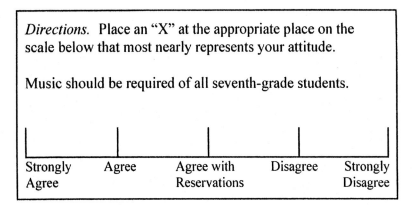

Directions. Place an "X" at the appropriate place on the scale below that most nearly represents your attitude.

Music should be required of all seventh-grade students.

| Strongly | Agree | Agree with | Disagree | Strongly |
| Agree | | Reservations | | Disagree |

Figure 5.2.   Likert-Type Scale

eight. With an odd-number of points the middle item always is neutral. Many different variables can be measured by a rating scale, including evaluation of instruction, adequacy of facilities, perceptions of program effects, among others.[71]

Rating scales have limitations. One of these is conveying to the rater exactly which "quality one wishes evaluated." Perhaps the most critical is the halo effect, which causes raters to transfer qualitative judgments from one factor to another.[72] A respondent who displays a pleasing personality may rightly or wrongly be judged as "intelligent," or an individual who is artistic may be judged as a "liberal," which may or may not be a valid assessment. The halo effect is very difficult to control and usually is prevalent when uncertainty exists in choice of behaviors displayed by a particular respondent.

Rating scales reflect the judgment of persons who may be subject to various influences, and thus reveal inconsistencies or errors. One way to determine consistency of judgments is to use two or more raters.[73]

The next chapter will focus on the hypothesis and on precise statistical measurements in which interaction between dependent and independent variables becomes an exact comparison.

FOR REVIEW, DISCUSSION, AND IMPLEMENTATION

- What are some of the concepts and methods that relate to qualitative research?

- What factors distinguish qualitative from quantitative research?
- Why is the designation nonexperimental research used rather than some others to classify concepts and methods of research?
- Why is survey research such an important concept to consider for a research project?
- What are possible weaknesses of longitudinal research?
- What is the concept behind ex post facto research?
- Identify and explain the different kinds of sampling.
- Why is the questionnaire such a widely useful tool for researchers? What distinguishes a questionnaire from an opinionnaire?

NOTES

1. John W. Best and James V. Kahn, *Research in Education,* 9th ed. (Boston: Allyn & Bacon, 2003), 240.

2. Best and Kahn, 115.

3. Paul D. Leedy, with Timothy J. Newby and Peggy A. Ermer, *Practical Research Planning and Design,* 6th ed. (Upper Saddle River, N.J.: Prentice-Hall, 1987), 189.

4. Leedy, 105–6.

5. Mildred L. Patten, *Understanding Research Methods,* 2nd ed. (Los Angeles: Pyrczak, 2000), 19.

6. Bruce W. Tuckman, *Conducting Educational Research,* 5th ed. (Belmont, Calif.: Wadsworth, 1999), 395.

7. Joyce P. Gall, M. D. Gall, and Walter R. Borg, *Applying Educational Research: A Practical Guide,* 4th ed. (New York: Longman, 1999), 173.

8. Emanuel J. Mason and William J. Bramble, *Research in Education and the Behavioral Sciences: Concepts and Methods* (Madison, Wis.: Brown & Benchmark, 1997), 38.

9. Melvyn N. Freed, Joseph M. Ryan, and Robert K. Hess, *Handbook of Statistical Procedures and Their Computer Applications to Education and the Behavioral Sciences* (New York: Macmillan, 1991), 16.

10. Donna Mertens, *Research Methods in Education and Psychology: Integrating Diversity with Quantitative and Qualitative Approaches* (Thousand Oaks, Calif.: Sage, 1998), 60.

11. Gerald R. Adams and Jay D. Schvaneveldt, *Understanding Research Methods* (New York: Longman, 1999), 107.

12. William O. Aydelotte, Allan G. Bogue, and Robert W. Fogel, eds., *The Dimensions of Quantitative Research in History* (Princeton: Princeton University Press, 1973), 263.

13. Paul D. Leedy and Jeanne E. Ormrod, *Practical Research Planning and Design*, 7th ed. (Upper Saddle River, N.J.: Prentice-Hall, 2001), 102.

14. Ronald C. Martella, Ronald Nelson, and Nancy E. Marchand-Martella, *Research Methods: Learning to Become a Critical Research Consumer* (Boston: Allyn & Bacon, 1999), 258.

15. Mertens, 60.

16. Leedy, 163.

17. Leedy and Ormrod, 154.

18. Norman K. Denzin and Yvonne S. Lincoln, *Handbook of Qualitative Research* (Thousand Oaks, Calif.: Sage, 1994), 273.

19. Jeanette S. Young, "A Grounded Theory Study of the Values and Beliefs That Shape the Teaching Strategies of Middle-Level Music Educators" (Ph.D. diss., University of Nebraska, 2002).

20. Gall, Gall, and Borg, 443–44.

21. Mason and Bramble, 363–64.

22. Gall, Gall, and Borg, 363–64.

23. Tuckman, 12.

24. Roger Sapsford, *Survey Research* (London: Sage, 1999), 4.

25. Best and Kahn, 117–19.

26. Best and Kahn, 117.

27. Leedy, 190–92.

28. Robert J. Knop, "A Study of the Internalization and Generation of Tempo by Replicating the Reciprocal Movements of Walking" (D.A. diss., University of Northern Colorado, 2002).

29. Best and Kahn, 117–18.

30. Best and Kahn, 119–20.

31. Tuckman, 13.

32. Best and Kahn, 249.

33. Best and Kahn, 250.

34. Michael D. Huff, "The School Chorus and Commercial Music Festivals: A Case Study" (D.M.A. diss., Arizona State University, 2002).

35. Catherine Hakim, *Research Designs for Social and Economic Research*, 2nd ed. (London: Routledge, 2000), 109.

36. Tuckman, 187–88.

37. L. R. Gay, *Educational Research: Competencies for Analysis and Application*, 5th ed. (Englewood Cliffs, N.J.: Merrill, 1996), 252–53.

38. Gall, Gall, and Borg, 468.

39. Robert D. Bogdan and Sari K. Biklen, *Qualitative Research for Education: An Introduction to Theory and Method*, 2nd ed. (Boston: Allyn & Bacon, 1992), 223.

40. Louis Cohen, Lawrence Manion, and Keith Morrison, *Research Methods in Education*, 5th ed. (London: Routledge-Falmer, 2000), 236.

41. Best and Kahn, 321.

42. William Wiersma, *Research Methods in Education: An Introduction,* 7th ed. (Boston: Allyn & Bacon, 2000), 158.

43. Gay, 321.

44. Best and Kahn, 129.

45. Benno P. Fritz, "A Qualitative Delphi Analysis on the Insights of Music Educator-Trained School Administrators on the Current State of Music Education in the United States" (Ph.D. diss., George Mason University, 1999).

46. Cohen, Manion, Morrison, 205.

47. Wiersma, 158.

48. Leedy, 227.

49. Natalie L. Sproul, *Handbook of Research Methods: A Guide for Practitioners and Students in the Social Sciences* (Metuchen, N.J.: Scarecrow, 1988), 321.

50. Sproul, 328.

51. Tuckman, 256.

52. Wiersma, 269.

53. Sapsford, 50.

54. Best and Kahn, 12.

55. Best and Kahn, 14.

56. Wiersma, 273.

57. Leedy, 206.

58. Wiersma, 280.

59. Best and Kahn, 16.

60. Wiersma, 276.

61. Wiersma, 279.

62. Best and Kahn, 17.

63. Adams and Schvaneveldt, 200.

64. Wiersma, 200.

65. Best and Kahn, 301.

66. Tuckman, 237.

67. Best and Kahn, 302.

68. Leedy, 191–99.

69. Best and Kahn, 308.

70. Best and Kahn, 317.

71. Wiersma, 311.

72. Best and Kahn, 298.

73. Tuckman, 224.

SUPPLEMENTARY SOURCES

Adams, Gerald R., and Jay D. Schvaneveldt. *Understanding Research Methods,* chaps. 5–11. New York: Longman, 1999.

Anderson, Gary. *Fundamentals of Educational Research*, chaps. 11, 13–15, 18. London: Falmer, 1990.

Balnaves, Mark, and Peter Caputi. *Introduction to Quantitative Research Methods: An Investigative Approach*, chaps. 3–5. London: Sage, 2001.

Barron, Ann E., Greg W. Orvig, Karen Ivers, and Nick Lilavois. *Technologies for Education: A Practical Guide*, chaps. 1–3, 8–9. 4th ed. Greenwood Village, Colo.: Libraries Unlimited, 2002.

Best, John W., and James V. Kahn. *Research in Education*, chaps. 5–9, 12. 9th ed. Boston: Allyn & Bacon, 2003.

Bogdan, Robert D., and Sari K. Biklen. *Qualitative Research for Education: An Introduction to Theory and Method*, chaps. 4–6. 2nd ed. Boston: Allyn & Bacon, 1992.

Byrne, David. *Interpreting Quantitative Data*, chaps. 1–2, 5–6. London: Sage, 2002.

Cohen, Louis, Lawrence Manion, and Keith Morrison. *Research Methods in Education*, chaps. 4, 6, 8–11. 5th ed. London: Routledge-Falmer, 2000.

Crowl, Thomas K. *Fundamentals of Educational Research*, chaps. 12–13. 2nd ed. Madison, Wis.: Brown & Benchmark, 1996.

Denzin, Norman K., and Yvonne S. Lincoln. *Handbook of Qualitative Research*, chaps. 14, 17, 22–23. Thousand Oaks, Calif.: Sage, 1994.

Freed, Melvyn N., Joseph M. Ryan, and Robert K. Hess. *Handbook of Statistical Procedures and Their Computer Applications to Education and the Behavioral Sciences*, chaps. 3–5. New York: Macmillan, 1991.

Gall, Joyce P., M. D. Gall, and Walter R. Borg. *Applying Educational Research: A Practical Guide*, chaps. 5, 7–8, 10, 15. 4th ed. New York: Longman, 1999.

Gay, L. R. *Educational Research: Competencies for Analysis and Application*. 5th ed. Englewood Cliffs, N.J.: Merrill, 1996.

Girden, Ellen. *Evaluating Research Articles*. 2nd ed. Thousand Oaks, Calif.: Sage, 2001.

Hakim, Catherine. *Research Designs for Social and Economic Research*, chaps. 1, 5, 7–8. 2nd ed. London: Routledge, 2000.

Keppel, Geoffrey. *Design and Analysis: A Researcher's Handbook*, chap. 2. 2nd ed. Englewood Cliffs, N.J.: Prentice-Hall, 1982.

Kerlinger, Fred N. *Foundations of Behavioral Research*, chaps. 2–3, 7–8, 12–13, 22–24. 3rd ed. Ft. Worth, Tex.: Harcourt Brace Jovanovich College, 1986.

Leedy, Paul D., with Timothy J. Newby and Peggy A. Ermer. *Practical Research Planning and Design*, chaps. 7, 9–10, 17. 6th ed. Upper Saddle River, N.J.: Prentice-Hall, 1997.

Leedy, Paul D., and Jeanne E. Ormrod. *Practical Research Planning and Design*, chaps. 7, 9–11. 7th ed. Upper Saddle River, N.J.: Prentice-Hall, 2001.

Levine, Gustav. *A Guide to SPSS for Analysis of Variance*, chap. 3. Hillside, N.J.: Erlbaum, 1991.

Martella, Ronald C., Ronald Nelson, and Nancy E. Marchand-Martella. *Research Methods: Learning to Be a Critical Research Consumer*, chaps. 4–9. Boston: Allyn & Bacon, 1999.

Mason, Emanuel J., and William J. Bramble. *Research in Education and the Behavioral Sciences: Concepts and Methods*. Madison, Wis.: Brown & Benchmark, 1997.

Mertens, Donna. *Research Methods in Education and Psychology: Integrating Diversity with Quantitative and Qualitative Approaches*, chaps. 3–5, 7, 10–12. Thousand Oaks, Calif.: Sage, 1998.

Patten, Mildred. *Understanding Research Methods*, pts. A, C–F. 2nd ed. Los Angeles: Pyrczak, 2000.

Salkind, Neal J. *Exploring Research*, chaps. 4–5, 7–11. 4th ed. Upper Saddle River, N.J.: Prentice-Hall, 2000.

Sapsford, Roger. *Survey Research*, chaps. 1, 3, 5, 10. London: Sage, 1999.

Schloss, Patrick J., and Maureen A. Smith. *Conducting Research*, chaps. 5, 7, 9. Upper Saddle River, N.J.: Merrill, 1999.

Sproul, Natalie L. *Handbook of Research Methods: A Guide for Practitioners and Students in the Social Sciences*. Metuchen, N.J.: Scarecrow, 1988.

Stake, Robert J. *The Art of Case Study Research*. Thousand Oaks, Calif.: Sage, 1995.

Tuckman, Bruce W. *Conducting Educational Research*, chaps. 4–10. 5th ed. Belmont, Calif.: Wadsworth, 1999.

Wiersma, William. *Research Methods in Education: An Introduction*, chaps. 4–8, 11–12. 7th ed. Boston: Allyn & Bacon, 2000.

Wilkinson, David W. *The Researcher's Toolkit: The Complete Guide to Practitioner Research*. London: Routledge Falmer, 2000.

Chapter 6

Quantitative Research: Experimental Methods and Statistical Techniques

PURPOSES OF EXPERIMENTAL RESEARCH

The goal of experimental (or quantitative) research is to determine cause and effect.[1] Experimental research, write Freed, Ryan, and Hess, is concerned with studying the relationship between independent and dependent variables. Variations that occur on the dependent variable may be attributed to the independent variable.[2] Echoing the remarks of Leedy, Anderson states that the experimental method is the only one that can "truly test for cause and effect relationships."[3] The probability laws of applied statistics, a characteristic of quantitative research, indicate whether relationships observed are likely to occur by chance alone.[4] Experiments attempt to "measure observations directly to ensure that *confounding* and *extraneous* variables are removed."[5] Wilkinson avers that quantitative data usually can be reduced to numerical form, which is a strong feature for handling them.[6]

The three concepts usually associated with experimental research are (1) controlled observations, (2) reliability, and (3) validity. Controlled observation refers to "precision of conditions under which data are collected."[7] Reliability of results is important because they are tested by a hypothesis or hypotheses. Validity means conclusions reached are an indication that the results, based on statistical analyses, are valid and indicate what they are supposed to.[8] Cause and effect, also known as causation, has its roots in philosophy. Nineteenth-century English philosopher John Stuart Mill (1806–1873) postulated some canons that became the basis of causation, widely used in experimental research. These five canons are (1) method of agreement,

(2) method of difference, (3) joint method of agreement and difference, (4) method of residues, and (5) method of concomitant variations.[9]

Best known and simplest of these canons is the first, which states that factors relating to a certain event have one characteristic in common, that variable is the cause of the effect. According to the second canon, when two or more sets of circumstances are identical except for one factor, and when a given effect is noticed, only when that factor is present, the factor is said to be the cause of the effect. Both the first and second canons are methods of elimination. Methods of canons 1 and 2 are combined in the procedures for the third canon, in which the common factor is isolated first, then withdrawn to determine if the effect is dependent upon the presence of the common factor. A more complex canon, the fourth, is the method of residue, in which causes are determined by the process of elimination. When specific factors are known to affect certain parts of a given effect, the other aspects of the total effect must be due to the remaining factors. The fifth, and final canon, states that when two factors change consistently or when they vary together, the variations in one are caused by the other, or both are affected by the same cause.[10]

The premise of experimental research is that a preconceived plan is developed for manipulating "certain stimuli, treatments, or environmental conditions" to ascertain the nature of the condition or behavior that is changed.[11] Strict control is the key to the success of experimental research.

Leedy maintains that the experimental method is a procedure to account for the "influence of a factor or factors conditioning a given situation."[12] Quantitative, or experimental, research makes use of measurement, statistical principles, and models to verify the phenomenon being studied.[13] Best and Kahn report that in an experiment the effects of a treatment are compared with those of a different treatment or no treatment at all. In a simple experiment these groups would be called experimental and control.[14]

EXPERIMENTAL RESEARCH CONCEPTS

Hypothesis

Critical to experimental research is hypothesis and hypothesis testing. Tuckman says that after a problem is identified you normally use the logical processes of deduction and induction to formulate an expectation of the outcomes of the study.[15] A hypothesis tests the relationship of two or more variables. Are they similar or are they different? A research hypothesis is a general statement about the assumed nature of the "world" that gets "translated into an experiment."[16] The null hypothesis, writes Keppel, indicates no "treatment effects are present in the population."[17] Kerlinger positively asserts that a hypothesis really is a prediction. It is one of the "most powerful tools yet invented to achieve dependable knowledge."[18]

Best and Kahn state that a good hypothesis has four characteristics. The hypothesis should be (1) reasonable, (2) consistent with known facts or theories, (3) stated so it can be tested to ascertain whether it probably is true or false, and (4) stated in the simplest terms.[19]

There are two types of hypotheses: research, or substantive, and statistical, or null. *Research* hypotheses are tentative statements of the outcomes of a study, usually stated in a direction (more, greater, lesser, etc). *Statistical* or null hypotheses are nondirectional, meaning there is no difference or relationship.[20] (Hypothesis testing will be discussed later in this chapter in conjunction with statistical techniques.)

Variables

A variable is a condition or characteristic that you can control. "Independent" variables can be controlled or manipulated; "dependent" variables are conditions or characteristics that are subject to change as the independent variable is introduced or changed.[21] A characteristic or condition that is the same for all subjects (Ss) in a study is called a *constant*. On the other hand, a variable is a characteristic whose values are different for different individuals.[22]

Tuckman identifies three other kinds of variables: moderation, control, and intervening. A moderation variable is a special type of secondary independent variable. It is manipulated to discover whether it "modifies the relationship of the independent to an observed phenomenon."[23] Control variables are factors controlled by the researcher to neutralize or negate any effects that might occur on the observed phenomenon.[24] Commonly controlled dispositional control variables are gender, intelligence, and socioeconomic status. Situational control variables are noise, task order, and task content.[25]

Intervening variables theoretically affect "observed phenomena that cannot be seen, measured, or manipulated," It is inferred from the effect of the independent and moderator variables on the phenomenon.[26]

Tuckman sums up the discussion of variables by stating that after you decide which variables to include and exclude, theoretical, design, and practical considerations must be given attention.[27]

Standardized Tests

Standardized tests are useful tools to obtain data for experimental and nonexperimental research. The most frequently used tests are aptitude, achievement, and personality, among others. The prime source for information on various kinds of tests are *Mental Measurements Yearbooks (MMY)* and *Tests in Print (TIP),* published by the Buros Institute of Mental Measurements at the University of Nebraska at Lincoln. For example, *The Thirteenth Mental Measurements Yearbook* was published in 1999.[28] *Validity* indicates whether an instrument or device measures what it is supposed to measure. *Reliability* is an indication of whether an instrument or device will show the same results under identical or similar conditions. In a research setting the terms used are *internal validity* and *external validity.* Internal validity is the extent to which "results can be interpreted accurately," whereas external validity is the extent to which "results can be generalized to populations, situations, and conditions."[29]

Measures of Central Tendency

The most important and most frequently used measures of central tendency are mean, median, and mode. The formula for *mean* is

$$\bar{X} = \frac{\Sigma X}{N}$$

where Σ = uppercase Greek letter sigma, meaning "the sum of," X = each score or measurement in the array, and N = number of measurements.

Median represents the middle point in a distribution of scores. Half are above and half are below. Either Mo or Mdn is the symbol for median. *Mode,* indicated by the symbol Mo, represents the most prevalent interval in a distribution of scores.[30]

BASIC STATISTICAL CONCEPTS AND TECHNIQUES

Statistics, write Best and Kahn, is a set of mathematical techniques or procedures for "gathering, organizing, analyzing, and interpreting numerical data."[31] When statistical treatments are applied, data fall under one of two categories: *parametric* (or descriptive) statistics and *nonparametric* (or inferential) statistics. Parametric statistics assume data are normally distributed, or nearly so. Nonparametric statistics produce results that are normal or ordinal. Nonparametric statistics do not assume the populations are normally distributed. [32]

The normal distribution curve is employed in many statistical computations. Associated with German mathematician Carl Friedrich Gauss (1777–1855), it is also called the bell-shaped or Gaussian curve. (See figure 6.1.) It is assumed that scores of all individuals may be plotted along a normal probability curve. As an example, it is hypothetically assumed that the *mean,* or most critical value, is 0. Deviations from the central point are listed as either positive or negative. The total for all components of the curve equals *approximately* 100 percent. In Figure 6.1 approximately 68 percent of all scores in a normal curve fall between +1.0 and −1.0 standard deviations, and 95 percent of all scores will be found between +2.0 and −2.0 standard deviations (68

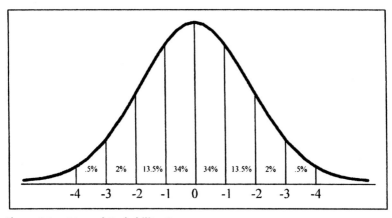

Figure 6.1. Normal Probability Curve

percent + 27 percent). Approximately 99 percent of all scores in a normal distribution will fall between +3.0 and −3.0 standard deviations.

Standard Deviation

Standard deviation and *variance* are the most useful and most frequently used measures of variability or variance. To determine standard deviation, each score is subtracted from the mean or average, then the differences are squared. The squared differences are added and the total is divided by the number of scores, which results in the amount of variance from the mean. Variance, according to Best and Kahn, is a value that "describes how all of the scores in a distribution are dispersed or spread about the mean."[33] The formula for standard deviation is

$$\sigma = \sqrt{\frac{\Sigma X^2}{N}}$$

where σ = lowercase Greek letter *sigma*, meaning standard deviation, ΣX^2 = sum of squared deviations from the mean, N = number of measurements, or scores. For example, 3, 15, 6, 10, 5, and 9 total 48, divided by 6 or N, results in X = 8. Subtracting each score from X results in 5, −7, 2, −2, 3, and −1. When deviations from X are squared they become 25, 49, 4, 4, 9, and 1, which signify an arithmetic total of 92. When 92 is divided by N (or 6) the *variance* is 15.33. The σ, determined by taking the square root of 15.33 is 3.92. Calculation of σ is a necessary first step for many advanced statistical techniques.

Variance

The sum of the "squared deviations from the mean, divided by N, is known as variance."[34] The formula for variance is

$$\frac{\Sigma X^2}{N}$$

where ΣX^2 = sum of squared deviations, and N = number of deviations. Variance determines how all the scores in a distribution are spread or disbursed about the mean.

Measures of Relationship or Correlation

Measures of relationship is concerned with determining whether or not a correlation exists between two or more variables, and if one does exist, the amount of that correlation or relationship. Correlation may vary from a positive +1.0 to a negative -1.0. The more the scores agree, the more positive the correlation, conversely the more disagreement there is, the more negative the correlation.

The most frequently used formulas for determining correlation are the Pearson product moment correlation, or *r*. Another is *the Spearman rank difference*, or *rho*, designated by the Greek letter ρ. Product-moment correlation, which shows deviation from 0 in a frequency distribution, may be computed by the formula

$$r = \frac{\Sigma Z\,(Z_x)\,(Z_y)}{N}$$

where r = product-moment correlation coefficient, Σ = sum of, Z_x = mean standard of x variable scores, Z_y = mean standard of y variable scores, and N = number of measurements. Product-moment correlation can help you pinpoint the variance evident between two observations for each subject. In other words, the two variables are compared.

When it is desirable to show correlation between persons by rank rather than by variables, the Spearman rank-difference correlation may be used, applying this formula,

$$\rho = \frac{1 - 6\Sigma D^2}{N\,(N - 1)}$$

in which ρ = rank-difference coefficient, ΣD^2 = sum of differences between rankings of the two variables squared, and N = number of paired ranks.

Standard Scores

Another measure of variance is standard scores. Standard scores, posit Best and Kahn, provide a method of "expressing any score in a distribution in terms of its distance from the mean in standard deviation units."[35] The most useful measure of standard scores is the Z score. By definition a Z score has a mean of 50 and a standard deviation of 10. The formula for Z scores is

$$Z = \frac{10\,(X - \bar{X}) + 50}{\sigma}$$

where Z = standard score, X = a student's raw score, $\bar{X}$ = mean of group, and σ = standard deviation of scores of the group.

Variance, standard deviation, Pearson product-moment correlation, Spearman *rho*, and Z scores fall under the heading of "descriptive statistics" because the results are generalized to a particular group beyond which results can not be extended.

Inferential Statistics

Wiersma writes that inferential statistics are measures of the sample, while parameters are measures of the population.[36] In inferential statistics a sampling is done with a small group that is assumed to be related to the population from which it is drawn. The sample is the small group and the large group is the population.[37] Included among the formulas of inferential statistics are the *t* test, analysis of variance (ANOVA), analysis of covariance (ANCOVA), and *chi square*.

The *t* test allows you to compare two means to determine the "probability that the difference between them reflects a real difference between the groups" of Ss and not a chance variation in data.[38] A *t* test can be run using SPSS (Statistical Package for the Social Sciences) for Windows.[39] When using a *t* test you compare the actual mean differences observed with the mean differences expected by chance. The formula for the *t* test is

$$t = \frac{\bar{X}_1 - \bar{X}_2}{\dfrac{S^2_1 + S^2_2}{N_1 \quad N_2}}$$

where X_1 = mean of experimental sample, X_2 = mean of control sample, S^2_1 = variance of experimental sample, S^2_2 = variance of control sample, N_1 = number of cases in experimental sample, and N_2 = number of cases in control sample.

Analysis of Variance (ANOVA)

Wiersma writes that the analysis of variance (ANOVA) "test the null hypothesis that two or more population means are not equal."[40] An advantage of using ANOVA is that it can examine the simultaneous effect of two, three, or four independent variables. The SPSS program can be used to compare ANOVA results. Using ANOVA procedures Kenneth Smith, in a doctoral study, used CAI (computer-assisted instruction) to assess development of rhythm reading skills among middle school instrumental music students. Students' abilities to read and perform rhythm skills improved in the experimental group when compared to the control group.[41]

Analysis of Covariance (ANCOVA)

By using ANCOVA, statistical adjustments are made to a dependent variable. ANCOVA is similar to ANOVA except scores of the dependent variable are "adjusted on the basis of the dependent variable's relationship to some other relevant variable."[42] Wiersma posits that ANCOVA is especially needed when experimental or design control over an "extraneous or mediating variable is impossible or undesirable."[43] Eppink, in a doctoral study, used a Web-based assessment of attitudes and self-perceived growth in music learning by general classroom teachers in a basic music course. When ANCOVA was used for the pretest, the results were calculated using SPSS.[44]

Chi Square (X^2)

The *chi square* distribution is used for statistics generated by nonparametric analysis. Chi square distribution is not symmetrical; it can vary from 0 to infinity. Two or more variables can be analyzed, although two is the number most frequently applied. The X test compares obtained frequencies to expected frequencies.[45] Formula for the chi square test is

$$X^2 = \frac{\Sigma\Sigma\,(o - e)^2}{e}$$

where $\Sigma\Sigma$ = calculation of sums across rows and columns of the contingency table, o = obtained frequencies, and e = expected frequencies.

The statistical techniques discussed in this chapter are examples of those most widely used. For more extensive and in depth coverage please refer to any standard statistics book and to texts by Best and Kahn, Leedy, Tuckman, and Wiersma, as well as others listed at the end of this chapter.

DESIGNS FOR CONDUCTING EXPERIMENTAL RESEARCH

Campbell and Stanley have developed a taxonomy for conducting experiments that has been widely used by educational researchers. They include three tables that list sources of invalidity for the sixteen designs discussed. Preexperimental designs are 1–3; true experimental designs are 4–6; and, quasi-experimental designs 7–16. In each of the sixteen designs the notation and discussion of the factors that could jeopardize internal and external validity are discussed. Tests of internal validity determine whether the independent variable actually effects a change on the dependent variable. To put it another way, are the results obtained due to the effect of the independent variable? Internal validity is the *sine qua non* for ideal research designs, according to Campbell and Stanley.[46]

Experimental Validity

To make a significant contribution to knowledge an experiment must be valid. Two types of experimental validity described by Campbell and Stanley are defined by Best and Kahn as *internal validity* and *external validity*. In internal validity do the factors that have been manipulated (independent variables) actually have an effect on the observed consequences (dependent variables) of the experiment?[47]

The threats to internal validity listed by Bet and Kahn are (1) maturation, (2) history, (3) testing, (4) unstable instrumentation, (5) statistical regression, (6) selection bias, (7) interaction of selection and maturation, (8) experimental mortality, and (9) experimenter bias. These essentially are the same as those listed by Campbell and Stanley.[48]

External validity relates to the generalizability of research findings to "other settings, persons, variables, and measurement instruments."[49] The five threats to external validity listed by Best and Kahn are (1) interference of prior treatment, (2) the artificiality of the experimental setting, (3) interaction effect of testing, (4) interaction of selection and treatment, and (5) the extent of treatment verification.[50]

The experimental design you select for your research must be valid to test hypotheses and to determine the relationships between independent and dependent variables. The adequacy of experimental designs is the extent to which threats to experimental validity are eliminated or minimized, as categorized by Best and Kahn: (1) preexperimental design, (2) true experimental design, and (3) quasi-experimental design.[51] The Campbell and Stanley symbols included in these designs are

R random assignment of Ss to groups or treatments
X exposure of group to experimental or treatment variable
C exposure of group to control or placebo condition
O observation or test administered.

The designs for each of these categories will be listed without explication. Specifics for each may be found in Best and Kahn (172–87).

Preexperimental Designs

The least useful of these designs is the one-shot case study, which lacks a control group or an equivalency of one. The formula is

$$X\ O$$

where X = treatment, and O = measurement.

The second design, the one-group pretest-posttest design, shows slightly more validity because treatment effects are compared between pretest and posttest scores, but no provision is provided to test control group scores. Its formula is

$$O_1\ X\ O_2$$

where O_1 = pretest , O_2 = posttest, and X = treatment.

The third of the preexperimental designs, according to Tuckman, is "the static-group comparison design.[52] A group that has received treatment is compared with one that has received none. The equivalence of the experimental and control groups, however, has not been established. The formula for this design is

$$X \; O$$
$$O$$

where X = treatment, and O = measurement.

True Experimental Designs

The equivalence of experimental and control groups is validated by their assignment to experimental and control treatments. The three true experimental designs listed by Best and Kahn are the pretest-only, equivalent-groups design, the Solomon four-group design, and the posttest-only control group design. The pretest-only, equivalent groups design is effective in minimizing threats to experimental validity. It differs from the static-group comparison design because the experimental and control groups are equated by random assignment. [53] The formula for the pretest-only, equivalent groups design is

$$R \; O_1 \; X \; O_2$$
$$R \; O_3 \quad\; O_4$$

where R = random assignment, X = treatment, O_1 and O_3 = pretests, and O_2 and O_4 = posttests.

The Solomon four-group design is a combination of two-group designs, posttest only and pretest-posttest. This design, report Best and Kahn, permits the "evaluation of the efforts of testing, history, and maturation." The formula for the Solomon four-group design is

$$R \; O_1 \; X \; O_2$$
$$R \; O_3 \; C \; O_4$$
$$R \quad\;\; X \; O_5$$
$$R \quad\;\; C \; O_6$$

where R = random assignment to four groups, X = two groups receiving experimental treatment, O_1 = experimental group receiving pretest, O_3 = control group receiving pretest, C = control groups not receiving treatment, O_2, O_4, O_5, O_6 four groups receiving posttest.

ANCOVA can be used to compare the four posttest scores and for changes in O_1 and O_2.[54]

The posttest-only, control group design is the last of the true experimental designs. This design effectively minimizes threats to experimental validity. The experimental and control groups are equated by random assignment.[55] The formula for the posttest-only group design is

$$R \quad X \quad O_1$$
$$R \quad C \quad O_2$$

where R = random assignment of Ss, X = experimental group, C = control group, O_1 and O_2 = posttests.[56]

Quasi-Experimental Designs

Five designs are classified as quasi-experimental: the pretest-posttest nonequivalent-groups design, time series, equivalent time samples design, equivalent-materials samples design, and counterbalanced design. The equivalence of these designs has not been verified because random assignment to experimental and control groups has not been manifested.[57] Notation for the pretest-posttest nonequivalent-groups design is

$$O_1 \quad X \quad O_2$$
$$O_3 \quad C \quad O_4$$

where X = experimental group, C = control group, O_1 and O_3 are pretests, and O_2 and O_4 are posttests.

Time Series

Measurements are taken periodically for individuals or groups. An experimental variable (X) is introduced and its effect determines the change immediately before and after the experimental variable has been introduced. The formula for time series is

$$O_1 \quad O_2 \quad O_3 \quad O_4 \quad X \quad O_5 \quad O_6 \quad O_7 \quad O_8$$

where O = various observations and X = experimental treatment.

The equivalent materials, pretest, posttest design uses the same procedure for both experimental and control groups, involving two or more cycles.[58] The order of exposure to experimental and control groups can be reversed. In other words, the group used for the first measurement can be used for the last, and the last for the first. The formula for this test is

$$O_1 \; X_{MA} \; O_2 \; O_3 \; X_{MB} \; O_4$$

where X_{MA} = teaching method A, X_{MB} = teaching method B, O_1 and O_3 = pretests, and O_2 and O_4 are posttests.

In counterbalanced design, sometimes called Latin square, all the Ss receive the same treatment. The formula is

	Time 1	Time 2	Time 3	Time 4
Group A	X_1 O	X_2 O	X_3 O	X_4 O
Group B	X_2 O	X_4 O	X_1 O	X_3 O
Group C	X_3 O	X_1 O	X_4 O	X_2 O
Group D	X_4 O	X_3 O	X_2 O	X_1 O

where X = treatment occurs only once in each row and each column, O = tests.

Best and Kahn report that the counterbalanced design has excellent internal validity because "history, maturation, regression, selection, and mortality are all generally well controlled."[59]

The final test is the factorial design, which makes it possible to measure the effect of two or more independent variables simultaneously and examine their interaction with one another. Figure 6.2 is a hypothetical example involving four groups that were treated with two kinds of musical instruction, CAI and traditional, and two levels of musical aptitude, high and low. Group A, high musical aptitude students, get computer-assisted instruction; high-scoring group B receive traditional instruction; low-scoring group C students get CAI; and low-scoring group D students receive traditional instruction. High-scoring students are randomly assigned to groups A and B, and low-scoring students to Groups C and D. In figure 6.2, musical aptitude is the control variable, the one that is not manipulated.

The next chapter looks at the role history plays in music and music education.

Musical Aptitude Scores	CAI Instruction		Traditional Instruction
High	Group A	Group B
Low	Group C	Group D

Figure 6.2.   2 × 2 Factorial Design

FOR REVIEW, DISCUSSION, AND IMPLEMENTATION

- What are the goals of quantitative or experimental research?
- Why is a hypothesis so important for experimental research? What are the limitations of a hypothesis stated by Best and Kahn?
- What is a variable? Differentiate between an independent and a dependent variable.
- Identify the two kinds of statistics listed in this chapter. What is the difference between parametric and nonparametric statistics?
- What are the most important measures of central tendency? Identify what each one signifies.
- Campbell and Stanley list several threats to internal validity. What are they? What is the difference between internal validity and external validity, as stated by Campbell and Stanley?
- Could you use either ANOVA or ANCOVA (or both) in a research study you have in mind? Explain why you would or would not use either of these (or both of them).
- For the research you have in mind, could you use a factorial design? If not, why not?

NOTES

1. Paul D. Leedy, with Timothy A. Newby and Peggy A. Ermer, *Practical Research Planning and Design*, 6th ed. (Upper Saddle River, N.J.: Merrill, 1997), 230.

2. Melvyn N. Freed, Joseph M. Ryan, and Robert K. Hess, *Handbook of Statistical Procedures and Their Computer Applications to Education and the Behavioral Sciences* (New York: Macmillan, 1991), 16.

3. Gary Anderson, *Foundations of Educational Research* (London: Falmer, 1990), 127.

4. Anderson, 14.

5. Mark Balnaves and Peter Caputi, *Introduction to Quantitative Research Methods: An Investigative Approach* (London: Sage, 2001), 79.

6. David Wilkinson, ed., *The Researcher's Toolkit: The Complete Guide to Practitioner Research* (London: Routledge Falmer, 2000), 81.

7. Ellen R. Girden, *Evaluating Research Articles,* 2nd ed. (Thousand Oaks, Calif.: Sage, 2001), 2.

8. Girden, 85.

9. John S. Mill, *A System of Logic: Ratiocinative and Inductive* (London: Longmans, Green, 1919), 253–66.

10. Mill, 253–66.

11. John W. Best and James V. Kahn, *Research in Education,* 9th ed. (Boston: Allyn & Bacon, 2003), 159.

12. Leedy, 229.

13. Emanuel J. Mason and William J. Bramble, *Research in Education and the Behavioral Sciences: Concepts and Methods,* (Madison, Wis.: Brown & Benchmark, 1997), 38.

14. Best and Kahn, 161.

15. Bruce W. Tuckman, *Conducting Educational Research,* 5th ed. (Belmont, Calif.: Wadsworth, 1999), 77.

16. Geoffrey Keppel, *Design and Analysis: A Practical Handbook,* 2nd ed. (Englewood Cliffs, N.J.: Prentice-Hall, 1982), 23.

17. Keppel, 25.

18. Fred N. Kerlinger, *Foundations of Behavioral Research,* 3rd ed. (Ft. Worth, Tex.: Harcourt Brace Jovanovich College, 1987), 23.

19. Best and Kahn, 38.

20. William Wiersma, *Research Methods in Education: An Introduction,* 7th ed. (Boston: Allyn and Bacon), 39.

21. Best and Kahn, 162–63.

22. Wiersma, 32.

23. Tuckman, 47.

24. Tuckman, 100.

25. Tuckman, 100.

26. Tuckman, 101.

27. Tuckman, 107.

28. Wiersma, 304.

29. Wiersma, 4.

30. Wiersma, 325–26.

31. Best and Kahn, 340.

32. Best and Kahn, 340.

33. Best and Kahn, 350.

34. Best and Kahn, 350.

35. Best and Kahn, 359.

36. Wiersma, 345.

37. Best and Kahn, 342.

38. Tuckman, 300.

39. Wiersma, 357.

40. Kenneth H. Smith, "The Effectiveness of CAI Instruction on the Development of Rhythm Reading Skills among Middle School Instrumental Students" (Ph.D. diss., University of Illinois, 2002).

41. Wiersma, 367.

42. Wiersma, 368.

43. Joseph A. Eppink, "The Effect of Web-based Portfolio Assessment Strategies on the Attitudes and Self-Perceived Growth in Music Learning of Non-Elementary General Classroom Educators in a Basic Music Course" (D.A. diss., Ball State University, 2002).

44. Tuckman, 316.

45. Donald T. Campbell and Julian C. Stanley, *Experimental and Quasi-Experimental Designs for Research* (Chicago: Rand McNally, 1966).

46. Best and Kahn, 166.

47. Best and Kahn, 166–70.

48. Best and Kahn, 170.

49. Best and Kahn, 170–71. For more specific explanation of threats to external validity, see Best and Kahn, 166–71.

50. Best and Kahn, 172.

51. Tuckman, 160.

52. Best and Kahn, 174.

53. Best and Kahn, 177–78.

54. Tuckman, 161.

55. Tuckman, 161.

56. Best and Kahn, 178. A summary chart listing sources of internal and external validity may be seen in table 6.1.

57. Best and Kahn, 184.

58. Best and Kahn, 186.

SUPPLEMENTARY SOURCES

Adams, Gerald R., and Jay D. Schvaneveldt. *Understanding Research Methods,* chaps. 7–8. 2nd ed. New York: Longman, 1991.

Anderson, Gary. *Foundations of Educational Research,* chaps. 12–13, 15. London: Falmer, 1990.

Balnaves, Mark, and Peter Caputi. *Introduction to Quantitative Research Methods: An Investigative Approach,* chaps. 3–5. London: Sage, 2001.

Barron, Ann E., Gary W. Orvig, Karen Ivers, and Nick Lilavois. *Technologies for Education: A Practical Guide.* 4th ed. Greenwood Village, Colo.: Libraries Unlimited, 2002.

Best, John W., and James V. Kahn. *Research in Education,* chaps. 6–7, 9–11. 9th ed. Boston: Allyn & Bacon, 2003.

Byrne, David. *Interpreting Quantitative Data,* chaps. 1–2, 5–6. London: Sage, 2002.

Cohen, Louis, Lawrence Manion, and Keith Morrison. *Research Methods in Education,* chaps. 10–13. 5th ed. New York: Routledge Falmer, 2000.

Freed, Melvyn N., Joseph M. Ryan, and Robert K. Hess. *Handbook of Statistical Procedures and Their Computer Applications to Education and the Behavioral Sciences,* chaps. 3–5. New York: Macmillan, 1991.

Gall, Joyce P., M. D. Gall, and Walter R. Borg. *Applying Educational Research: A Practical Guide,* chaps. 5–9, 14–15. 4th ed. New York: Longman, 1999.

Gay, L. R. *Educational Research: Competencies for Analysis and Application.* 5th ed. Englewood Cliffs, N.J.: Merrill, 1996.

Girden, Ellen. *Evaluating Research Articles,* chap. 1. 2nd ed. Thousand Oaks, Calif.: Sage, 2001.

Johnson, Burke, and Leroy Christensen. *Educational Research: Qualitative and Quantitative Approaches,* chaps. 1–2. Boston: Allyn & Bacon, 2000.

Keppel, Geoffrey. *Design and Analysis: A Researcher's Handbook,* chap. 2. 2nd ed. Englewood Cliffs, N.J.: Prentice-Hall, 1982.

Kerlinger, Fred N. *Foundations of Educational Research,* chaps. 2–3, 8, 12–13, 22. 3rd ed. Ft. Worth, Tex.: Harcourt Brace Jovanovich College, 1987.

Leedy, Paul D., with Timothy J. Newby and Peggy A. Ermer. *Practical Research Planning and Design,* chaps. 9–10, 12. 6th ed. Upper Saddle River, N.J.: Merrill, 1997.

Leedy, Paul D., and Jeanne Ellis Ormrod. *Practical Research Planning and Design,* chaps. 10–11. 7th ed. Upper Saddle River, N.J.: Prentice-Hall, 2001.

Levine, Gustav. *A Guide to SPSS for Analysis of Variance,* chap. 3. Hillside, N.J.: Erlbaum, 1991.

Mason, Emanuel J., and William J. Bramble. *Research in Education and the Behavioral Sciences: Concepts and Methods,* chaps. 2–4, 6–8. Madison, Wis.: Brown & Benchmark, 1997.

Mertens, Donna M. *Research Methods in Education and Psychology: Integrity and Diversity with Qualitative and Quantitative Approaches,* chaps. 3–4, 11–12. Thousand Oaks, Calif.: Sage, 1998.

Patten, Mildred. *Understanding Research Methods,* pts. E, F, J. 2nd ed. Los Angeles: Pyrczak, 2000.

Salkind, Neil J. *Exploring Research,* chaps. 5, 7–8, 10–11. 4th ed. Upper Saddle River, N.J.: Prentice-Hall, 2000.

Sapsford, Roger. *Survey Research,* chaps. 5, 10–11. London: Sage, 1999.

Schloss, Patrick J., and Maureen A. Smith. *Conducting Research,* chaps. 5, 9. Upper Saddle River, N.J.: Merrill, 1999.

Sproul, Natalie L. *Handbook of Research Methods: A Guide for Practitioners and Students in the Social Sciences,* chaps. 2–3, 5, 13, 15. Metuchen, N.J.: Scarecrow, 1988.

Tuckman, Bruce W. *Conducting Educational Research,* chaps. 4–9. 5th ed. Belmont, Calif.: Wadsworth, 1999.

Wiersma, William. *Research Methods in Education: An Introduction,* chaps. 4–6, 12–13. 7th ed. Boston: Allyn & Bacon, 2000.

Wilkinson, David, ed. *The Researcher's Tool: The Complete Guide to Practitioner Research,* chaps. 1–2. London: Routledge Falmer, 2000.

Chapter 7

Historical Research: Concepts and Techniques

The focus of historical research for years has been the collection of data, recording and interpreting past events to determine how they impinge on the present and may portend the future. Usually labeled chronological or narrative history, this kind of reporting is called historiography. Breisach states that the task of the historiographer is to trace the way persons have reflected on the past as a key to helping them ascertain the present and predict the future.[1] Many educational researchers, including Wiersma, subscribe to a long-held belief that thinking about the past enables one to project what will happen in the future.[2] Leedy considers the task of a historical researcher to report what has happened and why these events took place.[3] The key to successful historical research, not unlike that of other modes of inquiry, is the researcher. Barzun and Graff spell out six virtues needed by a historical researcher: (1) accuracy, (2) love of order, (3) logic, (4) honesty, (5) self-awareness, and (6) imagination.[4] Keeping in mind Barzun and Graff's suggestions, historical research should be easier to pursue, whether it is chronological history or interdisciplinary in approach.

HISTORICAL RESEARCH APPROACHES

Almost from the beginning of time the human race has recorded events in many ways. Archaeologists have been able to decipher cuneiform wedge-shaped characters of the ancient Behistun Rock, the pictures and characters of the Egyptian Rosetta Stone, and the

Babylonian wedge-shaped cuneiform characters, some dating back as far as 2300 B.C., of the tablets of Ugarit.

Origins of the modern historical method date back to the Greek historian Herodotus (c. 484–c. 420 B.C.), who is referred to as the "Father of History." Another Greek, Thucydides (second half of the fifth century B.C.), was known for his eyewitness accounts of the Peloponessian War (434–401 B.C.). That approach has been the cornerstone of history for hundreds of years—and still is. Josephus Flavius (c. A.D. 37–100) chronicled early Jewish and Christian events preceding and following the fall of Jerusalem to the Romans in A.D. 70. For hundreds of years thereafter historians emphasized Christianity, science, and philosophy in their reporting of history.

Origins of modern music historiography go back to eighteenth-century humanism of the Renaissance, according to Pruett and Slovens.[5] British historian Arnold Toynbee (1889–1975), in his monumental ten-volume *A Study of History*, chronicled the rise and fall of civilizations of all ages. His approach has been referred to as "chronological history," or reporting on events over time, with little or no attempt to interpret the causes.

The early and middle twentieth century saw historians using interdisciplinary approaches to relate the events of history to their causes and effects. As a result, the objective of history is to accurately report worldwide events using media such as TV, radio, the Internet, and print media (newspapers and journals). These reports enable history to "come alive," rather than remain a mere "happening" reported long after the event has taken place. The chronological narrative approach still has validity and comprises the bulk of historical research in music education and the arts.

For several years revisionist historians have emphasized interdisciplinary approaches such as those listed by Shafer: psychohistory, comparative history, cooperative history, and intellectual and literary history.[6] Even though Rainbow and Froehlich admit that chronological is still an important technique to use, they identify psychohistory, quantitative-social scientific history, comparative history, and oral history as significant newer approaches, but not as commonly as the traditional or chronological method.[7]

Cunningham, in a doctoral historical social-cultural study, reviewed the role that the Long Beach (California) Municipal Band has played in the social, political, and musical lives of the citizens of

Long Beach. Originally subsidized by tax revenue, the band existed as a professional organization from 1911 to 1978.[8]

Barzun and Graff de-emphasize the stranglehold that "narrative" history has had on the past, largely due to some of the scientific claims attributed to interdisciplinary methods.[9] Writing several years ago, Brickman, a strong advocate of the narrative approach, says the historian's responsibility is to report accurately what has taken place, but often he is not in a position to be a firsthand observer.[10]

In a doctoral study, "A History of the Dorian Band Festival by Weston Henry Noble at Luther College," De Sotel researched and documented the Dorian Band Festival instituted by Noble in 1950 at Luther College, Decorah, Iowa. Dorian was the first band festival sponsored by a college or university in Iowa. In addition to tracing the life of Weston Noble, De Sotel listed guest artists, soloists, guest bands, and literature performed.[11]

For a music researcher interested in tracing early string instrument class instruction, a historical review of Albert G. Mitchell's teaching methods might be studied. Some questions to be posed are as follows: What impact did Mitchell's teaching methods have on the fledgling instrumental music movement in the United States in the early twentieth century? What are the antecedents of the Mitchell method? Did Mitchell expand his teaching procedures to wind and percussion instruments? What procedures did Mitchell use to determine that all students in a class were at the same performance level? Was Mitchell's class approach heterogeneous or homogeneous?

Comparative history, which made its appearance in the early 1960s, according to Frederickson, systematically compares the same events in different social settings. Most of the completed research has been concerned with civil rights, slavery, and race relations. A comparison is made of how an event may be in the same or different in various settings.[12] Shafer gives an example of the treatment of slaves in English-, French-, Spanish-, and Portuguese-speaking Americas.[13]

Cooperative history, in the words of Shafer, refers to historical reference works.[14] An example in music education is Keene's seminal work, *A History of Music Education in the United States.*[15]

In a doctoral study, Frontera combined a quantitative social-historical approach with aesthetic inquiry to examine the output of nineteenth-century Puerto Rican composers. She reviewed the political, social, and economic conditions in the time period covered in her research to find out how these affected the musical contributions of Gutiérrez, Tavárez, Compos, and Quintón. Also traced were Indian, African, and Spanish cultural influences on these composers to determine if they developed a nationalistic style based on the indigenous Puerto Rican *danza*.[16]

NARRATIVE OR CHRONOLOGICAL HISTORY

As already noted, collection of data pertaining to the past has been referred to as history. According to Vincent, this narrative is a statement of what persons do in various fields such as law, politics, music, or other arts.[17] Nevins presents a different viewpoint, stating that history is a bridge that connects the past and present and leads to the future.[18]

Historical research, as is true with all methods or procedures for obtaining data, must employ the scientific method to solve problems in history. This might be the inclusion of approaches from other methods (e.g., quantitative) or the generally accepted tenets of narrative history that are concerned with external and internal criticism of data. Defining an approach that is predicated on the scientific method, Fischer states that history is involved with solving problems. The historian, continues Fischer, asks open-ended questions about events of the past. Answers to these questions are based on facts that are arranged according to some type of paradigm to explain the phenomenon being studied.[19]

Historical research has not always been done by professional researchers and historians. Some of the more interesting and meaningful historical research has been done by amateurs and history buffs, whose purpose has been to preserve artifacts, literary works, and other items that may be gone forever. Witness the spate of historical journals, pamphlets, and brochures generated by local historians in cities and towns and even in rural areas during the bicentennial of the United States in 1976 and since. As further evidence, note the ever-increasing interest and attendance at Civil War Roundtables. Most of these feature new facts and relatively obscure insights into the Civil War (also called the War Between the States) by professional historians who spend years ferreting out information on skirmishes and battles that largely have been bypassed or treated lightly by other historians. Amateur historians often bring a fresh insight into local history. Some of them have used oral history techniques to preserve important information for posterity. Another example of the interest by the general public, as well as that of Civil War history buffs, was the blocking of a proposed shopping mall on lands contiguous to the Manassas National Battlefield Park in Virginia. Manassas is one of the most famous unspoiled battlefields, where the bloody First and Second Battles of Manassas (or Bull Run) were fought and won by Confederates in July 1861 and August 1862. The U.S. Congress in December 1988, at the urging of citizens groups and the National Park Service, bought six hundred acres of the threatened territory.[20] In North Carolina, unspoiled parcels of land are being purchased by agencies who want to preserve more of the Bentonville battlefield, the last major confrontation between Union and Confederate forces in North Carolina.

A long-held view of history consists of several objectives and purposes. Shafer lists three: (1) to review past happenings, (2) to maintain a record of current events, and (3) to develop methods to evaluate evidence and provide a meaningful documentation of events.[21]

Study of the past often serves as the basis for understanding the present or for predicting the future. Although this concept is not used as extensively in music education as it is in the social or political sciences, researchers, for example, could review stylistic periods in music. The simpler and emotionally restrained classical period may be better understood when compared with the highly chromatic, introspective, and less formal romantic era. Concepts of neoclassicism might become more evident when compared with classicism. Such research could be labeled comparative history because of comparisons in musical style.

Applying Shafer's second point, keeping a record of current events, could result in recording the life and influence of important music educators, the development and contributions of a performing group, or the influence of a professional organization. This kind of research might be classified as psychohistory, as an example, the contributions of Charles H. Congdon (1856–1928).

Patrick Sarsfield Gilmore (1829–1892) was the subject of a psychohistorical study by Cipolla. In "Patrick S. Gilmore: The Boston Years," Cipolla reports on the influence the legendary P. T. (Phineas Taylor) Barnum (1810–1892) had on Gilmore, the best known bandmaster of the nineteenth century before John Philip Sousa (1854–1932) came on the scene. Gilmore played an important role in musical activities just prior to and during the Civil War. The band performed at the Democratic Convention in Charleston, South Carolina, when delegates adjourned because they could not agree on a proslavery platform, resulting in the departure of delegates from eight southern states. Gilmore's band also performed at the Republican Convention in Chicago the same year, when Abraham Lincoln (1809–1865) was chosen to head the Republican ticket. During the Civil War the Gilmore band was on active duty for the Union at New Bern, North Carolina, and in New Orleans, Louisiana.[22]

Another doctoral study with psychohistorical implications is Ferguson's "The Bands and Musicians of the Confederate States of America," which was discussed in the first chapter.

Howe, in a doctoral dissertation, traced the life and influence of Luther Whiting Mason (1828–1896), an important figure in American music education. In "Luther Whiting Mason: Contributions to Music Education in Nineteenth Century America and Japan," she reviewed Mason's authorship of the first graded music textbook series and the first program to train classroom teachers to supervise elementary school music teaching. Mason also assisted in the establishment of music education in Japan by editing the first graded series of music textbooks for Japanese students.[23]

The third meaning for history given by Shafer is only partially applicable to music education research. Music researchers usually do not develop methods, but they do evaluate historical evidence and then present it in a meaningful context.

Although historical research in music often has been guarded jealously by scholars in musicology, there really is little justification for this exclusiveness, as an examination of historical research in music education over the past four dozen years will reveal. Garrett, in defining the function of the musicologist, insists that researchers must use scholarly procedures to locate and organize data relating to the evolution of all types of music.[24] These same conditions are incumbent upon the music educator engaged in historical research today. There is no need for investigators who use the scientific method to be classified according to some narrow, arbitrary distinction like historian, musician, or educator. Rather, they should all be regarded as research scholars. This is in harmony with the views of Hockett, who considers history as the pursuit of honesty in any field, when there is a temptation to do otherwise.[25]

HISTORICAL RESEARCH PROCEDURES

Historical research is based on certain steps or procedures that Hockett avers are (1) collecting data, (2) evaluating the data collected, and (3) presenting and interpreting the facts in readable form.[26] Hockett's first point is closely related to sources and kinds of data needed for the research. External and internal criticism, to be discussed later, are used respectively to determine the truthfulness and the trustworthiness of the data collected. Hockett's final step, relating to the exposition and interpretation of data, already has been referred to as historiography, but will continue to be discussed throughout this chapter.

Gottschalk's historical research focus involves (1) obtaining the facts, (2) placing the facts in appropriate order, (3) determining the accuracy of the data collected, and (4) assuring that certain items follow seriatim.[27] Gottschalk's first two steps relate to what Hockett calls "gathering of data," but with positive or negative implications. Finally, Gottschalk's sequence of data placement is closely allied to Hockett's "interpretations and conclusions." Barzun and Graff record a more succinct statement about research procedures applicable to historical research. The subject or topic is defined by "that group of associated facts and ideas which, when clearly presented in a prescribed amount of space, leave no questions unanswered WITHIN the presentation, even though many questions could be asked OUTSIDE it."[28]

Historical researchers often are criticized for being too subjective because historiographers are not always in a position to exercise the rigid controls that natural scientists regard as absolutely essential. Historiographers, unlike scientists, normally are concerned with more than an observation of the present. When involved in the preservation of today's chronology, which tomorrow will be history, historiographers must be just as accurate and precise as natural scientists in order to realize the ultimate objective of presenting the truth. A music critic attending the world premiere of a composition, by either a renowned or largely unknown composer, is on the threshold of history, as it were. The critic's responsibility to the musical world in accurately reporting the performance of a new work is essentially no different from that of the reporter who writes the proceedings of a conference of the world's leaders for dissemination to the general public. Both have an obligation to provide information that is as objective, truthful, and unbiased as possible.

The classic who, what, when, where, why, timeworn as it may seem, is another way to look at procedures for collecting historical data. Researchers in history, however, should always be aware that they may never be able to acquire all the data needed and that additional sources may be discovered later that will refute what they believe to be true based on the evidence at hand

Probability

The concept of probability, in its simplest terms, may be stated as, What is the likelihood that evidence I am considering is valid? For the historical researcher it is as important to establish the truth or probability as it is to determine the veracity of other kinds of information. Barzun and Graff stress that truth is arrived at by the historian through probability. An examination of evidence that has been reviewed and without question is truthful.[29] The same historians further state that the historical method verifies truth by using common sense.[30] Probability can be ascertained by applying external criticism to establish its validity.

Bringing probability down to a personal level, when Phelps was a docent at the North Carolina State Capitol in Raleigh, he continually asked himself, What is the probability that the legends reported to tour groups are true? One example will suffice. Were the so-called secret rooms in the Capitol actually used by Confederate spies in the closing days of the Civil War as the Union Armies converged on Raleigh? These second floor rooms were unfinished when the Capitol was completed in 1842, were inaccessible, and contained no flooring until recent renovations of the building in the 1970s. The probability of the truth of the legend of the secret rooms thus is very remote.

On a more positive note, a press dispatch from Israel in 1989 indicated that archaeologists had uncovered a two-thousand-year-old flask from the caves at Qumran that may have been used to anoint ancient Israelite kings. The reddish oil found in a small clay juglet had a honeylike consistency and apparently came from a perfume known as persimmon oil extracted from a now extinct bush. The probability of the genuineness of this oil is very strong, according to chemists and scholars who examined it.[31] Barzun and Graff sum up the concept of probability by concluding that "truth rests not on possibility nor on plausibility but on probability."[32]

Source Materials

Source materials used by the historiographer normally consist of two kinds: *primary* and *secondary*. A primary source of data is firsthand information. It is an account by an observer on the spot, as it were. When data are not original to the one reporting them they are secondary sources. Also possible is procuring information from a "tertiary" or other source even further removed from the original. Every effort should be made to ferret out original data because the basis of historical research is a primary or firsthand source. Historiographers recognize the necessity of directing their energies discretely to obtain valid data, state Mason and Bramble, in concord with Barzun and Graff.[33]

If you are preparing a biography or an article about a living person, e-mail and/or personal interviews could serve as primary sources of information. Also, primary would be publications by the subject, legal and personal documents, such as contracts and diaries, newspaper items, photographs and photocopies, concert programs, oral and written reports by contemporaries, as well as other primary sources.

Secondary sources often have value but should be used only when primary sources are untrustworthy or difficult to procure. Brickman says, however, that reliable secondary sources are preferable to primary sources that are questionable or incomplete.[34] Secondary sources worthy of merit will be documented since they should be based on primary materials. Accounts of a concert written by someone other than the person actually present to hear the concert are secondary, as are specially prepared summary accounts of the minutes of meetings. History books and many encyclopedia articles are secondary even though their authors may have had recourse to primary materials. Likewise, publications by an individual may be primary sources, but when excerpts from them are quoted by another person they become secondary.

Biographical accounts of composers frequently include an analysis of some of their music to indicate how events in their lives may have influenced their contributions to the field of music. As an example, Madeja, in a doctoral dissertation entitled "The Life and

Work of Herbert L. Clarke (1867–1945)," gathered data on the life and influence of this important trumpet soloist, conductor, and teacher. Clarke's style of playing, concert programming, and his cornet method book all have left their mark on many of today's trumpet and cornet players.[35]

Selection of Topic

General considerations in the selection of a topic have been discussed at considerable length earlier in this book. Five factors that Brickman considers to be significant for a historical researcher are (1) interest, (2) source materials available, (3) time factor, (4) relevance to course, and (5) specialized knowledge.[36] A music researcher, like any researcher, is expected to direct his or her energies toward a topic in which an intense interest has been manifested. A high school choral director, for instance, might want to write a history of the high school choral festival movement in the United States. Preliminary investigation may reveal that primary source materials are so limited that it would be impractical to continue with the original idea without expanding its scope. Such expansion obviously would require additional time, a factor that might not be feasible in a situation where a deadline becomes an external factor imposed by the duration of the instructional period.

One aspect has not been mentioned yet. Brickman states emphatically that a historical research topic must bear relevance to the objective of the research class.[37] While there are exceptions, it is not illogical for music education researchers to select a topic that can be pursued, even if it exceeds a deadline, imposed or anticipated. One of the principal objectives of a music education research course is to give students experience in making practical applications of the precepts they learn there, be they historical or other. Taking Brickman's rejoinder more seriously could result in fewer unsuitable research studies in music education.

In the realm of specialized knowledge, if you propose to tackle a history of music education in Germany, to cite a possibility, you must possess both knowledge of the history of music education in general and an adequate reading comprehension of German, the language in which most primary sources likely would appear. It would be impractical to attempt logical and free-flowing translations with the use of a German-English lexicon exclusively, especially if you are unfamiliar with music education terminology and philosophical principles, and with technical terms and idioms that appear often in the German language.

An intriguing topic for a music researcher might be to determine why so many musicians are interested in railroads and railroad songs. Some questions that might be posed are as follows: What is there about railroad songs that fascinate some musicians? Is the fascination the rhythm of the wheels as they cross the gaps between the jointed rails? Are the frequencies of the air horns on diesel locomotives or frequencies of the steam whistles on steam locomotives intriguing? Why have so many songs been written about railroads? Here are some examples that come to mind: "The Atchinson Topeka, and Santa Fe" (now part of BNSF), "The Chattanooga Choo-Choo," and "Casey Jones," among others.

The author of this chapter knows a professional cellist and a retired physician with musical skills who regularly volunteer at the North Carolina Transportation Museum in Spencer, restoring railroad equipment no longer in active service. Rail fans volunteer for nonoperating duties as hosts on Amtrak trains operating in North Carolina. Evidence of a link between railroads and music is the recent publication of *The Great Locomotive Chase*.[38] This composition is based on the bizarre attempt by Union raiders in 1862 to hijack the Confederate locomotive "The General" in North Georgia and take it to Chattanooga, Tennessee, burning bridges as they traveled north to foil the Confederate supply line of the Western and Atlantic Railroad. The plan was foiled when Confederate troops captured the Union raiders and the bridges remained intact.[39] Then, who does not know the anonymous railroad folksong "I've Been Working on the Railroad?" Studwell and Scheunemann state that the song appeared in a collection of Princeton University songs.[40] The unflappable Casey Jones is said to have devised a six-ton calliope-type whistle for his locomotive, number 382, on which he played various melodies and bird calls, especially the whippoorwill.[41]

ORAL HISTORY

The purpose of oral history, states Ritchie, is to collect "spoken memories and personal commentaries of historical significance through recorded interviews."[42] Columbia University's Alan Nevins is generally conceded to be the first person to formally identify, in 1948, and use techniques of oral history. However, Hoover reports that the Forest History Society, in 1947, began to report on the history of forest products in the United States and Canada.[43] In 1948, Nevins conducted an oral history interview with George McAney, a New York City civic leader. The Columbia University Oral History Collection, begun by Nevins, now includes the memoirs of several thousand persons and over 400,000 pages of transcripts. Oral history data now are being collected by e-mail and the Internet. Verbal evidence can be a primary source when written evidence is not readily available. Data gathered through oral history interviews are largely intended for use by historians rather for the substantiation of hypotheses, as would be true in experimental research or even in psychohistory. Cutler reports that knowledge which passes from one generation to another must be scrutinized to distinguish important from inconsequential and fact from fiction.[44]

Collection of data in oral history is based on a well-planned procedure rather than on spontaneous or random interviews, following these steps: (1) researcher's invitation to individuals to participate, (2) preparation for the interview, (3) preinterview visit, (4) the interview (recorded), (5) preparation of verbatim transcript of the interview, (6) submission of transcript to interviewee for additions and corrections, along with legal draft agreement, (7) conclusion of the legal agreement, and (8) preparation of final copy of interview.

Before sending an invitation to prospective interviewees, purpose and problem of the research to be addressed must be identified. If the oral history project involves working in a remote area, persons able to provide the desired information must be identified, then necessary preparations arranged, such as housing for the researcher (if required), equipment to be used (portable battery-operated recorder or VCR and adequate supply of discs or tapes), and mode of transportation to reach the interviewee. The researcher meets and establishes rapport with the interviewee, indicating purpose of the interview and arranging a time and place for the next meeting. Portable equipment must be used to record remarks of the interviewee because the researcher will not have time to write down everything of importance said by the interviewee. Most portable recording systems are easy to transport. An additional advantage is that a recorded interview may be replayed as many times as necessary to obtain a literal transcript of the interview. A verbatim transcript permits the interviewee to make additions, corrections, or deletions to protect parties from legal action that might result. Occasionally an interviewee will not permit the interview to be recorded. If this be the case, wishes of the interviewee must be respected; some kind of subterfuge by the investigator must not be sanctioned. In case of a refusal, the interviewer needs to write down as much information as possible at the completion of the interview. The danger is that something of importance may be left out when the researcher tries to recall everything of significance.

Legal documents should be worked out with an attorney. After editorial and legal details have been clarified, the final document is submitted for signatures, and a statement is made indicating amount of remuneration, if any, the interviewee is to receive. The oral history process culminates with the preparation of a copy to be deposited in a central repository or archive for the benefit of other researchers.

Oral history studies in music education have not been numerous. This could change when music researchers become involved in sociological and cultural research that impinges on music, when qualitative research techniques are used. With greater attention being given now to minority groups, what a nascent area for oral history research this can be! Hoover states that one of the early oral history music studies was completed in the 1960s at Tulane University in New Orleans, Louisiana, consisting of tapes to supplement manuscripts (MSS) on the history of jazz.[45] Regional and national meetings of the Music Educators Conference often include sessions devoted to oral history. These should help to kindle interest, enthusiasm, and support for oral history research.

An oral history study in music education was completed by Brobston.[46] In the first part of his doctoral research Brobston presented the antecedents of gospel music, music by evangelists in the nineteenth and twentieth centuries, and the status of gospel music in the South at the time of his research. Also included were singing conventions, publishers of gospel music, and gospel music performers. The second part of his research, "A Brief History of White Southern Gospel Music and a Study of Selected Amateur Family Gospel Music Singing Groups in Rural Georgia," contained in the field research, or oral history. Conducted in twenty-five counties in South Georgia, selected at random, twenty-five family singing groups were interviewed and recorded in actual performance. Brobston concludes that there appears to be no significant diminution of gospel singing in the geographical area included in his research.

Two important sources for oral history research are *The Oral History Manual* [47]and Ritchie's *Doing Oral History*, mentioned earlier.

The Oral History Association publishes two sources of information that should be helpful to music education researchers: *Oral History Association Newsletter* and the annual *Oral History Review*. Both contain articles, abstracts of recently completed oral history studies, plus a listing of recent publications dealing with oral history.

Oral history, if carefully conducted, can be a useful procedure to collect data that otherwise probably would be unobtainable. Handlin, however, offers a caution that the oral historian needs to be aware that the tape recorder can be an instrument to encourage an interviewee to resort to "uninhibited reminisce." The oral historian must be resourceful enough to be able to expunge all but the most important statements.[48]

HISTORY RESEARCH DATA GATHERING

Musicians involved in historical research likely will find their data falling into one or more of the following categories: (1) heretofore unknown information about an individual, group, object, or era; (2) uncovering heretofore unknown creativity of someone; (3) discovering an authentic copy of a work or a more complete one; (4) locating creative efforts that were known to have been written but not believe to be extant; (5) collecting, codifying, or analyzing data of historical import from diverse sources; (6) verifying that documents, statements, or creativity of a reputed creative artist are spurious; and (7) rectifying incorrect statements, dates, or information previously accepted as true.

Referring to the first point, one of the most gratifying by-products of historical research is the discovery of heretofore unknown information. Although such data usually result from serendipity, opportunities for revelations of this kind are rare in music, music education, and the arts. The most likely sources of such information are newly discovered MSS, personal letters, or documents that previously were unavailable to scholars or the general public. Barzun and Graff give an interesting account of Barzun's discovery of a previously suppressed letter of Hector Berlioz (1803–1869) that appeared shortly after the performance of his "Rakoczy March" in 1846. The original not only was misdated but also distorted from a letter basically musical in content to one with political implications.[49]

Even more significant than the Berlioz discovery is identifying heretofore unknown creativity, the second category. Richard L. Crocker, while professor of music at the University of California at Berkeley, reported on the deciphering of a song on clay tablets that shunted the history of music back a thousand years to the second millennium B.C. Unearthed by French archaeologists in the 1950s in Ugarit, in what is now Syria, the cuneiform symbols were undecipherable until 1972. The song is based on the same heptatonic scale in use today in Western music. Crocker states that it sounds like a lullaby, hymn, or gentle folk song.[50]

Discoveries of heretofore unknown creativity are of two kinds: items that have been identified positively as authentic, and those about which some questions remain regarding authenticity. Newspapers and journals such as the *Journal of the American Musicological Society* and the *Music Quarterly* frequently report on the discovery of previously lost items. A case in point: a lost MS containing two movements of a Franz Joseph Haydn (1732–1809) *Mass* (1786) was found in a cupboard in a northern Ireland farmhouse a few years ago The renowned Haydn scholar H. C. Robbins Landon identified the work as an important find. Among the clues used for identification, Robbins Landon reported the ink had faded and the paper is from a mill on the Esterhazy estate. The folder has a handwritten note by Vincent Novello, indicating that it was an unpublished work by Haydn that Novello bought in Vienna in 1829.[51]

The American pianist Byron Janis identified a heretofore lost copy of Chopin's Waltz in G-Flat Major, op. 70, no. 1. Found in the Chateau de Thoiry in Yvelines, France, the MS was unearthed in a box marked "old clothes" by the mansion's owner, Count Paul de la Panouse, who showed it to Janis. The connection between Chopin and the Panouse Family is that Chopin's friend French writer Eugene Sue (1804–1857) was in love with the second wife of one of Count Paul's relatives. Janis recognized the importance of the manuscript and had it authenticated by Chopin expert Francois Lesure of the Societe Francaise Musicologie.[52] Discovered at the same time and in the same place was the E-Flat Waltz, op. 18, "The Grand Valse Brillante."[53]

The discovery a few years ago of a Violin Concerto in C Major, reputedly by Ludwig van Beethoven (1770–1827), is an example of a composition the authenticity of which remains uncertain. Only further investigation will reveal whether the work indeed belongs to Beethoven's catalog.

Another source of personal satisfaction to a researcher is to uncover a more complete or authentic copy of a musical composition or other creativity, the third category of data. While examining stacks of uncataloged instrumental music in the Moravian Archives in Old Salem (now part of Winston-Salem, North Carolina), Phelps located a complete set of Three Trios, op. 3, of John Antes (1740–1811) minus the last page of the violoncello part. John Bland published these charming, undated trios, about 1785, because Antes was known to have been in England then. Prior to their discovery, the only known set in existence consisted of a second violin and a violoncello part owned by the Sibley Music Library of the Eastman School of Music in Rochester, New York. A comparison of the Eastman and Old Salem copies revealed exact duplication. Thus, by using the Old Salem first- and second-violin parts and the Eastman violoncello part, it was possible to present the first modern performance of Trio in D Minor, op. 3, no. 2, the second of these delightful Haydnesque trios at the University of Iowa, Iowa City, on May 19, 1950, with violinists Stella Hopper and Joanne Dempsey and violoncellist Charles Becker as performing artists.

Antes, whose surname is the Greek equivalent of von Blume, was born at Fredericktrop, Montgomery County, Pennsylvania, on 24 March 1740. In accord with the prevailing philosophy of the Moravians at that time, Antes intensively pursued musical instruction in his youth, in addition to other studies. In 1769, after being ordained to the ministry at Marienborn, Germany, he served in Egypt as a missionary. While recuperating from an illness, Antes composed some quartets and other works before returning to Europe in 1782, where in Vienna, according to Grider, Antes met Haydn, who assisted other musicians in the performance of some of his early compositions.[54] It was during his convalescence in Cairo that the trios apparently were written, as indicated by the inscription on the title page, which states in part, Composti a Grand Cairo dal Sigre Giovanni A-T-S. Dilettante Americano, Op. 3 (composed in Grand Cairo by Mr. John A-T-S, American dilettante, op. 3). Quite in keeping with the custom of the time. Antes perplexingly listed himself as A-T-S, a factor that resulted in his anonymity until 1940, when the late Carlton Sprague Smith, former chief of the Music Division, New York Public Library, revealed the identity of this important Moravian composer.[55]

When any work is unearthed its importance ultimately may rest on its value when viewed in light of its historical perspective. Under ordinary circumstances the discovery of works by someone such as Antes, who is relatively unknown, probably would go unheralded. In terms of historical perspective, however, the Antes trios assume a new dimension. They represent, as far as Phelps has been able to discern, the earliest extant chamber music written by a native-born American.[56]

Another phase of historical research in music and music education relates to the fourth category, locating works previously believed not to be extant. At the Moravian Archives in Old Salem, in the same pile of uncataloged instrumental compositions containing the Antes Trios, the MS of "Parthia IX," by David Moritz Michael (1751–1825) was discovered. Michael is generally regarded as the most important nineteenth-century American Moravian instrumental composer. Rau and David, in their seminal catalog of American Moravian music, report that "Parthia IX" was not to be found in Bethlehem or in Lititz, Pennsylvania.[57] They also state that the collections at Lititz and Bethlehem contained thirteen wind *partien*.[58] With the finding of "Parthia IX" it may safely be stated that Michael composed at least fourteen *partien*, all of which exist in the Moravian Archives either in Bethlehem, Pennsylvania, or in Old Salem (Winston-Salem, North Carolina).[59] Since Bethlehem and Salem served as the ecclesiastical headquarters for the northern and southern divisions of the Moravian Church, respectively, the MSS duplication of some compositions in the archives of the two cities may be explained by the constant interchange of personnel. Michael, however, confined his activities to Bethlehem and Nazareth, Pennsylvania.

These *partien*, in accordance with the meaning of the word, were meant to be performed out of doors. Grider notes that they usually were performed from a balcony of the home of the Moravian Brethren on Wednesday evenings during the summer for the benefit of citizens of the community.[60]

In four short, technically easy technical movements, "Parthia IX," except for the second movement, is scored for two B♭ clarinets, two B♭ French horns, and bassoon. The first (Allegro), third (Minuet), and the fourth (Allegro) are in the key of B♭ major. The second (Andante), in F major, is scored for two B♭ clarinets and bassoon.

A recent discovery of music hidden for more than a century and thought to be lost, was four string quartets from Haydn's Op. 50. The disclosure was announced by Dr. Georg Feder, director of the Joseph Haydn Institute in Cologne, Germany, during an interview in Sydney, Australia, in conjunction with 250th anniversary celebrations for the birth of Franz Joseph Haydn (1732–1809). Feder affirmed that these works were authentic and that they were autographed by Haydn himself.[61]

Polish-born violinist Henryk Szeryng, after a seven-year search, finally located a MS copy of Concerto no. 3 in E Major, by violin virtuoso Nicolo Paganini (1782–1840). It was known that Paganini had written five violin concertos, but prior to Szeryng's announcement, Concerto no. 3 was the only one that had not been found. Authenticity of the work was verified by French musicologists, according to Henahan.[62]

Collecting, codifying, or analyzing data from diverse sources, sometimes known as "documentary research," represents the fifth category for historical research in music and music education. An example of "documentary research," the Mendelssohn Quintet Club was the subject of an investigation by Phelps.[63] This New England–based ensemble must be considered to be the first professional group organized in the United States to devote itself to the performance of chamber music, unless other evidence subsequently proves to the contrary. Remaining in existence for forty-nine years, from 1849 to 1898, the ensemble performed in many parts of the United States, Hawaii, Australia, and New Zealand. Also, the group is reputed to be the first ensemble to organize a conservatory of music.[64] Its focus on the performance of music by American composers is noteworthy.

Spearhead and driving force behind the Mendelssohn Quintet Club was Irish clarinetist, flutist, and violist Thomas Ryan (1827–1903), who emigrated from Ireland in 1844. Original members of the ensemble were August Fries, first violin; Frances Riha, second violin; Ryan, viola and clarinet; Edward Lehmann, viola and flute; and Wulf Fries, violoncello. Ryan was the only member who remained with the group through its forty-nine-year existence.[65] Three New England composers whose chamber works were featured by the quintet were Boston-born Charles Callahan Perkins (1823–1886),

James Cutler Dann Parker (1828–1916), and Vermont-native Edward Jerome Hopkins (1836–1898).

In documentary research investigators assemble data from all available sources, codify them, and present their interpretations. Value of this kind of study for both the musical layperson and the professional music educator is obvious. Someone who has neither time nor the inclination to ferret out answers to questions usually welcomes the opportunity to acquire detailed and comprehensive information from one codified source. This is one of the reasons dictionaries and encyclopedias of musical biography, terminology, and other kinds of information are so widely used by music educators and others who are seeking ready references.

The sixth category is documents, statements, compositions, or other items that, although they have been accepted at one time or another as authentic, subsequently have proven to be spurious. An oft quoted example is the account of the fantastic and fanciful Cardiff Giant, unearthed in upstate Cardiff, New York, in the late nineteenth century. Buried by a scheming entrepreneur, the Cardiff Giant became a tourist attraction in central New York State. The "giant" was an eight-foot gypsum image of a man, even attracting the attention of the flamboyant P. T. Barnum (1810–1891), who wanted it for his circus. Unable to obtain it, Barnum had another one made!

Good tells of another kind of chicanery involving a person who received a baccalaureate degree from a music school in 1950 and who, by 1963, through extensive forgery, was able to fabricate a transcript, complete with official registrar's seal, indicating this person had earned an Ed. D.[66] Phelps's evaluation of the authenticity of a string quartet allegedly by Benjamin Franklin (1706–1790), and a copy of a composition attributed to Sidney Lanier (1842–1881) will be discussed later in this chapter under "External Criticism or Authenticity."

Rectifying incorrect statements or data is the seventh category of information for historical research to be discussed in this book. Numerous examples exist in music as well as in history for the rectification of statements, dates, or beliefs that previously have been accepted as correct. Brickman, Gottschalk, Hockett, and Nevins present several accounts to show that anecdotes and statements attributed to George Washington (1732–1799), Thomas Jefferson (1743–1826), and Abraham Lincoln (1809–1865), among other distinguished Americans have proven to be illusory. Of local interest to

Phelps has been the name of Bennett Place, near Durham, North Carolina, site of the surrender on April 26, 1865, of the ninety-thousand-man Confederate Army of the Carolinas, Georgia, and Florida of General Joseph E. Johnston (1807–1891) to Union General William T. Sherman (1820–1891). This humble farmhouse of James and Nancy Bennett was the site of the largest troop surrender of the American Civil War. Historians of the North Carolina Division of Archives have found that the correct spelling of the surname should be *Bennitt* rather than *Bennett,* although many historical accounts still spell the family name as *Bennett.*

Correction of an improperly dated musical example, well known to students of music history, is cited. Hockett, in reporting on the English round "Sumer is icumen in," writes that the use of unskilled evidence led nineteenth-century historians to believe it was written about 1240 because that was the date of another MS in the collection. In the 1940s an American musicologist pointed out that the hand-writing of the two pieces was not the same, and that the notation of "Sumer" did not "come into use until long after 1240, making the probable date of *Sumer* about 1310."[67] The rectification of this date was made by the late Manfred Bukofzer (1910–1955).

Another interesting example of misdating is the claim that Boston University, in 1876, awarded the first Bachelor of Music degree in the United States. Eells, however, relates that the U.S. commissioner of education for 1873 confirms that the distinction properly belongs to Adrian College in Michigan. Trustees' Minutes of Adrian College, dated June 1873, list Mrs. Mattie B. Pease Lowrie as the first recipient of a Bachelor of Music degree in 1873.[68] Eells also writes that the first honorary degree in music was awarded by Georgetown University in Washington, D.C. to one Henry Zielman, by Zachary Taylor (1784–1850), twelfth president of the United States. Eells reports this apparently was the first time a sitting president of the United States was privileged to award honorary degrees.[69]

While reviewing archival records at New York University, Phelps found the listing of an earned doctorate in music education awarded by New York University in1895 to John J. Dawson, for his Ped.D. dissertation "The Education Value of Vocal Music." The Ped.D. designation was a common one for degrees in education at that time. Since the listing of doctoral degrees in music education have shown none earlier than 1912, Dawson must be recognized as the first recipient of an earned doctorate in music education with the designation "Doctor of Pedagogy."[70] Dawson's seventeen-page, single-spaced document contains the following divisions: Vocal Music Has Been Overlooked; Vocal versus Instrumental Music; the Elements of Music; Reasons for Neglect of Music Culture, Character and Conduct in Education, in Physical Culture, in Emotional Culture (Song as a Means of Culture); Aesthetics; Conclusion. His closing statement is still largely applicable today: "Song is a fundamental process in education—a true humanity subject—fitted to produce beneficial results in the evaluation and development of a more perfect manhood. The curriculum of elementary education is imperfect without it, while the curriculum of Higher Education cannot but be improved by it."[71]

Evaluating results of data has been discussed to some extent in conjunction with the seven categories of information mentioned earlier in this chapter. The historical method, however, is more explicitly concerned with external and internal criticism, or the "how" techniques.

External Criticism

Through the process of external (or lower) criticism you can learn whether or not the object of your inquiry is authentic or genuine. Many factors constitute the approach to external criticism, but the prime objective is to determine whether or not an item is genuine. Hockett, in defining external criticism, states: "It examines *documents*—a comprehensive term which . . . includes not only manuscripts but books, pamphlets, maps, even ancient inscriptions and monuments."[72] Verification of authenticity also is part of the external criticism procedure. Fischer, insisting that the successful outcome of factual verification may rest on the skill of the researcher, remarks that the historian must not only tell the truth, but verify its truthfulness as well. The historian's veracity and skill at verification are important.[73]

Some of the questions that might be asked in the process of applying external criticism are (1) Where was the item originally located? Where is it now? (2) Is the document (item) an original or a copy? If a copy, where is the original? (3) What is the estimated age of the item? Does it appear to be as old as it should be to be authentic? (4) Are there autographs or other identifications that will make the process of verification easier? (5) Is the handwriting (in the case of MSS) consistent with other writings by the reputed author? (6) Are there any indications (diaries, newspaper accounts, etc.) that such an item existed? and (7) Is there any reason to suspect that the item may be a hoax?

In the process of external criticism it often is necessary to probe auxiliary areas of knowledge. Some of the fields musicians frequently consult are photography, paleography, semantics, chronology, genealogy, and cartography. With the recent explosion in the use of the Internet, this important tool should not be overlooked. Sometimes you may even find yourself trying to determine the watermark on a document as well as age and kind of paper used. A typewritten document might be located, reputedly written before 1868. Such information would be inaccurate, because, according to Murphy, the typewriter was not patented until 1868 by Milwaukean Christopher Scholes.[74]

Applying the principles of external criticism, consider an intriguing and beguiling flute and piano composition, allegedly by Sidney Lanier (1842–1881), entitled "Danse des Moucherons." Phelps has in his possession a negative photostat of this short, rhapsodic, chromatic work obtained from Johns Hopkins University in Baltimore, Maryland. In an attempt to locate the original MS he checked the holdings of the Lanier Room at Johns Hopkins, along with those of Georgia's Oglethorpe University, and other repositories without success. In addition, personal correspondence with each of Lanier's children, each of whom courteously replied, failed to shed any light on MSS other than those at Johns Hopkins, where Lanier was known to have been, but which, as just noted, does not possess the original to "Danse des Moucherons." Henry W. Lanier, one of Lanier's sons, indicated his MSS had been given to the Lanier collection at Johns Hopkins. Henry, writing about his father, a self-taught flutist and poet, remarked that his father's problem was not writing down music. When he had time and strength songs were ready to come forth.[75] Several brief sketches may be found in the Lanier room at Johns Hopkins, including his projected "Quartette," "Tuno Religioso" (for two flutes or violas), "La Reve" (three flutes and bass flute), and "Trio for flute, pianoforte[,] and violoncello."

Applying the tools of external criticism resulted in inconclusive answers to the first two questions. As to the third, Phelps was informed that his copy was reproduced directly from the original MS. The date 1873 appears after Lanier's name, yet style of handwriting for tempo and dynamics is inconsistent and suggests it came from another hand. The tempo markings, in particular, appear to be in a more contemporary hand, especially on the last two pages of the six-page composition. In addition, the twelve-line MS paper on which the work was written bears this inscription: "Carl Fischer, New York, Monarch Brand Warranted." It is true that Lanier spent some time in New York from 1870 to 1872, the year in which Carl Fischer arrived in the city. Fischer's first venture, moreover, was in musical instruments, according to city directories of that time. It was not until 1880 that the publishing phase of the company began, so the colophon in question did not exist in 1873.

There are no autographs, holographs, or others identifications on Phelps's copy to suggest a positive answer to the fourth question. The composer's name is written in a combination of upper- and lowercase hand lettering. The tempo and dynamic terms appear to be from different hands, making them difficult to compare with the written form of the composer's name and therefore making it difficult to identify the composition. Starke, in his biographical and critical account of Lanier's life, includes a photostatic copy of the flute part of the second and concluding pages of Lanier's "Gnat Symphony," which consists of only three-and-one half lines.[76] The copy does include Lanier's account, in a very neat and unhurried handwriting, of the composition, which he describes as a "translation of the sound," but this does not necessarily mean this description is in Lanier's handwriting. Phelps's copy of *"Danse des Moucherons"* contains six pages including the piano part, but the last twelve measures of the flute part in the versions do not agree.

In response to the fifth question, a comparison was made of the item just cited and another by Lanier, his unaccompanied flute solo "Wind Song," which Starke relates was performed in October 1874, but apparently written earlier.[77] There is a strong similarity of handwriting; both appear in a style that shows a lighter, more delicate, and less hurried stroke than that in "Danse des Moucherons."

That such a work by this Georgia-born poet-musician may have existed, the object of the sixth question, has already been established in conjunction with the previous discussion, and the title is listed in Starke's bibliography under "Music by Lanier." [78] It also is listed in *Centennial Edition of the Works and Letters of Sidney Lanier.*[79]

In answer to the seventh question, it would appear that the authenticity of the copy of "Danse des Moucherons," is open to serious question because of the discrepancies that exist, although the composition is listed by both Starke and Graham. Perhaps additional research will result in more convincing data to suggest otherwise. Hockett pinpoints the universal dilemma faced by historians who must pass judgment on a document—especially if there are some questions about its veracity—by prudently noting that additional evidence may appear to alter accepted ideas.[80]

Another example of external criticism is an item that appeared in a now defunct New York City newspaper. A dispatch from Lynchburg, Virginia, stated in part that a previously unknown quartet for strings by Benjamin Franklin (1706–1790) was soon to have a performance in Philadelphia, Pennsylvania, largely through the efforts of a woman who was an associate professor of French at a woman's college in Lynchburg, Virginia (Randolph Macon Woman's College). The professor's attention was called to this work by the owner of a Parisian bookstore in which she was browsing. The quartet was discovered, according to the article, by an unnamed musicologist in a pile of forgotten items, but their location was not disclosed.[81]

Several factors should be noted relative to this quartet. The original MS, in tablature, was reported by the unidentified transcriber to be housed in the Bibliotheque Nationale in Paris. In correspondence with the music librarian, it was learned that the Bibliotheque and the Conservatory Bibliotheque possessed neither the quartet nor any other item by Franklin.[82]

The real motive behind the use of tablature would be interesting to learn. In the preface to the transcription, which was published in 1945, the transcriber reports that the original was in the hand of a professional copyist of the late eighteenth century, who otherwise remains unidentified. Franklin served as U.S. ambassador to France from 1776 to 1785, and it is known that he attended concerts in Paris, including performances of chamber music at the salon of Madame Helvetius d'Auteil. It does seem rather strange, though, that tablature would be used for a string quartet so late in the eighteenth century. This type of writing, except for guitar and other fretted instruments, had largely been replaced by the conventional system of notation currently in use. Also unexplained is the rationale for placing each of the instruments (three violins and violoncello) in *scordatura.* Use of this system of mistuning by Heinrich Biber (1644–1704) is well known, but the simple, uninteresting, single melody line employed for each instrument in the alleged Franklin quartet suggests no need for *scordatura*, because the instrumentalists can play each of the parts entirely on open strings, another curious circumstance. Also unorthodox for a string quartet is the instrumentation: three violins and violoncello.

In five short movements, the first bears no subtitle, but appears to be march tempo. The second is *menuetto*, the third *capriccio*. A *menuetto* and a *siciliano* complete the work. The *capriccio* and *siciliano* are tripartite, while the others are in two parts structurally. Unusual too, is a five-movement quartet in this period of musical history.

Information from the Franklin Institute, where the first contemporary performance of the quartet was scheduled, was to the effect that the work had yet to be presented. All attempts to communicate with the discoverer and the transcriber of the quartet proved fruitless. These repeated attempts continued for approximately two years. Review of a performance of the alleged Franklin quartet appeared in a New York City newspaper, but no additional information was provided to suggest that the work was genuine, except that the 1945 version had further been edited and corrected by yet another unidentified hand.[83]

Finally, no definite proof has been advanced to show that Franklin actually knew enough about the techniques of musical composition to write a quartet, or any other musical work for that matter. True, he is credited with the invention of the *armonica,* or musical glasses, a distinction he disclaimed. Franklin admittedly did make many improvements on the instrument, whose sweet and pleasant tinkling sounds were produced by moistened fingers massaging rotating tumblers of different frequencies. Even Mozart and Beethoven were so intrigued by the soothing sounds of the *armonica* that they composed several pieces for the instrument.

In view of the consistent negative evidence, coupled with lack of affirmative data, it must be concluded that this is a spurious work. The alleged Franklin quartet appears to be a musical joke, the product of an anonymous jester. Always possible, of course, is that more positive data may be forthcoming in the future that could result in a more exact evaluation.

Internal Criticism or Credibility

Had evidence for the Lanier and Franklin works been more positive, investigation of other factors, known as internal (higher) criticism, could have proceeded. There are many occasions when this additional step is necessary. Even though external criticism may establish that a document, item, or statement is authentic, there may be inaccuracies or inconsistencies within. Nevins says that although it is time-consuming to establish authenticity of a historical source, to establish integrity is more difficult.[84] Gottschalk states the purpose of internal criticism is to determine how credible the data may be.[85] Experienced researchers frequently engage in external and internal criticism simultaneously, in which they will use information from one to assist the interpretation of the other.

Some historiographers divide internal criticism into positive and negative phases. Making a distinction between them, Brickman writes that through positive criticism a researcher tries to ascertain the true meaning of a statement, whereas negative criticism concerns a researcher's rationale for discrediting them, as evidenced by the partially or inefficiency displayed by the writer.[86]

In dealing with internal criticism you must ask such questions as the following: (1) Is the document consistent stylistically with others by the writer? Are there major inconsistencies? (2) Are there any indications the writer's reporting was inaccurate? (3) Does the writer actually mean what is said? (4) Could this work have been written by someone else in the style of the individual? (5) Is there any evidence the writer is biased or prejudiced?

It is generally conceded that artists do change their manner of expressing themselves stylistically due to the natural process of artistic growth and development. For example, students of music literature often are called upon to compare various characteristics of a composer's stylistic periods. Witness three distinctive epochs in the creative life of Ludwig van Beethoven (1770–1827): the first ending in 1802, the second in approximately 1815, and the third in 1827.

Although composers may show drastic style changes during their lifetime, the musical idioms they favor usually persist throughout their creative life. Characteristic idioms serve as guides when an attempt is made to determine whether a composition in question is consistent with others by the same composer. Major inconsistencies result when a composer deliberately alters his or her style by using different idioms. On the other hand, the incongruent features suggest that these works are indeed by two different composers. In the instance of a composer like Arnold Schoenberg (1874–1951), a change in both stylistic characteristics and musical idioms is apparent in his transition from the postromantic style of *Verklärte Nacht* to the dodecaphonic *Pierrot Lunaire*.

Occasionally inaccuracies will be suspected in a document. Barzun and Graff describe the incorrect dating of a letter by Hector Berlioz (1803–1869) to his publisher indicating that he was forwarding the table of contents for a book. Berlioz dated his communication Thursday June 23; Barzun and Graff point out that the year must have been 1852, in which case June 23 fell on Wednesday. It was not unusual for Berlioz to mistake the day of the week, according to Barzun and Graff.[87]

A third question relative to internal criticism is whether or not the writer actually meant what he or she said. Some confusion understandably could come from a writer's assumption that readers comprehend and agree with their definitions and certain terminology. Misunderstandings often are more than merely problems of semantics. Observe persons who use "cornett" when "cornet" is intended. Despite the difference of only a single *t* the instruments are vastly different in nature. The former refers to an obsolete fifteenth- and sixteenth-century instrument, normally made of wood, containing six finger holes and played with a cup-shaped mouthpiece. The contemporary cornet is a three-valved instrument constructed of metal, similar to the trumpet, but shorter. The cup-shaped mouthpiece of the *cornett* is larger and deeper than that of the *cornet*.

Applicable more to music than other disciplines, the next question is concerned with works that may have been written by an imposter in the style of another composer. Especially suspect are newly discovered works claimed to be by such well known composers as Haydn and Mozart. Reasons for this type of deception vary, but one of the most common is to enable a person who is unheralded to capitalize financially and prestigiously on the name of an esteemed composer. Then, there are numerous examples of musicians, in good faith and with no attempt at deception, who have completed works left unfinished by composers at the time of their death. Witness the *Requiem* by Wolfgang Amadeus Mozart (1756–1791), which was completed by his protégé and intimate friend Franz X. Sussmayer (1766–1803).

Despite the best of intentions, it is difficult to be completely unbiased or unprejudiced. Some writers deliberately present a unilateral point of view, as evidenced by some early textbooks on the history of music in the United States. *Music in America*, for example, by

Frederic L. Ritter, is generally considered to be strongly prejudiced in the direction of German Romanticism. Another oversight is the absence of references in many music texts to the role the Moravians played in the early musical life of the United States.

In a general sense, the realm of aesthetic judgment is characterized by personal predilection and prejudice, just as is the choice of a musical instrument, automobile, computer, or Internet provider. Normally it would be more difficult for a critic who prefers the piano music of Franz Liszt (1811–1886) to that of Frédéric Chopin (1810–1849) to present an unbiased account when reviewing the works of both composers than it would be for one who has no strong preference. Likewise, two concert artists do not perform the same composition in precisely the same way. Gottschalk believes differences of interpretation are not bad. Musicians, he says, really are historians who interpret past events in a particular manner.[88]

Historical research can provide many challenging opportunities for one to make significant contributions to human knowledge. It should be remembered, however, that history is more than facts. Winks succinctly states that a balance must be maintained between historical facts based on research and history that involves analysis, interpretation, and generalization.[89]

Applying the principles of historiography, a researcher in music and the arts can employ the scientific method to obtain and evaluate facts objectively, especially if some of the newer technologies discussed in the next chapter are used.

FOR REVIEW, DISCUSSION, AND IMPLEMENTATION

- What is the meaning of the term "historiography?" Give examples of research focusing on "historiography."
- Barzun and Graff identify certain "virtues" needed by a historical researcher. What are these "virtues?"
- Identify and explain some of the approaches used by historical researchers to obtain data. Which of these approaches is/are useful for your proposed research?
- Differentiate between "primary" and "secondary" sources as applied to historical research. Give examples of each.
- How might a music education researcher apply techniques of oral history?

- Using the Internet, locate research studies that apply external and internal criticism techniques.

NOTES

1. Ernst Breisach, *Historiography: Ancient, Medieval, and Modern,* 2nd ed. (Chicago: University of Chicago Press, 1994), 3.

2. William Wiersma, *Research Methods in Education: An Introduction,* 7th ed. (Boston: Allyn & Bacon, 2000), 220.

3. Paul D. Leedy, with Timothy J. Newby and Peggy A. Ermer. *Research Planning and Design,* 6th ed. (Saddle Rock River, N.J.: Merrill, 1997), 173.

4. Jacques Barzun and Henry F. Graff, *The Modern Researcher,* 5th ed. (Boston: Houghton Mifflin, 1992), 44–47.

5. James W. Pruett and Thomas P. Slovens, *Research Guide to Musicology* (Chicago: American Library Association, 1985), 16.

6. Robert J. Shafer, *A Guide to Historical Method,* 3rd ed. (Homewood, Ill.: Dorsey, 1980), 15.

7. Edward L. Rainbow and Hildegard C. Froehlich, *Research in Music Education: An Introduction to Systematic Inquiry* (New York: Schirmer Books, 1987), 108.

8. Gregory M. Cunningham, "A History and Socio-Cultural Examination of the Long Beach Municipal Band (California)" (Ed.D. diss., University of Illinois, 2002), AA 1304407.

9. Barzun and Graff, 192.

10. William W. Brickman, *Research in Educational History* (Norwood, Pa.: Folcroft Library Editions, 1975), 91.

11. John R. De Sotel, "A History of the Dorian Band Festival Founded by Weston Henry Noble at Luther College (Iowa)" (Ph.D. diss., Florida State University, 2001), 3004421.

12. George M. Frederickson, "Comparative History," in *The Past before Us: Contemporary Historical Writing in the United States,* ed. Michael Kammen (Ithaca, N.Y.: Cornell University Press, 1980), 409.

13. Shafer, 15.

14. Shafer, 15.

15. James A. Keene, *A History of Music Education in the United States* (Hanover, N.H.: University Press of New England, 1987).

16. Nélida Munoz de Frontera, "A Study of Selected Nineteenth-Century Puerto Rican Composers and Their Musical Output," vols. 1–4 (Ph.D. diss., New York University, 1988), UMI 8812518.

17. John M. Vincent, *Aids to Historical Research* (New York: Appleton-Century-Crofts, 1934), 139.

18. Allan Nevins, *The Gateway to History,* rev. ed. (Garden City, N.Y.: Anchor, 1962), 14.

19. David H. Fischer, *Historian's Fallacies: Toward a Logic of Historical Thought* (New York: Harper & Row, 1970), xv.

20. The Confederacy referred to the battleground as Manassas, whereas the Union, which lost both battles, preferred the term Bull Run, the name of the small stream that runs through the battlefield. The Manassas battlefield is located about twenty-six miles southwest of Washington, D.C.

21. Shafer, 2.

22. Frank J. Cipolla, "Patrick S. Gilmore: The Boston Years," *American Music,* Fall 1988, 281–92.

23. Sandra Wieland Howe, "Luther Whiting Mason: Contributions to Music Education in Nineteenth Century America and Japan" (Ph.D. diss., University of Minnesota, 1988), UMI 8826463.

24. Allen M. Garrett, *An Introduction to Research in Music* (Washington, D.C.: Catholic University of America Press, 1985), 2–3.

25. Homer C. Hockett, *The Critical Method in Historical Research and Writing* (New York: Macmillan, 1955), 4–5.

26. Hockett, 9.

27. Louis Gottschalk, *Understanding History,* 2nd ed. (New York: Knopf, 1969), 207.

28. Barzun and Graff, 166.

29. Barzun and Graff, 166.

30. Barzun and Graff, 130.

31. Associated Press dispatch, February 15, 1989.

32. Barzun and Graff, 166.

33. Emanuel J. Mason and William J. Bramble, *Research in Education: Concepts and Methods,* (Madison, Wis.: Brown & Benchmark, 1992), 36.

34. Brickman, 108.

35. James T. Majeda, "The Life and Works of Herbert L. Clarke (1867–1945)" (Ed.D. diss., University of Illinois, 1988), UMI 8823188.

36. Brickman, 3–5.

37. Brickman, 14.

38. Robert W. Smith, *The Great Locomotive Chase* (Miami: Warner Brothers Publications, 2000). The writer of this chapter conducted the Raleigh (N.C.) Concert Band in a performance of this work on July 14, 2002.

39. *Spies, Scouts, and Raiders: Irregular Operations* (Alexandria, Va.: Time-Life Books, 1989), 111–12. See also Stan G. Cohen and James G. Bogle, *The General and the Texas: A Pictorial History of the Andrews Raid, April 12, 1862* (Missoula, Mont.: Pictorial History Publishing, 1999).

40. William E. Studwell and Bruce R. Schuenemann, *State Songs of the United States: An Annotated Anthology* (New York: Haworth, 1997), 65. Later the song was adapted as "The Eyes of Texas" (1903).

41. Richard Sheppard, "Casey Jones Killed in Train Wreck," *Old News,* July 2002, 9.

42. Donald A. Ritchie, *Doing Oral History* (New York: Trayne, 1995), 1.

43. Herbert T. Hoover, "Oral History in the United States," in Kammen, 393.

44. William W. Cutler, "Oral History: Its Nature and Uses for Educational History," *History of Education Quarterly,* Summer 1971, 184.

45. Hoover, 394.

46. Stanley H. Brobston, "A Brief History of White Southern Gospel Music and a Study of Selected Amateur Family Gospel Singing Groups in Rural Georgia" (Ph.D. diss., New York University, 1977), UMI 7808451.

47. Barbara W. Sommer and Mary Kay Quinlan, *The Oral History Manual* (Walnut Creek, Calif.: Alta Mira, 2002).

48. Oscar Handlin, *Truth in History* (Cambridge: Harvard University Press, 1979), 127.

49. Barzun and Graff, 116.

50. Lacey Forsburgh, "World's Oldest Song Reported Deciphered," *New York Times,* March 6, 1974.

51. "A Hidden Haydn Found in Farmhouse," *Newsday,* February 20, 1984, 9.

52. Harold T. Schonberg, "Byron Janis Discovers Chopin MSS in a Chateau," *New York Times,* December 21, 1967.

53. Muriel Brooks, "Chopin/Janis," *American Music Teacher,* April–May 1979, 7–8. The waltzes were published in 1978 by Envolve Music Group, New York, under the title *Chopin/Janis: The Most Dramatic Discovery in Ages.*

54. Rufus A. Grider, *Historical Notes on Music in Bethlehem, Pennsylvania* (Philadelphia: John L. Pile, 1873). Foreword by Donald M. McCorkle (Winston-Salem, N.C.: Moravian Music Foundation, 1957), 57.

55. These trios were reissued by Boosey and Hawkes and recorded for the first time on New Records, "Instrumental Music in Colonial America: The Moravians," on Record NRLP 2016. They also are listed in the Schwann Catalog: NWW2, s 0507 DDD 2997.

56. See the microcard version of Phelps's doctoral dissertation, *The History and Practice of Chamber Music in the United States from Earliest Times up to 1875* (Rochester, N.Y.: University of Rochester Press, 1980), 241–57, 579–80, 654–726.

57. Albert G. Rau and Hans T. David, *A Catalogue of Music by American Moravians (1742–1842)* (Bethlehem, Pa.: Moravian College and Seminary for Women; New York: A. M. S. Press, 1970), 102.

58. Rau and David.

59. Regarding the Michael *partien,* see the Phelps dissertation, 277–381, 820–57.

60. Grider, 9.

61. "Four Haydn Scores Surface after More Than 100 Years," *San Juan Star,* June 20, 1982.

62. Donald Henahan, "Paganini's Concerto No. 3 Rediscovered," *New York Times,* January 14, 1971, 44.

63. Roger P. Phelps, "The Mendelssohn Quintet Club: A Milestone in American Music Education," *Journal of Research in Music Education,* Spring 1960, 8,

64. Phelps, "Mendelssohn Quintet Club," 40.

65. Phelps, "Mendelssohn Quintet Club," 40.

66. Carter V. Good, *Essentials of Educational Research: Methodology and Design,* 2nd ed. (Englewood Cliffs, N.J.: Prentice-Hall, 1972), 1764.

67. Hockett, 26.

68. Walter E. Eells, "First American Degrees in Music," *History of Education Quarterly,* March 1961, 36.

69. John G. Shea, *Memorial of the First Century of Georgetown College, Washington, D.C.* (New York: Collier, 1891), 164; quoted by Eells, 39.

70. Roger P. Phelps, "The First Earned Doctorate in Music Education," *Bulletin of Historical Research in Music Education,* January 1983, 2.

71. John J. Dawson, "The Education Value of Vocal Music" (Ped. D. diss., New York University, 1895), 16, UMI 7233518.

72. Hockett, 14.

73. Fischer, 40.

74. Richard W. Murphy, *The Nation Reunited* (Alexandria, Va.: Time-Life Books, 1987), 82.

75. Henry W. Lanier, personal letter to researcher, March 17, 1949.

76. Audrey H. Starke, *Sidney Lanier* (Chapel Hill, N.C.: University of North Carolina Press, 1933), opposite 174.

77. Starke, 184.

78. Starke, 462.

79. Philip Graham, ed., *Centennial Edition of the Works and Letters of Sidney Lanier* (Baltimore, Md.: Johns Hopkins University Press, 1945), 6:389.

80. Hockett, 8.

81. *New York Tribune,* November 10, 1946.

82. E. Lebeau, personal letter to researcher, November 10, 1949.

83. Harold C. Schonberg, "Music: American Oddities," *New York Times,* September 24, 1968, 54.

84. Allan Nevins, *The Gateway to History* (Boston: Heath, 1938); Nevins, *Gateway to History,* ed. Robin Winks (New York: Garland, 1984), 122.

85. Gottschalk, 138.

86. Brickman, 95.

87. Barzun and Graff, 126.

88. Gottschalk, 219–20.

89. Winks, 276.

SUPPLEMENTARY SOURCES

Ary, Donald, Lucy Cheser Jacobs, and Asghar Razavieh. *Introduction to Research in Education*, chap. 13. 5th ed. Ft. Worth, Tex.: Harcourt Brace College, 1996.

Barzun, Jacques, and Henry F. Graff. *The Modern Researcher*, chaps. 9–13. 5th ed. Boston: Houghton Mifflin, 1992.

Baum, Willa K. *Transcribing and Editing Oral History*. Nashville, Tenn.: American Association of State and Local History, 1997.

Best, John W., and James V. Kahn. *Research in Education*, chap. 4. 9th ed. Boston: Allyn & Bacon, 2003.

Breisach, Ernst. *Historiography: Ancient, Medieval, and Modern*. 2nd ed. Chicago: University of Chicago Press, 1994.

Cohen, Louis, Lawrence Manion, and Keith Morrison. *Research in Education*, chap. 7. 5th ed. New York: Routledge Falmer, 2000.

Crowl, Thomas K. *Fundamentals of Educational Research*, chap. 10. 2nd ed. Madison, Wis.: Brown & Benchmark, 1996.

Duckles, Vincent H., ed., with Ira Reed and Michael A. Keller. *Music Reference and Research Materials: An Annotated Bibliography*. 5th ed. New York: Schirmer Books, 1997.

Dunaway, David R., and Willa K. Baum, eds. *Oral History: An Interdisciplinary Anthology*. Walnut Creek, Calif.: Alta Mira, 1996.

Fraenkel, Jack R., and Norman E. Wallen. *How to Design and Evaluate Research in Education*, chap. 18. 2nd ed. New York: McGraw-Hill, 1993.

Gall, Joyce P., M. D. Gall, and Walter R. Borg. *Applying Educational Research: A Practical Guide*, chap. 13. 4th ed. New York: Longman, 1999.

Gay, L. R. *Educational Research: Competencies for Analysis and Application*, chap. 6. 4th ed. New York: Macmillan, 1992.

Handlin, Oscar. *Truth in History*, chaps. 5–6. Cambridge: Harvard University Press, 1979.

Heller, George N. *Music and Music Education History: A Chronology*. 3rd ed. Lawrence, Kan.: Department of Music Education and Therapy, 1996.

Higham, John. "The Historian as Moral Critic." In *The History and Climate of Opinion*. Ed. Robert A. Skotheim. New York: Garland, 1985.

Hopkins, Charles D., and Richard L. Antes. *Educational Research: A Structure for Inquiry*, chap. 9. 3rd ed. Itasca, Ill.: Peacock, 1990.

Johnson, Burke, and Leroy Christensen. *Educational Research: Quantitative and Qualitative Approaches*, chap. 12. Boston: Allyn & Bacon, 2000.

Leedy, Paul D., with Timothy J. Newby and Peggy A. Ermer. *Practical Research Planning and Design*, chap. 8. 6th ed. Upper Saddle River, N.J.: Merrill, 1997.

Maripou, Henri. *The Meaning of History*. Baltimore, Md.: Helicon, 1976.

Mark, Michael L., and Charles L. Gary. *A History of American Music Education*, pt. 5. New York: Schirmer Books, 1992.

Martella, Ronald C., Ronald Nelson, and Nancy E. Marchand-Martella. *Research Methods: Learning to Become a Critical Research Consumer,* chap. 13. Boston: Allyn & Bacon, 1999.

McMillan, James H., and Sally Schumacher. *Research in Education: A Conceptual Introduction,* chap. 15. 5th ed. New York: Longman, 2001.

Pruett, James W., and Thomas P. Slovens. *Research Guide in Musicology.* Chicago: American Library Association, 1985.

Ritchie, Donald A. *Doing Oral History.* New York: Twayne, 1995.

Sommer, Barbara W., and Mary Kay Quinlan. *The Oral History Manual.* Walnut Creek, Calif.: Alta Mira, 2002.

Wiersma, William. *Research Methods in Education,* chap. 9. 7th ed. Boston: Allyn & Bacon, 2000.

Chapter 8

Technology and Music Education Research

The use of new technologies for research in music and music education has increased dramatically in recent years. Reinforced by ongoing commercial development, and near universal use of personal computers and the Internet among researchers and educators,[1] music technology has revolutionized the way we listen, perform, compose, teach, and research music.[2] In today's world, technology is widely considered an essential tool of research.

The purpose of this chapter is to provide an overview of the relationship between technology and music education research. We describe how students and faculty might use technology in their research and scholarly work, addressing its basic functions in research. By first concentrating on broader concepts and applications, and then reviewing specific applications in music, this chapter serves both as a companion to earlier chapters and a handy reference for investigators.

Specifically, this chapter examines three areas pertinent to research in music education:

- Computer-based research: An overview of search engines, databases, and tools for organizing and facilitating qualitative and quantitative research. Practical methods of securing and structuring bibliographies, sources, and references are presented.
- Technology in the classroom: MIDI, music software/hardware, and CAI—MIDI (musical instrument digital interface) software and digital instruments: Their current state, development, and relevance in research. Implementation via music composition

and performance in the classroom. An in-depth presentation of specific computer applications and digital instruments offer insights into the breadth and limitations of this environ. CAI (computer-assisted instruction): Assessing adjunct and alternative means of teaching theory, ear training, class piano, and composition. CAI represents the most fledgling of software. What can actually be expected of CAI applications? Where is the current development headed?

- Future directions: online research projects and forums. Online forums and listservs are critiqued in terms of their methodologies and fecundity. Multimedia and synergistic constructs via Web-authoring and team-facilitated research will be explored. How do new media improve on conventional technologies of the recent past (i.e., video conferencing).

CONCEPTS IN TECHNOLOGY-AIDED RESEARCH

Traditionally, the process of doing research has been considered a solitary one, a "person solo" endeavor. The lone investigator develops a research proposal, executes a study or series of studies, and disseminates the findings to the wider field. Although the principle of individual, unique contributions to the research literature remains intact, the notion of "person solo" work has been challenged recently by new models of intelligence that emphasize the *distributed* nature of cognition.[3]

The idea of distributed cognition assumes that the resources which shape and enable intelligent activity are "distributed in configuration across people, environments, and situations."[4] Thus knowledge is not just in one's head; it is also in the notes that one puts into a book, in the social intellectual world in which one lives and works, and in the information sources one locates via the Internet. In this view, the process of research is more aptly described as a "person plus" endeavor.

Nowhere is the idea of distributed "person plus" cognition more evident than in the uses of computers in research. Mainframe and personal computers are employed routinely in a range of research activities, from delimiting the questions asked and controlling the experimental situation to managing data collection and organizing data analysis. Typically, mainframe computers are used for large quantitative databases requiring complex statistical procedures. For example, the Biomedical Computer Programs, P-Series (BIMED) is one of the oldest (begun in 1961) and probably the most widely used mainframe statistical package. Alternatively, microcomputers are generally programmed to be used for controlling data collection and recording, such as physiology laboratories where a premium is placed on regulating the conditions of exercise, controlling the time intervals, and calculating various measurements.

However, the most commonly used computer environment is the personal computer (PC). PCs combine the power of a mainframe with the functionality of microcomputers in a "point and click"—a quintessentially "person plus"—environment (e.g., Windows for IBM or compatibles, Macintosh). PCs can use sophisticated data analysis software and allow the use of several programs simultaneously, exporting and importing data among programs. Over the years, the demand for PCs and software applications for research purposes has grown exponentially. Thus, numerous programs have been developed to store, sort, reduce, retrieve, analyze, write, and edit research data.

USING COMPUTERS FOR DATA MANAGEMENT, ANALYSIS, AND WRITING

Searching the Literature

In chapter 1, we reviewed music reference materials and databases to facilitate your search for relevant sources and materials. As noted there, library information systems are being updated continually. Thus the card catalog—with little trays of cards containing bibliographic information by author and subject—is being phased out rapidly. As finances permit, libraries are computerizing catalog systems. Most universities and colleges already have made the shift.

Though some librarians may bemoan the loss of card catalogs, literature searches are faster and more productive with computers. Imagine trying to find a specific article by browsing through random issues of periodicals. This is akin to finding a needle in a haystack. In contrast, with a computerized database, you can use key words to find articles on specific topics, providing more effective and efficient access to indexes and information than does manual searching.

At present, many college, university, and public libraries allow us to do computer searches from a terminal in the library, either online or on CD-ROMS (Compact Disc-Read Only Memory), or remotely from home, work, or a local Internet café. Such widespread availability provides access to a myriad of source materials including books, doctoral dissertations, international documents, magazines, media sources, newspapers, periodical articles, scholarly journals, government documents, and World Wide Web sites.

With all this information at your fingertips, reviewing the literature becomes exciting and easy, if you know how to search. Yet the prospect of beginning a literature search can be daunting. How and where do you begin? What kind of sequence or strategy should you use to find relevant literature? While jumping into the fray via a computer search has its drawbacks (e.g., depending on the database), only the more recent references are available for computer searching. Computerized catalogs abound and automated searching can greatly expedite the literature search.

Computer-aided literature searching begins with clearly defined descriptors and preliminary (general) sources, such as abstracts and indexes; searching ends with a list of related references that you must obtain, read, and record. The first step is to use your research problem statement to help formulate a list of descriptors: terms that help you locate sources pertaining to a topic. For example, for researching the topic of the effect of student teaching on the attitude toward teaching music, obvious descriptors would be attitude (toward teaching), changes in attitude, student teaching, and music education.

The next step is to narrow or broaden one's search by using key words called "Boolean operators." The two most common operators (or connectors) are the words "and" and "or." To narrow your search, you connect two terms with the word "and." In the study of attitudes toward teaching music, you will find thousands of references listed under the descriptor "attitude change," but only a few hundred items using "attitude and teaching." As you connect all the key descriptors together with the word "and," you will find your search has been narrowed to a more manageable number of references. In contrast, the word "or" broadens your search; the computer will search for more than one descriptor. For example, if you seek information about "practice teaching," you could broaden your search by using "student teaching," or "internship" to raise your total references. Finally, if you want to learn how practice teaching influences attitudes toward teaching music, you can use the Boolean search to yield relevant results: music AND attitude AND (student teaching OR internship).

A good computer search strategy uses a combination of key word descriptors and Boolean operators to locate recent sources of information in relevant databases and then works backward. For the example above, you might consult recently published articles and bibliographies in the Educational Resources Information Center (ERIC) or the Music Psychology databases. This way, you would save time and profit from the searches of others.

Computers and Qualitative Data

As suggested in earlier chapters, qualitative research is a very broad term. It involves different forms of data collection—from field notes to interviews—and requires a wide variety of data analysis techniques. The use of computers for qualitative data analyses has increased dramatically in the last two decades,[5] and numerous software programs have been developed to work with data generated by qualitative studies.[6] Whether a researcher works collaboratively or individually, the computer facilitates data management to the point that we now have a wide choice of programs designed for this purpose. This section explains how computers are being used, describes one software application called the Ethnograph, and discusses the advantages and disadvantages of using computers for such analyses.

Beginning investigators are often surprised by the large volumes of data that are generated in qualitative research and by how much detailed, careful work is involved in analysis. Most researchers agree that the best uses of computers in qualitative research are for storing, coding, and retrieving data for future analysis. As Gerson famously said, "Imagine a situation in which every researcher has a full-time clerk with three exceptional capabilities: a perfect memory, the ability to retrieve any document immediately, and the capacity of an untiring and very fast typist."[7] Twenty years ago, the response of most qualitative researchers would be to hire that person immediately. Today, most researchers buy a PC and specialized software. As described in chapter 3, computer programs vary according to the general functions and more specialized features offered for dealing with qualitative data. Most programs are a combination of six types: word processors, text retrievers, text base managers, code and retrieve programs, code-based theory builders, and conceptual network builders.[8] Below, we describe one such program: the Ethnograph.[9]

The Ethnograph Version 5.0 is a typical code and retrieve program designed to import and organize data, code and retrieve data, and manage files. The program includes on-screen coding, analytic memos, a text editor, master list of codes, and a codebook of definitions. Getting started with the Ethnograph is straightforward. Returning to our earlier example, let's assume you have designed a qualitative case study to explore the role of student teaching on attitudes toward teaching music. You collected interview data from student teachers, supervisors, and collaborating teachers. You transcribed the interviews from audiocassettes into a word processing program like Microsoft Word. Now you are ready to begin data analysis. The Ethnograph allows you to copy and paste your document directly into the program, importing and saving it as a project, such as Project Attitude. In the blink of an eye, the program translates your data into a line-numbered ETH file format, and then automatically produces up to ten associated files that record your code applications, code master list, header information, speaker/section identifiers, memos, and others. These files are regularly updated as you add codes, even while your basic data files remain untouched.

After uploading data into the Ethnograph, you are ready to begin dividing text into meaningful segments (i.e., chunks), attaching codes to chunks, finding and displaying all the chunks with a green code (or combination of codes), and writing analytic memos. For example, you might want to find in your interviews that student teachers consistently mention the cooperating teacher's approach to teaching music as important to their experience. Within minutes of opening a new file in the Ethnograph, you choose a code name, such as CTAPPROACH, and begin coding all such instances in the interview text. You define relevant text segments to which you are applying this code by specifying a start line and a stop line.

As you work on the data, a master code list is automatically created and code words are added to the code book, where you can also attach definitions of your codes. The master code list keeps track of all the code words used and acts as a tool for selecting codes to be entered for code sets and quick code procedures. If you choose the code sets option, you can apply a number of codes at once; the quick code procedure allows you to key in one code to a segment that can be applied to other segments. As you add your codes, the program inserts the code name and code symbol at the top of each coded segment, providing on-screen verification.

While the coding functions, codebook, and master lists help segment the data, the Ethnograph's memos function allows you to pull your thoughts together into one place. For instance, during coding, you may find substantial connections between students' beliefs about teaching (code name STBELIEF) and cooperating teachers' approaches to teaching music (CTAPPROACH). You may begin to hypothesize that STBELIEF and CTAPPROACH are related factors in the development of student teachers' attitudes toward teaching music. This is the time to write an analytic memo.

The memo function allows you to develop questions, hypotheses, and tentative theories as they occur in the course of your analysis. By attaching memos to specific lines in a data file, directly to the data file or to the project, the Ethnograph helps you to keep ideas close to the actual data source. In this way, the program supports the development of data-driven ideas, hypotheses, and theories that eventually you will build into a logical and well-supported argument about the setting.

The use of computers to search for relevant information and communicate results is not controversial today, but the same cannot be said for the use of computer in qualitative research. Unlike areas of quantitative research, such as psychometric or survey research, the issues of validity and reliability have no mutually agreed upon meaning in the context of qualitative inquiry. Indeed, some qualitative researchers argue against qualitative software analysis packages, like the Ethnograph and NUD*IST, precisely because the sophisticated code and retrieval and memo functions characterize one approach to, and theoretical perspective on, qualitative research. These critics contend that such computer programs push one toward the uncritical adoption of a single approach to analysis-grounded theory, which carries implicit assumptions about, and very real implications for, the validity and reliability of our findings.[10]

Ultimately, the decision about whether to use computers in qualitative research depends on the researchers' perspective and purpose. The key is to remember that computers do not think, and they cannot understand the meaning of your qualitative data. At the same time, programs differ in the amount and kind of strategies and supports they offer to your questioning, theory building, and argumentation. Thus, before you choose a software package, it behooves you to take the time to consider seriously the philosophical foundations of your work, the nature of project(s) and database(s) that you will be working on, and how you expect to go about data analysis.

Computers and Quantitative Data

In stark contrast to the ongoing debate about computer use in qualitative research, computers are the sine qua non of contemporary quantitative research. Computers were designed originally to process the large volume of socioeconomic data generated by government agencies. Over the past quarter century, computer programs have become ubiquitous in the data analysis and reporting of descriptive and inferential statistics.[11]

Today, investigators have a wide choice of computer programs, software applications, and statistical packages to use in quantitative research. Unlike the situation for word processing where a handful of packages have captured a large share of the market, there are numerous statistical packages available. Some packages are written for a particular area of application (e.g., survey analysis) and others are quite general. One feature that distinguishes among statistical packages is whether they are written for mainframe computers or the PC. Among the most popular general purpose statistical packages available on both the mainframe and PC are SAS (Statistical Analysis System), SPSS (Statistical Package for the Social Sciences), and BMDP.[12]

Each of these three packages offers a comprehensive set of procedures that allow users to enter data—edit, manipulate, and screen data for erroneous values—and perform statistical analyses and display the results. These programs perform all of the basic univariate, bivariate, and multivariate analyses that are covered in earlier chapters, but have very different approaches. Both BMDP and SPSS adopt the philosophy of offering a number of *comprehensive* programs, each with its own options and variants for performing portions of the analyses. The SAS package, on the other hand, offers a large number of limited-purpose procedures, with the philosophy that the user should string together a sequence unique to the specific analysis.

Most recent versions of SAS, SPSS, and BMDP are implemented in the Windows environment. They include a graphical interface that allows the user to conduct statistical procedures without detailed knowledge of the relevant programming language. For example, all of the basic statistical techniques in SAS are implemented through programming syntax, most of which can be generated through menu-driven options in SAS/ASSIST, the graphical interface to SAS procedures. SAS/ASSIST facilitates data management and analysis without the requirement of programming SAS instructions. Syntax generated by SAS menus is recorded in a "log" file. The contents may then be copied to an interactive window, edited, and run. In this way SAS/ASSIST enables you to create or import data files, run data analysis procedures, view and graph the results, print and save to a new file.

Finally, there are a number of important considerations when buying a statistical package. First, as suggested above, you must keep in mind the differences between these programs when purchasing a software package. With SAS you need to buy entire sets of procedures. At minimum, you need the basic package and the statistical package to perform the major analyses. To run SAS you need nearly 10 megabytes (MB) disk storage for basic SAS and statistics, and less than 1 MB for data entry. SPSS is similar to SAS, but only requires 4.5 MB of storage space for the Base Package, with an additional 1.6 MB for the Advanced Statistics module. BMDP programs can be purchased either in sets or individually. There is a Base Package set of programs and an Advanced Statistics set. For BMDP, about one-third of 1 MB is needed for storing BMDP system files, and each program takes an additional MB.

Secondly, with commercial packages, you need to know which version you are using. These updates may be different than the version your institution uses. Program upgrades are often corrections or errors discovered in earlier versions and corrections that may be relevant to some of your previous programming and data analyses.

Once you have purchased and installed a package, you are on the verge of using a powerful tool for statistical analysis. It is at this crucial juncture that you must recall the following caveat: the trick in doing statistics is not in computation or data display. Commercial computer programs do the computing for you; with their beautifully formatted tables and graphs, even simple statistical programs can make ugly duckling "data" look like a beautiful swan "result." The trick is in the selection of reliable and valid measurements, the choice and correct use of an appropriate package, and the knowledge of how to interpret the output. Given these preconditions, the real "statistical" power always resides with the researcher and not the computer.

Writing the Research Document

Despite growing demand, use of computers for qualitative and quantitative research pales in comparison to the near universal use of word processing software for writing and editing documents. Anyone who has ever composed and spell-checked an e-mail message has used a rudimentary form of word processing. Anecdotes abound about friends and family members who buy expensive office software—bundled with the latest programs for creating spreadsheets, presentations, movies, and photos—but rarely end up using anything other than e-mail and the word processor. This situation makes perfect sense given our society's reliance on the written word for communicating and disseminating ideas. This is especially true in academia, where a well-written document is the gold standard of scholarly accomplishment.

Word processing programs, such as Microsoft Word or WordPerfect, make writing and editing much less time-intensive than before. Instead of laboring over mechanical typewriters like our forefathers in the early to mid-twentieth century—with the inevitable use of correction fluid, new ink ribbons, and multiple hard copies—we write, edit, and revise our documents instantaneously. I just rewrote the prior sentence in a matter of seconds not minutes. Once I finish this section, I might spell-check, change the format and perhaps the font, check the margins, and use the thesaurus to double-check the connotation of a word. I will do all this in a matter of minutes not hours. While computer word processors will not make us better writers, they facilitate the process of actually getting words onto paper, which is half of the battle.

Recently, software designers have turned their attention to another of the most time-consuming, laborious activities in writing a research document: the bibliography. One example is Endnote, a program that helps you prepare a bibliography of a paper or report by building reference databases.[13] Basically, Endnote is a bibliography maker. It specializes in storing, maintaining, and searching for bibliographic references in a private reference library that you create.

You use Endnote to insert citations into word processing documents and later scan those documents for in-text citations to compile a bibliography in any format that you need. You can also use Endnote as an online search tool—it provides a simple way to search online bibliographic databases and retrieve the references directly into it. Endnote can also import data files saved from a variety of online services, CD-ROMs, and library databases. For example, if you use Microsoft Word, Endnote's "cite while you write" feature integrates seamlessly with Word so that your bibliography is automatically built and updated as you write and insert citations.

As the title of this section suggests, a growing number of researchers use computers and software programs as tools for gathering, managing and analyzing data, and reporting research results. Computer programs provide tools that have made the process of research and dissemination easier and faster than before. While such tools have become for most researchers an indispensable part of their academic lives, the same assertion is true of computer applications in music. In the following sections, we invite you to consider computers in music by exploring key issues in the implementation and uses of computers in the music classroom and for research in music education.

IMPLEMENTING COMPUTERS IN THE MUSIC CLASSROOM

Issues and Philosophies

Logically, prior to any recommendations for classroom uses of technology are three basic philosophical questions: What is music education? Why teach music? Should we teach music? The aesthetic philosophy of music education, long in practice, envisions education via a formal understanding and appreciation of "masterpieces," of the Western European tradition, culminating in achieving the aesthetic experience.[14] It holds the work of art as a self-contained, verifiable act of genius, a stand that has contributed to "legitimizing" music education as a worthy field. Praxial philosophies are relativist, dynamically forged from the musical practices of various cultures and assessed via the social condition and intentions by which they derive meaning.[15]

Through "musicing" (developing music-making and listening skills as defined from within their cultures), it is surmised that students engender an enhanced consciousness, self-knowledge, and self-esteem.[16] The current technology is increasingly more sophisticated and malleable, capable of an implementation reflective of either approach. Conversely, technology tools are often utilized in ways that are divergent from their intended design. Hence, software functionality, which may initially appear unrelated to the task at hand, may embody the seeds of theory as mediated through the prism of educational philosophies.

Technology has begun to effect some curricular modifications. Current thought in music education questions some traditional pedagogical approaches. This is apparent in a more proactive stance toward teaching composition in the classroom.[17] Music composition has attained serious attention largely through the inclusion of computers and digital music instruments. While this has opened the floodgates of interest and enthusiasm, it raises fundamental questions: To what extent are teachers trained to teach conventional composition? Should composition be defined and limited by traditional values, or should it also include composing and performing popular music and the music of world cultures?

The venerable mode of traditional music education lies in the teaching of performance (vocal, solo, and instrumental ensemble), where each instrument and its respective repertoire possesses clearly identifiable attributes of standardized performance practices and methods of teaching "techniques." However, sophisticated technology tools, such as the sequencer and digital reproductions of acoustic instruments, have made composition accessible to the untrained musician. The implementation of technology is provoking pedagogical perspectives that reflect salient elements of aesthetic and praxial philosophies. Sara Kiesler sees the potential impacts of technologies in two terms: amplicative and transformative. "Amplicative" impact involves the completion of tasks and activities with increased efficiency when new technologies are used. "Transformative" impact "shows a qualitative change in how people think and react."[18]

Computer-assisted instruction (CAI) is in a fledgling state, essentially comprised of task-oriented modules under the aegis of conventional pedagogical models.[19] As tutoring aids in theory or ear training programs, CAI programs embody ideas in accordance with aesthetic philosophy. Much akin to the way a word processor assumes the function of pen and paper, CAI programs simply transpose existing materials to the software's environs. The fluency and effectiveness of these programs have vastly improved, but they continue to respond to the same call. Also, Vocal and Instrumental instruction tend to isolate very specific task-oriented constructs. However, this is an area where future directions may bring about profound change. The challenges will be formidable.

- Creating software that synergizes the current Balkanized approach—designing programs that interweave skills in theory, ear training, keyboard harmony as a dynamic and practical classroom application.
- Transforming CAI into an integral curricular partner, as opposed to its present adjunct state.
- Creating software for teaching composition and performances that draws on the multicultural approach inherent in the dedicated programs of sequencing, notation, and object-oriented programs like MAX.

Finally, from a broad educational perspective, extramusical factors will require a researcher's apt assessment in addressing the emerging, multicultural complexion of the classroom, and the cross-fertilization of interdisciplinary approaches: "interdisciplinary dialogues among scholars in anthropology, psychology, sociology, political science, and other disciplines have fundamentally altered their curricular content of these fields."[20] In sum, grand perspective must be holistic. In formulating integrated technology-assisted curricula, research must attend to a collage of technology and pedagogical modalities, as filtered through educational philosophies and eclectic cultural landscapes.

TECHNOLOGY DIRECTIONS IN THE CLASSROOM: MIDI, MUSIC SOFTWARE, AND DIGITAL INSTRUMENTS

The Musical Digital Interface Protocol: From Commerce to Curricular Transformation

MIDI, an acronym for Musical Instrument Digital Interface, and its periphery is ubiquitous—entrenched in nearly all music environs.

However, its range and functionality are often exalted in hyperbole, masking its limitations and clouding its efficiency for research design. For these reasons, we dedicate a substantial inquiry to illuminating aspects that may inform your research.

MIDI is the music industry's standard protocol that enables interactive control of computers and digital musical instruments. For clarity, we will use the term MIDI as a catch phrase of collective reference to interactive computers, software, and digital musical instruments. Developed by the MIDI Manufacturers Association and implemented in 1983, it is a paradigm example of how commercial interests inadvertently define a path by which a vast range of related technologies may emerge. An awareness of current technological developments in commercial contexts is a necessity, in that it functions as a barometer of music software and hardware trends, often revealing technologies that may be germane to music research and education. For instance, sequencing software was originally modeled after Les Paul's 1960s multitrack recorder, which addressed the practical and aesthetic needs of rock and roll. This spawned the evolutionary development of sophisticated notation programs, CAI programs, and object-oriented programs like MAX. Peripheral to commercial development, proprietary software for alternative music genres and music education emerged in parallel. In a pragmatic sense, the sequencer, when used by a formally trained musician, merges and mediates the compositional processes of two cultures.

In the classroom, MIDI has become the facilitator in supporting a veritable toolbox of interrelated programs, seamlessly bridging software, hardware, digital audio, and video—a plethora of music programs intended for commercial environs and routinely applied to the classroom. In "The Systems Approach to Technology,"[21] Reese proposes a purposeful, task-oriented focus in selecting the various components that will effectively operate as an integrated workstation—the synergy of software, keyboards, MIDI modules, audio components, and computers. Attesting to music educators' effective inclusion of technology, he cites MENC's opportunity to learn standards, which call for computer and music technology equipment in the classroom. This has also given rise to a metamorphosis in music education's means and goals in the classroom

Software, spawned in MIDI's wake, has enabled accessibility to compositional skills, previously reserved exclusively for the formally trained. While performance has been the cornerstone of music education, current critical thought, in part mediated by the potential of MIDI environs, suggests that composition and improvisation will become the preferred pedagogical themes of the future. Elliott W. Eisner offers an overview that proposes an alternate pedagogical stance: "Musical problems are best, but not exclusively, addressed in the context of musical composition. Yet we have little musical composition going on in schools. Its virtual absence is rooted in traditions of performance. When we think of music in our schools, we think about performing music rather than creating it. Yet the act of creation in music, as in the other arts, is vitally important in promoting forms of thinking that demand attention to the ways in which sound or other qualities are modulated and organized. Without an opportunity to cope with problems, the forms of thinking that they would develop are simply unlikely to be promoted. Composition is a way to grapple with relationships, to imagine new musical possibilities, to pursue new musical ideas."[22]

RESEARCH DELIMITATIONS: A CASE STUDY OF INTERDEPENDENT SYSTEMS

MIDI possesses significant delimitations well worth examining in terms of its efficacy for research in music education. A priori, the MIDI protocol presents a rigid delineation of musical components, articulated in discreet commands for pitch, note-on, note-off, velocity, duration, and assigned sound. Unlike acoustic instruments, the actual source of sound is formally bifurcated from the sound source.[23]

Let's examine what transpires when we play and record using MIDI: we seamlessly transverse both analog and digital worlds. Initiated by keystrokes, the information is digitally converted and simultaneously transmitted to a sound source. In addition to the immediacy of tactile/aural responses associated with an acoustic instrument's behavior,[24] a sequence's "event list" subsequently collates a digital diary of performance events. All digital information is represented by zeros and ones, potentially capable of infinite manipulation and transformation. Every parameter is interchangeable and reassignable, readily available for transposition, tempo changes, reassignment of sounds, and rhythmic alterations. We may cut-and-paste performance data and integrate it elsewhere—assign pitch data in randomly selecting a separate sound for each note. We can begin with an existing work, and transform its elements into something unique and unrelated to the original. This stands in stark contrast to the notion of a masterpiece, penned directly from Mozart's mind to manuscript paper. Composition via MIDI sculpts a musical stone until the form of a lion emerges.

Taking a systems approach to MIDI, we will create a case study, providing a specific context for research in music performance and pedagogy. We will utilize two primary tools that offer a broad range of musical and analytical elements: the Yamaha Disklavier piano and Apple's Audio Platinum sequencing software. The quality of sound and wealth of data elicited by this collaboration has proven to be fertile ground for inquiry.[25]

Disklavier

The Yamaha Disklavier is an acoustic piano, fitted with fiber optic sensors, solenoids, and a MIDI enhanced microprocessor, enabling it as a modern player piano. A performance can be recorded by its on-board sequencer, and played back within the self-contained instruments; it triggers itself (acoustic piano) for playback. It can also be played as an acoustic piano via an external sequencer—available to receive all the transformational commands within the MIDI specification. The innovation and value of such an instrument lies in the fact that we can witness the reproduction of an acoustic instrument's actual sound in its playback, preserving the "live" quality and timbral changes of the performance. All physical attributes are (theoretically) replicated and mirrored in playback: keystrokes, key releases, speed of release stroke, hammers hitting strings, pedals depressed, pedals released, half pedals, and so on. This bears a difference from a synthesizer of sampled piano's playback, all of which are literally a recording of a piano as experienced through speakers.

There are limitations. While the Disklavier is generally sensitive in its replication, it can misinterpret and mildly alter rhythms and note velocities in pianissimo sections. Pedaling that generates vast amounts of information, like flutter pedaling, is not always accurately reproduced. At present, the instrument's recording capabilities are utilized most often in commercial studios and in popular venues. The ultrasensitive editing and playback necessary for a Beethoven sonata is not currently viable.

Logic Audio Platinum Sequencing Software

While the Disklavier's development is mediated by both its physical and MIDI constraints, a sequencer is devoid of any dependence on the resultant sound. Modeled after the 1960s analog multitrack recorders, and residing on a computer, its research and development curve is also far less restrictive. Of significance for performance and pedagogical related research is its ability to render accurate and useful representational performance data, as generated by the Disklavier or other MIDI controller device.

In highlighting technical functionality and limitations pertinent to performance and pedagogy, we offer a thumbnail presentation of a salient element within the sequencing environment: "quantization." It will serve to illuminate the need for a preassessment of individual components, in order to effectively evaluate their mediation of efficacy and delimitations within a technical ecosystem.

Quantization is an integral element of the digital landscape. Commonly understood in terms of CDs sampling rate of 44.1K per second, quantizing is the process by which "smooth" analog sound waves are converted into the "terraced" digital realm. In the case of CDs sampling rate, it has been argued that an analog sound wave possesses more information and is therefore more natural sounding, albeit with the associated distortions of tape hiss, flutter, and pitch inconsistencies. This criticism is supported by the emergence of archival digital systems that are capable of highly enhanced sampling rates, resulting in enhanced clarity and detail.[26] Quantization levels clearly affect the quality of sound replication.

The sequencer operates analogously in that it converts analog signals to digital ones during the recording process. In playback, there is an analogous process of quantization that mediates outgoing data. The key difference is that we are not recording sound. We are recording selected physical aspects of the "performance"—key-down, key-up, speed of keystroke, duration of a key-down, and so on. We are, in essence, extracting the physical gestures of the performance from the sound itself. Measurements concerning time are articulated in the pulse per quarter note (ppq). In the fledgling MIDI recording software of the early 1980s, this delineation was only 24 ppq, guaranteeing rhythmic alterations in recording and playback. In other words, values not perfectly divisible into, or a factor of twenty-four were altered, effectively distorting all rhythmic elements of the performance.

Current sequencer rates are quite high, capable of producing a far more accurate recording environment. However, this must always be considered in the context of the entire system. In the case of the Disklavier's microprocessor, whose recording quantization may be far higher than its sequencing host, it is now held hostage to MIDI's protocol and limitations, unavoidably introducing subtle to profound rhythmic distortions in playback. This can easily be misinterpreted as a performer's intentions or idiosyncrasies. Another similar factor lies in the quantization of velocity information, as mediated by the 127 steps of the MIDI specification. This can profoundly affect the interpretive range through inaccurate readings of volume, affecting subtle (and vital) musical elements like phrasing, shading, and color.

Quantization may also offer useful interpretive information. Notation is quantized—user defined but often resulting in a flawed or compromised blueprint. Notation renders all note values rigidly, as in the display of a series of quarter notes. Conversely, a "piano roll" editor displays a series of horizontal bars, which reveal precise velocities, start times, and durations for each note. Its controlled or lack of quantization levels may reveal performance practices. The piano roll may also define valuable interpretive information, such as how one performs legato at the piano. For instance, overlapping bars, which replicate keystrokes and releases, suggest a performer's physical motions in attaining legato at the instrument. Notation remains invaluable as a universal standard—a venerable de facto tool for realizing a composer's intent. However, it is not representative of a performance, instead offering a detailed performance guide, yet requiring interpretation as handed down history via pedagogy in the aural tradition.

In sum, through assessment and an understanding of interrelated technological elements, research design can be more accurately defined, delimited, and designed.

Computer-Assisted Instruction

Computer assisted instruction (CAI) has experienced a rapid growth and interest since the early 1970s, accelerated by powerful and inexpensive computers. This has been documented in concomitant research, often illuminating the efficacy of the software and the underlying principles toward music education. CAI, as authorized and utilized within music education environs, has come to address essential areas with increasing focus, although it remains in its early stages of development. The broad areas include the following:

- Literature and materials: Ear training, sight singing, music theory and analysis, music history
- Instrumental and vocal performance: Guided instruction for piano, instruments, and voice
- Accompaniment: Intelligent "music minus one" and improvisational programs
- Composition: Arranging, sequencing, notation-based software

Software Overview and Development

CAI has been earmarked by steady growth and focused interest, initiated by perhaps its first extended usage in Fred Hofstetter's 1975 Guido curriculum. As a testament to its significance, Guido was carefully documented, ultimately paving the path of the establishment of the Association of Technology in Music Instruction (ATMI).[27] The first microcomputers of the late 1970s and early 1980s spawned the first commercially available CAI suite of software by Micro Systems, featuring software for dictation and composition. The MIDI protocol of the mid-1980s brought about the most prolific development, fostering such programs as Band-in-a-Box (automated accompaniments for improvisation), Music Mouse (improvisation-based software), and Practica Musica (a music theory and aural skills program, authored for a pragmatic classroom).

In parallel development throughout the late 1980s and early 1990s were the corporate-funded commercial programs in sequencing logic (Audio, Digital Performer), notation (Finale), and audio editing (Pro Tools), their innovative embedding of a wealth of compositional tools plus the use of multiple programs within a single program, highlighted the interactive and synergistic possibilities. Related CAI and eclectic programs began to emerge on CD-ROM: Robert Winter's analytical exposé on Beethoven's Symphony no. 9,[28] and Morton Subotnick's *All My Hummingbirds Have Alabis,*[29] a composition that coalesced multimedia.

By the late 1990s, dedicated CAI programs in theory and ear training proliferated, among them Rising Software's Auralia and Musitron and MiBAC Music Software's suite of Music Lessons. A recent inventory of commercially available CAI music education software numbered twenty-three companies, offering 172 software programs as modules.[30] This is exclusive of any sequencing, digital audio, or notation programs, all of which are frequently utilized within the classroom.

Implications for Teaching Core Curriculum

Recent articles, dissertations, and tutorial books on CAI have appeared with regularity,[31] in a consensus of avid interest. The potential for CAI is largely accepted as viable and even integral, but its actual implementation and development as a curricular partner remains clouded by philosophical dichotomies. The playing field of CAI is an uneven terrain, with some areas nearly "ready for prime times," while others merely promising. The literature extols the creative values of Sequencing, Notation, and Digital Audio Editing software in promoting compositional skills, yet educators essentially "repurpose" these programs and create their own curricula in doing so.

Conversely, CAI, for enhancing performance skills via accompanying software like Vivace and Band-in-a-Box, has been the subject of many inquiries that attest to its practicality and effectiveness.[32] CAI, as guided instrumental and vocal instruction, is the least developed, generally focusing on ultraspecific quantitative issues like pitch accuracy, while ignoring complex, qualitative ones. CAI for ear training, music theory, and music history holds the middle ground, and perhaps the most promising and fertile ground for research. These programs, derived from formal, quantifiable musical elements and constructs, are readily available for verifiable CAI tasks. Many of these programs offer a host of tutorial and drill and practice cells, providing as adjunct tutor for theory and aural training courses.

MUSIC EDUCATION AND TECHNOLOGY: POLARIZED PERSPECTIVES

In many ways, music educators user computer technologies for teaching, learning, and research in much the same way as those in other disciplines. Music educators search libraries, manage and analyze data with qualitative and quantitative computer programs, and employ word processors to disseminate their findings. However, music educators also have a wealth of sophisticated technologies to conduct research and design instruction specifically for music. In particular, since the mid-1980s, MIDI and CAI technology have sparked much debate in the direction of alternative approaches for teaching music in the classroom. An essential divisiveness in modalities has erupted:

- Is CAI a tool of efficiency or transformation?[33] Will we remain beholden to the convention of the "score" as the primary window into composition, or will we approach music through a more intuitive "aural" mode, inherent in popular styles and in alternative visual representations of sound?
- "Will rote learning, memorization, and converging thinking . . . be likely to be augmented or replaced with discovery learning, problem solving, and divergent thinking? Cooperative learning, peer teaching, and project-oriented learning with the teacher as a facilitator or monitor are becoming more valued than teacher-dominated interaction."[34]
- Will the traditional, didactic, expository mode of teaching give way to a "discovery" mode, where methods focus on the student "discovering" what is to be learned, without being given the explicit information or content by the teacher.[35]
- Perhaps the most far-reaching goal will involve the integrated implementation of varied CAI programs within the larger curricular contexts. This will pose a serious challenge to music educators. An assessment of the major influences—pedagogical modalities and the breadth and design of software—is daunting. However, research will clearly be at the forefront in parsing, informing, and guiding CAI's development to fruition in the classroom and curricula.

NOTES

1. Edward C. Warburton, Xianglei Chen, and Ellen M. Bradburn, *Teaching and Technology: Use of Telecommunications Technology for Postsecondary Instructional Faculty in Fall 1998 (NCES 2002-161)* (Washington, D.C.: U.S. Department of Educational Research and Improvement, 2002).

2. David B. Williams and Peter R. Webster, *Understanding Music Technology*, 2nd ed. (New York: Schirmer Books, 1999), 10.

3. See Nina Granott, "Patterns of Interaction in the Co-Construction of Knowledge: Separate Minds, Joint Effort, and Weird Creatures," in *Development in Context: Acting and Thinking in Specific Environments*, ed. Robert H. Wozniak and Kurt W. Fischer (Hillsdale, N.J.: Erlbaum, 1993), 183–207; Roy D. Pea, "Practices of Distributed Intelligence and Designs for Education," in *Distributed Cognitions*, ed. Gabriel Salomon (New York: Cambridge University Press, 1993), 50–76; David Perkins, *Smart Schools: From Training Memories to Educating Minds* (New York: Free Press, 1992); Thomas Winograd and Fernando Flores, *Understanding Computers and Cognition: A New Foundation for Design* (Norwood, N.J.: Ablex, 1986).

4. Pea, "Practices of Distributed Intelligence," 50.

5. Jerry Willis and Muktha Jost, "Computers and Qualitative Research," in *Computers in Schools* 15, no. 3–4, ed. Leping Liu, D. LaMont Johnson, and Cleborne D. Maddux (1999): 21–52.

6. For an overview, see Eben A. Weitzman and Matthew B. Miles, *Computer Programs for Data Analysis: A Software Sourcebook* (Thousand Oaks, Calif.: Sage, 1995).

7. Evan Gerson, "Qualitative Work and the Computer," *Qualitative Sociology* 7, no. 1–2 (1984): 61–74.

8. For a more detailed description of this typology and excellent overview of software programs in the mid-1990s, see Weitzman and Miles.

9. One of the early code-and-retrieval computer programs for qualitative research, the Ethnograph was first released in 1985 with version 2.0 by Qualls Research Associates, P.O. Box 2070, Amherst, MA 01004. Phone: (413) 256-8835, e-mail: quails@ncimail.com. URL: www.quailsresearch.com. The Ethnograph is also distributed by Qualitative Research Management, 73425 Hilltop Road, Desert Hot Springs, CA 92240, phone: (619) 329-7026.

10. Willis and Jost.

11. Abdelmonia Affif and Virginia Clark, *Computer-aided Multivariate Analysis*, 2nd ed. (New York: Chapman & Hall, 1990); Barbara G. Tabachnick and Linda S. Fidell, *Using Multivariate Statistics*, 4th ed. (Boston: Allyn & Bacon, 2001).

12. For information and manuals, write: BMDP Statistical Software, Inc., 1440 Sepulveda Blvd., Los Angeles, CA 90025; SAS Institute, Inc., SAS Circle, Box 8000, Cary, NC 27512; SPSS, Inc., Suite 3000, 444 North Michigan Ave., Chicago, IL 60611.

13. EndNote version 6 is produced by ISI ResearchSoft, 2141 Palomar Airport Road, Suite 350, Carlsbad, CA 92009. For more information, phone (760) 438-5526, e-mail: info@isiresearchsoft.com, or visit www.endnote.com.

14. Bennett Reimer, *A Philosophy of Music Education*, 2nd ed. (Englewood Cliffs, N.J.: Prentice-Hall, 1989). Reimer's book provides a comprehensive exposé of the "aesthetic philosophy" in music education. While the aesthetic

philosophy is generally rooted in eighteenth- and nineteenth-century European repertoire, Suzanne Langer's theory provides a more specific rallying point. Langer surmises that music represents virtual feelings and defines art as the "creation of forms symbolic of human feeling." Suzanne Langer, *Feeling and Form* (New York: Scribner's, 1953), 27. Concomitantly, Reimer surmises that "music education is the education of feeling."

15. David L. Elliott, *Music Matters: A Philosophy of Music Education* (New York: Oxford University Press, 1995). The praxial philosophy exemplified in Elliott's writings is representative of educators and philosophers who oppose the narrow focus of the aesthetic philosophy. However, Elliott's notion of "musicing" may also subsume the essential canon of the aesthetic philosophy and its teaching modalities. Musicing is a priori open to unveiling salient and creative qualities of a culture's artistic production, inclusive of the eighteenth- and nineteenth-century classical canon and its mode of pedagogy.

16. Elliott, *Music Matters*.

17. Sam Reese, "Tools for Thinking in Sound," *Music Educators Journal*, July 2001; David Beckstead, "Will Technology Transform Music Education?" *Music Educators Journal*, May 2001, 44–49.

18. Elizabeth Burge, *Classrooms with a Difference* (Toronto: University of Toronto Press, 1993), 36.

19. Roger Dannenberg's Piano Tutor, an interactive piano-teaching system that combines an expert system with multimedia technology, offers a wealth of practical and potential implications for research into CAI. Its design, skillfully employing an aggregate of integral components, is a model of efficacy. An overview of the Piano Tutor can be found in Roger B. Dannenberg, Marta Sanchez, Annabelle Joseph, Robert Joseph, Ronald Saul, and Peter Capell, "Results from the Piano Tutor Project," *Proceedings from the Fourth Biennial Arts and Technology Symposium*, Connecticut College, March 1993, 134–50.

20. Marie McCarthy and J. Scott Goble, "Music Education Philosophy: Changing Times," *Music Educators Journal*, September 2002, 20.

21. Sam Reese, "The Systems Approach to Music Technology," *Music Educators Journal*, July 1998, 24–28.

22. Elliott W. Eisner, "Music Education Six Months after the Turn of the Century," *Arts Education Policy Review*, January–February 2001, 20–24.

23. It is interesting to compare this with an earlier technology that also placed a complex mechanism between the player and the actual sound production: the piano.

24. In the case of Yamaha's *Disklavier* and Boersendorfer's SE, one is actually playing an acoustic piano in addition to sending MIDI data.

25. Kathleen Riler-Butler, "Understanding Interpretive Nuance in Piano Performance through Aural/Visual Feedback" (Ph.D. diss., New York University, 2001). This study, in which Sadoff served as committee

member, suggested the tools utilized. It is an excellent example of combining an array of technology as governed by performance and pedagogical principles.

26. Sony's Super Audio CD (SACD), which uses direct stream digital (DSD) recording technology, features a sampling rate of 64 X 44.1 Khz. It was developed by Sony's engineers in order to archive Sony's vast catalog.

27. Peter Webster, "Historical Perspectives on Technology and Music," *Music Educators Journal,* September 2002, 38–43.

28. Robert Winter, *Ludwig van Beethoven's Symphony no. 9* (New York: Voyager Company), CD-ROM.

29. Morton Subotnick, *All My Hummingbirds Have Alabis* (New York: Voyager Company), CD-ROM.

30. *Electronic Musician,* "2003 Computer Music Products Guide," 44–48.

31. Peter R. Webster and David B. Williams, *Experiencing Music Technology,* 2nd ed. (New York: Schirmer, 1999). How-to books appear concomitantly with the release of popular programs in sequencing, notation, and digital audio. In providing an overview of CAI programs and offering guided tutorials, the most extensive exposé to date is *Experiencing Music Technology,* 2nd ed., which includes a text plus a CD-ROM with links to a dedicated website. See also Simon Holland, "Artificial Intelligence in Music Education: A Critical Review," in *Readings in Music and Artificial Intelligence,* volume 20 of *Contemporary Music Studies,* ed. E. Miranda (Netherlands: Harwood Academic Publishers). This publication is a special issue of *Contemporary Music Review.* Under the aegis of multiple approaches to using artificial intelligences in music education, this article presents a broad overview of Intelligent Tutoring Systems, Music Logo Systems, Cognitive Support Frameworks, highly interactive interfaces that employ A1 theories, and systems to support negotiation and reflection. This article illuminates the relationship between the software's functionality and its concomitant pedagogical philosophy.

32. Shan-Mei Amy Tseng, "Solo Accompaniments in Instrumental Music Education: The Impact of the Computer-Controlled Vivace on Flute Student Practice" (Ph.D. diss., University of Illinois, 1996); Susan Germaine Glenn, "The Effects of a Situated Approach to Musical Performance Education on Student Achievement: Practicing with an Artificially Intelligent Computer Accompanist" (Ph.D. diss., University of Georgia, 2000).

33. Beckstead, "Will Technology Transform Music Education?" 44–49.

34. Webster, "Historical Perspectives on Technology and Music," 38–43.

35. Michael T. Hopkins, "The Effects of Computer-Based Expository and Discovery Methods of Instruction on Aural Recognition of Music Concepts," *Journal of Research in Music Education,* Summer 2002, 131–44.

SUPPLEMENTARY SOURCES

Afifi, Abdelmonia, and Vivian Clark. *Computer-Aided Multivariate Analysis.* New York: Chapman & Hall, 1990.

Falk, J. D. "OCLC and RLIN: Research Libraries at the Scholar's Fingertips." *American Historical Association Newsletter Perspectives,* May–June 1989, 1, 11–13, 17.

Kelle, U. ed. *Computer-Aided Qualitative Data Analysis: Theory, Methods, and Practice.* London: Sage, 1995.

Weitzman, Even A., and Matthew B. Miles. *Computer Programs for Qualitative Data Analysis: A Software Sourcebook,* chaps 2–3, 9. Thousand Oaks, Calif.: Sage, 1995.

Index

About the Authors

Roger P. Phelps is professor emeritus of music and music education at New York University. He was a primary contributor to *A Guide to Research in Music Education, 4th Edition*.

Ronald H. Sadoff is an assistant professor of music at New York University.

Edward C. Warburton is an assistant professor of dance education at University of California, Santa Cruz.

Lawrence Ferrara is professor and chair of the Department of Music and Performing Arts at New York University. His previously published materials include *Philosophy and the Analysis of Music* and *A Guide to Research in Music Education, 4th Edition*.